sacred
SPARK

A Minister-mom's Quest to
Restore the Light in Her Son's Eyes
Inspires Her Church to Protect
Children from Harm and
Ignites a Global Debate about
Autism and Childhood Vaccines

Rev. Lisa K. Sykes

Epilogue by

Mark Geier, M.D., Ph.D. and **David Geier**

4th
LLOYD
PRODUCTIONS

Fourth Lloyd Productions, LLC.
Burgess, Virginia

For permissions write to:
Fourth Lloyd Productions, LLC
512 Old Glebe Point Road
Burgess, VA 22432

www.sacredsparkbook.com

ISBN: 978-0-971-78064-4 paperback
Library of Congress Control Number: 2009924001

Printed in the United States of America

Front cover photo: Wesley Sykes at age one.
Back cover photo: Lisa Sykes with Wesley Sykes at age thirteen.

sacred SPARK

Rev. Lisa K. Sykes

Joshua, Seth, Wesley, Lisa and Adam Sykes, 2009.

This book is dedicated
to my son, Wesley, and to all those like him,
who live heroically in spite of mercury poisoning

and to my husband, Seth, and our sons,
Adam, Wesley and Joshua,
and all those like them,
who love heroically in spite of mercury poisoning.

"The test of the morality of a society is what it does for its children."

Dietrich Bonhoeffer
1906-1945

CONTENTS

If you ever have the pleasure of meeting Reverend Lisa Sykes in person, the last thing that will cross your mind is that this soft-spoken woman with a gentle smile is really a firebrand of social reform, a person of great public resources and personal power. Through her public ministry in the United Methodist Church and her private fight for her son, Lisa's gift to other advocates for children is her ability to shine the intelligent light of ethical questioning on the vaccine safety issue, an issue that tends to bog down with political debates that obscure the real question of "When are we going to act as a nation with a conscience and do whatever it takes to protect and heal our children?"

In her search for answers to stopping the autism epidemic and healing her son, Lisa's path has taken her to discussions with scientists, national television journalists, state attorneys general and national politicians. In addition to her medical and political advocacy, Lisa is also a legal pioneer, having the courage to take her son's case out of our government's Vaccine Court and into Federal Court. Although her case was unsuccessful because of a legal doctrine called preemption, her effort will likely be seen as advancing the efforts of all those who seek to prevent the further poisoning of children by mercury in medicine.

While federal health agencies continue to spend billions of our tax-payer dollars in promotional efforts to shore up the public's trust of the ever expanding childhood immunizations schedule, there has yet to be funded one comprehensive study to assess the health impact of cumulative vaccine doses and the effects of their multiple toxicants. The glaring problems presented by the still present supply of mercury in our medicines and an ongoing sky-rocketing autism epidemic cannot be solved by marketing alone. This tired tactic failed in the not too distant past, when all the king's horses and all the king's men could not put "safety" back into tobacco products again. As history shows us, at some point the truth becomes too obvious to too many to be spun away with clever marketing. We have reached this point now with poorly manufactured and tested vaccines, especially those still containing mercury and other toxic ingredients, and the fact that they have not been and cannot be proven safe by our tax-funded federal health agencies.

It is now more than ever that parents, physicians and researchers supporting vaccine-safety must continue to hold our ground as we fight for our children and all those, born or unborn, who will benefit from our strength and unity. We need look no further than true stories like Lisa's for the inspiration to go forward in the coming months and years as the house of cards upholding the indefensible position of keeping mercury in our drug supply and children's bodies comes crashing down.

Books that chronicle the heartbreak and trials of families going through the ravages of autism are not uncommon, given the current high rate of autism. However, few stories have had an impact like the story of Lisa Sykes and her son, Wesley. With its impressive reach, *Sacred Spark* is a testimony of someone who stands fast in her faith that, when called upon, society will always act in the best interest of its children.

Lenny Schafer, Editor
The Schafer Autism Report

ACKNOWLEDGEMENTS

Paul G. King, Ph.D., Mary Megson, M.D., Boyd Haley, Ph.D., Elizabeth Mumper, M.D., Robert Krakow, Esq., Cliff Shoemaker, Esq., Robert F. Kennedy, Jr., Esq., Nancy and Richard Stodart, Lisa Reagan, Anne Geier, V. Karen Courtney, Mary L. F. Lang, Laura Ripol, Lenny Schafer, Bobbie Manning, Leslie Weed, Kelly Kerns, Teri Arranga, Brian Hooker, Lyn Redwood, J.B. Handley, Congressman Dan Burton, Congressman Dave Weldon, Estelle Pruden, Bishop Charlene Kammerer and the Virginia Annual Conference of the United Methodist Church, Julie Taylor, Harriett Olson, Lois M. Dauway, Sung-Ok Lee, Brenda Thompson, Barbara Wheeler, Beverly Irving, and the Women's Division of the United Methodist Church, James Winkler and the General Board of Church and Society of the United Methodist Church, *Mothering Magazine*, Autism Action Network, Autism One, Generation Rescue, Heal Every Autistic Life, Moms Against Mercury, National Autism Association, NoMercury, SafeMinds, Schafer Autism Report, Talk About Curing Autism, and the US Autism and Asperger Association, Don and Julianne King and Jennifer Davis-Lewis.

CHAPTER ONE

TOXIC

"In other words, Merthiolate (*Thimerosal*) is unsatisfactory as a preservative for serum intended for use on dogs. Occasional[ly] dogs do not show the local reaction but in some instances the reaction is extremely severe."

—Pitman-Moore Company to W. A. Jamieson, Director, Biological Division, Eli Lilly and Company, July 22, 1935

IT WAS LATE IN THE EVENING ON A FRIGID WINTER NIGHT WHEN NIKKI CALLED. For her to call me so late was as unexpected as it was uncharacteristic of her. Through hurried and jagged breaths, she begged me as her pastor to come over as quickly as I could.

The headlights of my car divided the darkness well into the rural outskirts of Richmond, Virginia. In the chill of the night I got out of my car and hurried to the door of a very modest home, feeling that something had to be very wrong. It was.

As soon as I entered the home, I saw Nikki's two children, their faces drawn, sitting shoulder to shoulder on the sofa, saying nothing, too scared to move. Nikki's face was tear-streaked, and the atmosphere in the room was painful and stagnant. I surveyed the chaotic situation, and suddenly it all made sense. Behind her, Nikki's husband, Sean, was seated, a loaded gun at his side. The smell of alcohol hung in the air around him.

"I didn't know whether to call you or the sheriff, Lisa. He's threatened to shoot all of us and then himself..."

I drew a long breath, knowing that the sheriff would have been the more appropriate choice. But I was here now, and could not leave, nor risk increasing the volatile dynamic that was reaching its pinnacle. Gently, as if waking a child, I began to speak.

"Sean," I almost whispered. "You have a disease, one that will kill you if you leave it untreated, as surely as cancer would... and this one may destroy your family, too..." I paused until his vacant eyes focused and registered comprehension. Every word I chose with the utmost care, and before the sun rose, the gun had been put away and help enlisted from the county's mental health department. Nikki called the next afternoon: "I didn't know you could be that strong," she said. I hadn't known it either.

I worked to dispel the frightening memory of this family's crisis by reassuring myself that as long as my husband, Seth, or I lived, our children would never face avoidable endangerment or jeopardy. With no alcoholism in the family and believing that we were not a part of that genetically vulnerable population, Seth and I could expect our children to be safe from disability or danger from intoxication.

What a fool I was to think I could safeguard my children so utterly or that it would be so simple. While I was not so naive as to believe that children were never sacrificed in contemporary society, I was naive to think that the tragedy was random, the result of illness and circumstance conspiring together. I had no reason then to imagine that I would soon, unwittingly and unknowingly, practice such profanity—sacrificing the well-being of my child. And that I would do so not because of any illness of my own, but because of a widespread and unrecognized sickness—the institutional and societal compulsion to inject susceptible infants with unseen but devastating mercury.

JANUARY 1996, RICHMOND, VIRGINIA

On a snowy day in January 1996, when the obstetrician placed our newborn son in his father's arms at the hospital, I was in no mood for love. Six hours of natural childbirth, the delivery, the exhaustion, the worry over how my two-year-old son, Adam, was... No, I had no time to fall in love. In fact, in my exhaustion I foreswore the possibility of any more children. I was done.

But then, my husband, Seth, entrusted the newborn infant into my embrace and I gently touched the baby's nose to my breast. He was docile, sweet, unassuming. The brilliant blue of his eyes upon their first opening would never fade, or so I thought. Here was as much magic and as great a miracle as I had ever hoped to see. I set my eyes on Wesley, and I vowed never to take them off.

The student nurse assigned to me on the maternity ward was fascinated that this thirty-year-old mother was an ordained minister. I shattered all the usual stereotypes of a clergyperson. No one ever first thought that I— a tall, slender woman with long wavy hair that bounced about the shoulders and who liked to giggle irrepressibly—was a clergyperson. Now, holding the child to whom I had given birth, I surprised strangers when I replied to their queries about my profession, saying I had been ordained six years earlier. Each time the student nurse came into the room to bring Wesley to me, or to return him to the nursery, she struck up a conversation.

"What did you do to have the perfect baby? He's so good."

I already took pride in the new nine-pound bundle that had so recently changed my life.

"I don't want him to be perfect. Just healthy and happy. That's all."

In that statement, had I already sought for too much, though I was blissfully unaware of the tragedy which had already begun.

The nurse, still searching to find her professional demeanor, addressed me again. "Lots of times, I worry about the babies. About whether or not they're getting the best. It's nice to see that this one is."

I smiled, in response, surprised by so searching a comment.

"I'll do everything I can to take care of him," I replied in answer, gently lifting the baby from the nurse's arms and holding him close.

He was perfect, still. The wondrous newness had not worn off my bewitching cherub-like son.

Summer 1997

Even the doctors in the pediatric office, who had seen little ones day in and day out for years, gawked at the rolling blue-green eyes, the neatly squared chin, and the plump cheeks that framed a precocious nose. After the doctor examined Wesley during each well-baby visit, the nurse took him out of the room while I spoke to the doctor about his progress. "Ninetieth percentile in height. Ninety-fifth percentile in weight." Wesley was thriving. "The picture of health, Ms. Sykes," said my old-school pediatrician.

"Is he still nursing?"

"No. He stopped at seven months."

"Why, that's just fine. Now, as for formula..."

The doctor went through his checklist. Wesley was crawling, saying "mamama" and "dadada" and giggling at his big brother's games of peek-a-boo. Wesley was so excited to see his father arrive home each day, and he ate only too well.

"You've got a fine boy there, Ms. Sykes..." I smiled in agreement.

"Now let me see, which shots is he due for today? He'll have..." The doctor began the list. "Any questions?"

"No."

"All right then, Ms. Sykes, just go down to the lab. Wesley is waiting there for you and his shots."

I wandered down the hallway with its bright and broad stripes of yellow, green, red and blue to discover Wesley was captivating several adults. I giggled.

"Come here, you flirt." I caressed his head.

"Oh, Ms. Sykes, if you could just sit him in your lap." I did so, dreading the prick of the needle for my son, but knowing it'd be over within only a second or two.

"Ms. Sykes, please initial right here, and then we can give Wesley his shots." I complied without question. Responsible parents, watchful parents, would do no less than get their children vaccinated against life-threatening infectious diseases.

"Now, there may be some redness, or swelling, or fever. If you see anything like that, just give him some Children's Tylenol, okay?" I nodded.

The nurse picked up the vial and inverted it. The syringe was inserted and a precise amount of clear liquid withdrawn into its cylinder. She then took the cotton swab and scrubbed a small patch of skin on Wesley's thigh. The air about this act was so keenly antiseptic. I winced as my baby boy was stuck with the needle. Two seconds. Maybe less. Wesley let out a wail of protest and a couple big tears. A cotton ball was placed over the site of the injection and secured with a purple Barney band-aid. Everything was clean, precise and efficient. Though my baby had cried, I felt an inner sense of security that Wesley would have the benefit of immunity from so many dreaded infectious diseases.

"It's going to be just fine," I cooed to Wesley.

I had been watching him resolutely. Protectively hovering, enjoying the inconvenience of a baby in my life. I reveled in his new discoveries. His coy smiles. His gentle soul. The special outfits for Christmas and Easter. His new-found abilities and newly-captured hearts. Wesley was a treasure, and each day was a joy. He played in the baby pool with the glee and abandon only a child knows. He crawled, and chased, and cuddled. Life seemed complete and perfect to me.

Wesley was slow in developing his language, but it was coming. My family had a history of late-speaking boys, especially on my father's side. Our pediatrician, when queried about it, replied with a laugh in his voice, "Why, Ms. Sykes, his big brother is doing all his talking for him!"

With reassurance given, I hadn't begun to worry until Wesley neared one-and-a-half. It seemed to me that I was hearing the few words he used regularly less and less. This social child, who loved to be adored, seemed suddenly stubborn about smiling. The portraits that had been so easy to make in his infancy and first year, now became difficult. He ate, but only soft foods, and ever since he had begun to walk at fourteen months, he didn't really stop to get into trouble. He just wandered and wandered happily about the house.

Oddly, he loved to be in his crib and was very contented there. I wrongly considered this a providential blessing because Seth was finishing his dissertation and each minute I could spare was spent editing his writing. I did ponder the fact that Wesley did not cry when Seth or I turned off the light in his room at night. I found this very strange because my eldest son, Adam, had been terrified of the dark at the age of one-and-a-half. Perhaps Wesley simply had a different, and more relaxed, disposition. Afterall, this seemed to be true of his teething also. When Wesley was getting a tooth through, he didn't seem to be in much pain. Adam, by contrast, had screamed and howled as if he were dying when his teeth broke through the gum. Occasionally this second son needed Tylenol to ease the pain of teething, but not very often.

OCTOBER 1997

Adam's fourth birthday party in 1997 was intended to be a brilliant celebration. A crystal clear October sky, the welcoming warmth of the sun, a park all to ourselves, and lots of little friends to bring presents and eat cake. As the children arrived, they played on the climbers and in the forts. Seth was supervising Wesley, now one-and-three-quarters years, amidst the kiddie climbers.

As I yelled that cake was ready, the children came running. Wesley, who was playing in the mulch beneath the playground equipment, angrily protested being removed from this diversion and bit his father hard. Wesley began sobbing and screaming and Seth literally had to hoist him up sideways so that Wesley's flailing arms and legs did not hit him in the face.

The party proceeded on, but from this day forward, Seth and I worried what might be wrong with our son.

I had watched over this child so carefully, how could it be that he seemingly had drifted away? One minute, there he is, right beside me, and I am the good mother. The next minute he disappears from sight as if he wandered into a cave, as black and vast as the darkest recesses of heaven's night. He is gone. At first, of course, I do not believe it. I dismiss the evidence. I reject it while tentatively holding onto the memory of a happiness that is already gone.

The cave is autism, and ten months after Wesley's first uncontrollable tantrum that October, he is diagnosed. He would soon cease to look at books and fall mute. He would become completely unpredictable, dropping to the floor and screaming without provocation, and more significantly, without warning. His eyes would become glazed and hollow, and despite my frantic searching, I would be unable to find the glint of recognition in his eye, the sacred spark of personality and spontaneity that had danced upon the brilliant blue and given me such joy. It was gone, and the vast emptiness which had replaced it was the measure of my sorrow.

I watched Wesley. This child, who had been the pride of his pediatrician, was now so sick. His skin had become sheet-white with pallor. His eyes were circled in purple and his ears were often bright red. The tale-tell hallmark of autism—chronic diarrhea—set in and lasted for a year. We gave up any attempt at toilet training.

Wesley wouldn't eat. I did not yet know why. He wouldn't look at toys or objects, just ceiling fans. Certainly, he seemed utterly deaf. But what devastated me to the point of being nearly inconsolable was the fact that Wesley would no longer permit me to touch him. I now had a child of two-and-a-half years who would not be rocked or held or caressed.

I could not bear it. And so I would wait... wait until Wesley fell deeply asleep. Because Wesley slept at odd hours, I did not dare intrude into his fragile slumber in the night, for upon waking he would scream and scream and scream. But occasionally, after one of those bad nights, he would fall asleep on the sofa, mid-afternoon, alone except for his tattered bear. And only then would I ease my body slowly, delicately, down beside his. I would slide one arm beneath his legs, the other, behind his back. Then, I would hoist him as softly as I could upon my lap, against my chest, and remember... remember he had not always been this way.

CHAPTER TWO

MERCURY

"My first reaction was simply disbelief, which was the reaction of almost everybody involved in vaccines," Halsey* says. "In most vaccine containers, Thimerosal is listed as a mercury derivative, a hundredth of a percent. And what I believed, and what everybody else believed, was that it was truly a trace, a biologically insignificant amount. My honest belief is that if the labels had had the mercury content in micrograms, this would have been uncovered years ago. But the fact is, no one did the calculation. "

"The Not-So-Crackpot Autism Theory" by Arthur Allen,
New York Times Magazine, November 10, 2002

OCTOBER 1998

WESLEY HAD NOT YET TURNED THREE YEARS-OLD. I FIRST HEARD THAT A LOCAL pediatrician, Dr. Mary Megson, theorized that children with autism were suffering a vitamin A deficiency and needed the fat soluble form of the vitamin, while sitting in a meeting of the Central Virginia Chapter of the Autism Society of America.[1] For three days thereafter, I gave Wesley the recommended daily allowance of vitamin A in cod liver oil. On the third day, Wesley was sitting aimlessly on the bottom step of the foyer stairs. I was hovering close

---

* Dr. Neal Halsey, Director, Institute for Vaccine Safety at the Johns Hopkins University, Former Chair of the Committee on Infectious Diseases of the American Academy of Pediatrics

by when the outlandish thought crossed my mind to simply speak his name. Not yell. Not scream. Almost whisper, in fact—whisper, in truth, for fear of being devastated one more time. "Wesley?" I cooed. "Wesley?" That was all. His head swung from center and down to right and up.

That week our home became a laboratory. Every move of his eyes, every positioning of his hands, every writhing tantrum upon the floor, I started writing in a log. Finally, I had so many minute but undeniable improvements recorded on paper that I could not keep a respectful distance or a polite silence from the unknown doctor whose protocol was helping my son. Without ever meeting or speaking to her, I was already convinced that this physician knew where the brightness in my son, the spark that until so recently shone in Wesley's eyes, had gone.

The road to accurate diagnosis and revelation began with Dr. Megson, a petite and insightful physician who was the Head Developmental Pediatrician at Richmond's Children's Hospital.

A "children's hospital", I thought as I looked up the number—a place I had assumed I would never need. I dialed the switchboard and got the receptionist.

"Excuse me," I said, "My name is Lisa Sykes. I just wanted to tell Dr. Megson how my son is doing with her treatment recommendations. His name is Wesley, and he has autism."

"Is he a patient of hers?" the receptionist asked.

"No," I gulped. "It's just that I heard about her new treatment," I stammered, "...and so I went ahead and started him on cod liver oil."

"And how is he?" a very intent voice asked from the other end of the line.

"He is better!" I burst out in declaration. "He is getting better!" I gasped, almost crying.

"Hold on please," said the receptionist, "I know Dr. Megson would like to talk with you."

I breathed in deeply, hoping Dr. Megson would listen to everything I had to tell her about Wesley.

"Hello," came an inquisitive, focused voice that sounded much too familiar and pleasant to belong to a medical specialist. "You have your son on cod liver oil? When did you begin?"

I told her, and began to recite a long litany of improvements.

"I'm going to call your pediatrician and have him order labs. Bring in the results. I want to see you and Wesley as soon as I am in my new office."

At that moment, I didn't know that Mary—a board certified pediatrician, Fellow of the American Academy of Pediatrics and mother of four children —was summoning the courage to walk away from her nine year-old medical practice and open an independent clinic. All I knew was that finally someone had told me something to do that had clearly helped my son.

As we finished our conversation, Dr. Megson did not give me her condolences for having a child with autism, as had other specialists. No, she had a radically different response. "Keep him on cod liver oil."

The hope in my soul now exploded upon my face in the first true smile I had felt cross my lips in months. My Wesley had a chance. Deeply thankful for a new-found taste of hope, I dared to wonder if Mary would be successful in finding what had disappeared? Could Mary, by restoring a simple vitamin to my son's body, rekindle the lively and sacred light that God had intended to illuminate his eyes?

January 1999

I realized at Christmas that my three-year-old didn't understand that presents were to be opened. Wesley's face filled with no joy to be given a gift; his hands moved in all directions, but with no intent to open the package. As the New Year began, my greatest gift was an appointment with the physician who had already helped my son without ever seeing him.

I had not quite sat down across the desk from Mary when she began asking me questions, not about Wesley but, instead, my family history.

"Do you have a family history of cancer?" Dr. Megson asked.

"Why is she asking me that?" I wondered in ignorance. It didn't matter; I would have told this woman my darkest confession, if I had one. Anything. Anything, I resolved.

"Yes, my father died of a rare form of leukemia at 44. It was called 'Hairy-cell.'"

Mary was visibly excited to hear my response. She picked up a medical reference book and flew through its pages.

"Here it is. Hairy-cell Leukemia. Inhibitory factor: vitamin A. You realize, Lisa, your father was also deficient? I bet I can tell you your father's favorite flavor of ice cream. Was it butter pecan?"

At that moment, I was ready to accuse Mary, the daughter of a Presbyterian pastor, of summoning spirits. Surely, it was not possible for her to diagnose my dead father's favorite flavor of ice cream when he had lain in his grave for nearly twenty years!

"How did you know that...?" I stammered, stunned.

"His body was craving the fat soluble forms of vitamins A and E, Lisa. You know what butter pecan ice cream has in it? The highest concentration of milk fat of any ice cream. It's loaded with fat-soluble, absorbable forms of vitamins A and E."

Though my father's waking mind had had no idea how sick and how deficient he was, his body did. He had craved butter pecan ice cream and now, two generations later, my son Wesley, who had inherited this genetic disposition, begged for fat-soluble vitamin A in cod liver oil, begged with hands that could not form the sign for "more" any faster, nor telegraph his demand any more repetitively, than he did.

"Anyone in the family with night blindness?"

"Yes, my mother and my grandmother. And my husband's mother has glaucoma."

"Anything else?"

"Well," I answered dutifully, "My brother Dan is red-green color blind. And Seth and I are night-blind, too."

"That's a vitamin absorption issue, too, Lisa."

I prayed for Mary. I prayed she could work a miracle on Wesley and every child that entered her office. In different ways, both our lives were about pulling children out of the darkness, she as a physician and I, as a mother and a minister. We both sought to renew the expressions and delight of childhood in children from whom autism had stolen these things.

With each consultation, this physician, who didn't mind if I called her "Mary," asked the most discerning questions about Wesley and the most unexpected questions about my father.

"Does Wes usually look at you sideways?"

"Yes."

"Could your father match his clothes or did they clash?"

"Mom matched them; Dad couldn't."

"Does Wes have chronic diarrhea?"

"Yes."

"Did your father have ulcers?"

"Yes, at age twenty, in college. We always assumed due to stress."

"Does Wesley spin?"

"Yes, and he is mesmerized by fans."

"Did your father have IBS?"

"What's IBS?"

"Irritable Bowel Syndrome"

"Oh, yes. So do my mother and brother."

"Does Wes crave milk or wheat?"

"Yes—milk, yogurt. He tantrums for them."

"Did your father have stomach troubles?"

I thought back. "He was always taking Gaviscon for his stomach. Is that important?"

"Does Wesley look out windows?"

"No."

"Did your father have unusual numerical or spatial abilities?"

I was lost for words. Again, how did she know that?

My father was a farm boy from Deshler, Ohio, whose numerical abilities propelled him to a remarkable career in the nation's capitol. Employed as a young man by a private engineering firm contracted to the United States Government, he had begun designing the guidance systems for the Atlas rockets. The federal officials with whom he collaborated and developed technology for national security purposes were so impressed with his abilities that they recruited him, and he quickly became one of this nation's leading counterintelligence engineers and scientists, receiving the Intelligence Medal of Merit by forty-two. By forty-four, he was dead.

Though he was stalwartly honest and ethical, throughout his life he was always accused of cheating at cards. Many people did not realize that Richard Courtney could remember every card played during a game.

My paternal grandfather was similar. Though he had no formal education, Paul Courtney was a Checker Champion in the state of Ohio. I never beat Grandpa Courtney at checkers. It was common knowledge that almost no one had. Grandpa, as if mystically, could see twelve moves ahead on the checkerboard.

"Spatial-numerical, Lisa." Mary said. "Your grandfather, your father. I'm telling you Wesley is incredibly gifted. You just can't see it yet."

"Yet..." I turned the word over in my mind, like a connoisseur moves a taste of wine upon his palate. "Yet..." Everyone else had told me to abandon all hope. All Mary did was fill me with it.

Only one mystery ever seemed to stump this physician who truly seemed to me a healer. "Mary, I need to show you something." I hugged Wesley to me, and pulled down his blue jeans. "Do you see it there on his right thigh?"

"Yeah, what's that?"

I laughed. "You're asking me? This odd patch of skin is thick and tough."

A patch of skin, two inches in diameter, high on Wesley's right thigh, was distinguishable by its stubborn texture.

Mary studied the skin somberly. "The texture is like orange-peel."

"Exactly," I concurred. "I don't know what to make of it."

"Neither do I," Mary admitted. It would take a year-and-a-half to decipher the stubborn patch of skin on Wesley's thigh, and many more years to resolve it.

SUMMER 1999

I sat once again in Mary's office as this physician poured hope and understanding, in equal portions, into my soul. The things she told me! Who ever heard of such absurdity? The gut as the second brain? Both formed of epithelial tissues that separated during the gestation of a child. News of this was only coming into medical textbooks in the 1990's.

"Lisa, you have a G-alpha-I protein defect," diagnosed the most gifted clinician I had ever met.[2] She didn't accuse me of being emotionally unavailable enough to cause my son's illness, as mothers of autistic children had been in the 1950's, and occasionally still were. She did not pity me or pronounce my child incurable. She did not discount my observations or suggestions, as had other physicians and textbooks.

"This protein defect produces a brilliant mind and a weak gut," Mary explained. "Wesley's gut is weak, and the tissue has become diseased. It can't absorb basic nutrients, especially water-soluble vitamin A, which we call palmitate. This form of vitamin A is about the only source of A in our diet. That's why Wesley craves the fat-soluble form of A in cod liver oil."

In a couple sentences, Mary explained to me what was to become the most fundamental truth of my universe.

"You know what vitamin A is?"

I stared stupidly ahead, eager to be educated out of my ignorance.

"It's the speech centers of your brain. It's the language. It's the social meaning. It's sensory input. It is the interconnections in the frontal lobe." There was a long pause. "It's the shots."

As Mary spoke these words to me, I did not yet appreciate the dogged courage by which she pronounced them.

"The shots?" I repeated, in a stunned and unsteady monotone.

"Yes, Lisa. Vaccines compromised Wesley's gut."

Slowly, I began to grapple with this revelation. Genetic vulnerability. Unforeseen consequences. Unpredictable reaction. I rubbed my head, which had suddenly begun to throb, with my hands. "The shots?"

Mary would eventually document and diagnose Wesley with deficiencies in Vitamin A, D, Calcium, Magnesium, Zinc, various enzymes, and with bacterial overgrowths of the gut, yeast overgrowths of the gut, viral infections, gluten intolerance and casein intolerance.[3] With each new identification of a breakdown in my son's body, I struggled with the knowledge that immunizations had created an unexpected catastrophe in Wesley's life.

During the next year and a half, I learned more and more from Mary's "biological approach to autism," and simultaneously, I learned more and more about vaccinations. I had not yet lost faith in them. I simply regarded Wesley as one of the rare and tragic failures of scientific know-how—that was, until one day, when Mary's office manager called me with an urgent request.

NOVEMBER 2000

Wesley had been in for another blood draw. I had lost count how many times his skin had been pierced by "butterfly" needles. In truth, I didn't want to count anymore. This had merely become a normal part of life, and I tried not to think about it.

The order Mary had written this time included seven different tests and would cost over seven-hundred dollars after insurance. But the results would cost more: they would cost me my faith in the American medical system and the country's national health agencies.

Mary had been out of town, speaking at a Defeat Autism Now! conference on her research. Mary's absence hadn't worried me. I knew I would hear from her office when the results came in. And I did.

But the message from Mary was unusual. "Lisa, Mary wants to see you in the office at 8:30 tomorrow morning."

"Okay," I answered, always grateful for the genuine care Mary had for my son.

"But what was this urgent," I wondered to myself, "that she must see me first thing tomorrow morning before the office opens?" The results had to be crucial, I knew, or she would not have demanded my presence so suddenly.

"I'll be there. I assume the blood came in."

"Yes," said the office manager, "Mary wants to go over the results with you in person."

Early the next morning, I sat in her waiting room, anxiously. What had Mary found?

Mary came out to the waiting room, a bounce to her step as always. "Come on back, Lisa. Sit down." She shut her office door behind us.

I noticed Mary's jaw was set. Something was very wrong.

From across her desk, I stared intently at Mary, one of the first physicians in the world to realize what physical anomalies to test for and to treat in autism, trying to anticipate what she found so difficult to utter. She grimaced, in utter disgust for the truth she had to tell me about my son.

"Lisa, he's toxic. I think he's toxic."

"Toxic? Toxic with what?" I stammered, more dumbfounded this time than any other before, when Mary had diagnosed what others couldn't see and deciphered what others had ignored.

"Mercury. He's toxic with mercury. If the shots hadn't had mercury in them, I bet he would have been fine." [4]

Mary was silent for a moment, waiting for my mind to comprehend what she had said.

"Mercury?" I repeated, hesitantly. "He's toxic from mercury in his baby shots?"

"The preservative used in them is half mercury. It's called Thimerosal. But there's something else, Lisa," Mary could see I was struggling with each word she pronounced.

"What more could there be, Mary?" My voice cracked.

"The shot that you were given when you were pregnant with Wesley for your Rh factor—it was loaded with mercury, too," Mary looked grim. "He was exposed to mercury before he was born; it crosses the placental barrier." [5]

I sat, speechless; my spirit reeling. Gently, Mary resumed the conversation. "Lisa, you know the patch on Wesley's leg?"

I looked up. "Yes?"

"It's a hypersensitivity reaction to mercury. Some of the metal pooled in the skin at the injection site. I was just reading about it in new medical science articles." [6]

My dazed mind finally settled on one horror and that one alone: my son had likely been poisoned by his baby shots. Worst of all, I had in ignorance held my baby down while he was repeatedly and regularly injected with enough mercury to devastate him for life. I was only in Mary's office for twenty or thirty minutes. But in that time, I aged. I grew old.

I spent the rest of the day going about my professional duties. I wept between hospital visits, phone calls and calendar appointments, when no one could see. That evening, I waited for Seth to return home from work. I had been married for eleven years to this quiet, strong Scot, whom I had met during a junior-year-abroad to the University of St. Andrews in Fife. After a fairy tale romance amid a medieval gray stone town on Scotland's east coast, we assumed when we married the years we spent having our family would be full of nothing but joy. Now, Seth struggled to take in the tragedy of what I was telling him as gently as I could.

"Seth, Mary thinks Wesley has been poisoned with mercury from his vaccines and my Rho(D) shot. No one ever told us, Seth. No one ever told us that there was mercury in those shots. If I had known there was a poison in them...." My voice trailed off momentarily, and my voice broke, as I fought back tears. I breathed in deeply, until the catch in my throat was gone.

"We'll learn soon enough if Mary's right. She's ordered tests to detect heavy metals, including mercury."

In order to test Wesley for heavy metals, Mary sent me to a specialist whose office was a half-an-hour drive away on the Southside of Richmond. The specialist was a distinguished man with a long-held belief that toxins were related to a myriad of chronic diseases. He regularly saw adult patients, but it was only after long conversations with Mary that he agreed to see her pediatric referrals. Under his direction we gave Wesley an initial dose of medication by mouth for three days and then collected a urine sample in a plastic container, which I drove to his office with the greatest of care as if it were a fragile piece of china. The nurse received it and prepared to ship it to the lab.

"We'll be in touch when the results are in, Reverend Sykes." I thanked her and drove home, willing the time to pass in an instant.

I picked up the phone, dialed the number and waited for her to answer. "Katherine, the test results are in. I can't get there today due to my work schedule and I'm desperate to find out the results. Could you run by the specialist's office and pick them up for me? I'll call and let them know you are coming."

In gaining the results, I hoped to regain peace of mind. What an immense favor I asked of Katherine this day. She agreed without a moment's hesitation.

For this reason, I prized her. Katherine had been one of the few friends from my old circle to weather the diagnosis and challenges of autism. She was beautiful, artistic and constant. Katherine's own son had struggled with epilepsy as a preschooler and, perhaps because of this, she offered no platitudes nor ever failed to inquire about my injured son. She lived some miles away from me but was always close in support and encouragement. As chance would have it, Katherine was also geographically close to the specialist who was overseeing Wesley's new test for heavy metals.

Within fifteen minutes, my cell phone rang. "Lisa, it's me. I have the results. They're in a sealed envelope. Do you want me to open them?"

"Yes, Katherine! Quick!"

"Okay, I've got them in my hand."

"Katherine, what do you see?"

"I see lots of dots... a line of them running off the page."

I knew from Mary that the succession of dots, in a straight line, was a reading. And a succession of dots running off the page was an unspeakably high reading. Dangerously high.

"Katherine, what word are the dots beside?"

"Mercury."

"That's it. That's my smoking gun. Katherine, Mary was right!"

When I sought to give Wesley's general pediatrician a copy of Wesley's lab report, he wouldn't see me. I was exasperated.

"Are you telling me that he could vaccinate my child with mercury-containing vaccines, but he is unwilling to discuss my son's off-the-chart mercury reading?"

Neither the receptionist nor the nurses behind her, who had become increasingly interested in our conversation, answered me.

"Do you see this?" I asked, handing over Wesley's dramatic test result. "I want to talk with him about this."

Though the nurses and receptionist eagerly received the lab report, no one moved to call Wes' pediatrician nor usher me back to his office.

Upset, I resigned myself to merely leaving the copy of the lab report at the front desk. I had no idea that as soon as I left this pediatrician would pick up the phone and call Mary.

"Mary, what the hell are you doing?" He gave her no opportunity to ask him what was so wrong. "I've got this mom, this autism mom, in my waiting room on the verge of tears! She starts talking about mercury, in the hearing of everyone in the room, and then hands my nurse this lab with a line running off the page! Do you know what that does for business?"

Mary did not know which she hated more: his complete disregard for a toxic result in one of his patients or his over-riding concern for his finances above all else.

Doctor's Data, Inc.
P.O. Box 111
West Chicago, Illinois 60186-0111
CALL TOLL FREE (800) 323-2784
Fax: (630) 587-7860
E-mail: inquiries@doctorsdata.com
Web site: www.doctorsdata.com
James T. Hicks, M.D., Ph.D., FCAP
Medical Director
CLIA ID # 14D0646470, Medicare Provider # 14849

Urine Toxic Elements

Lab #: 99678-0118		
Patient: Sykes Wesley	Age: 4	Sex: Male
Doctor:	Acct #: 18926	
c/o:	Collection Type: Random	
Collection Date: 5 Nov 2000	Time:	
Date In: 8 Nov 2000	Date Out: 9 Nov 2000	

ELEMENTS REGARDED AS TOXIC

Elements	Result (µg/g creatinine)	Reference Range* (µg/g creatinine)	Within Ref. Range	Elevated	Very Elevated
Aluminum	26	0 - 35	•••••••••••		
Antimony	.4	0 - 5	•		
Arsenic	98	0 - 100	•••••••••••••••		
Beryllium	< dl	0 - .5			
Bismuth	.8	0 - 30	•		
Cadmium	1.4	0 - 2	•••••••••••		
Lead	12	0 - 15	•••••••••••••		
Mercury	15	0 - 3	•••••••••••••••••	••••••••••••••••••	••••••••••••
Nickel	21	0 - 12	••••••••••••••••••		
Platinum	.2	0 - 2	•		
Thallium	.2	0 - 14	•		
Thorium	< dl	0 - 12			
Tin	5.5	0 - 6	••••••••••••••		
Tungsten	< dl	0 - 23			
Uranium	< dl	0 - 1			

OTHER TESTS

	Result (mg/dl)	Reference Range (mg/dl)	2 SD Low	1 SD Low	MEAN	1 SD High	2 SD High
Creatinine	43.4	21 - 76			•••		

Doctor's Data, Inc. urine lab report for Wesley at age four.

"The lab is a clinical result. I didn't order the result—just the test!"

"Well, Mary, stop ordering the damn tests! You're working the parents up and every time one of them brings their kid in for shots, I'm going to have to spend ages telling them not to worry about it! You keep slowing me down like this and I won't be able to afford my country club dues!"

Mary clenched her teeth. She was so sorry to have inconvenienced him!

From now on, she thought to herself, she would leave the toxic kids on the floor to writhe in pain so this physician could enjoy a nice Saturday morning on the green!

"I think you need to look at the mercury issue," Dr. Megson encouraged.

"I think you need to look at your medical license, Mary! You may find it's missing one of these days."

Compelled by her own convictions and clinical evidence, Mary would become more than a dissenter amidst the medical community. She would come to be considered a blasphemer. She would reveal to parents that their children had been injured, and could be injured again, by the mercury in the shots. To an institutional medical faith that tolerated no dissent, but rather demanded unquestioning assent to its central affirmation that all vaccines were safe and effective, Mary was now a threat. The faithful esteemed her as either lunatic or evil. The local pediatricians in Richmond, and many in the medical community where Mary taught at the Medical College of Virginia, ostracized her. At a great cost, weathering distress that was both professional and personal to her as a physician and mother, Mary learned to heal children discretely.

Miracle recoveries achieved by scientific breakthroughs were trumpeted in the medical community only when the illness healed was not one that the community itself had inflicted. In comprehending this, Mary became one of the first clinicians to begin a Copernican revolution in medicine. Though medicine instructs society that all vaccines encircle risk, protecting the public health, Mary was now convinced that risk encircled some vaccines, endangering the public health. She only hoped that, unlike Galileo, she would not end her professional career before an inquisition defending herself as an apostate from the one "true" faith.

DECEMBER 2000

With Christmas approaching, despite my busy pastoral calendar, I made time for yet one more unusual phone call to a perfect stranger.

"Hello. I'd like to speak with Mr. Cliff Shoemaker, please," I requested, seeking to be as articulate and calm as I could.

"Speaking," replied Cliff. His voice was deep, steady, and inviting.

"Mr. Shoemaker, I understand you are quite expert in legally representing children with vaccine injuries."

Cliff replied, a modest demeanor in his voice, "Well, thanks. It's been my area of specialty for years." Cliff was the leading attorney in the nation advocating for injured and damaged children in a special vaccine court established by the National Vaccine Injury Compensation Program.[7] "Call me Cliff. What did you say your name was?"

"Lisa Sykes. I have a son, Wesley, who is almost five. He has been diagnosed with mercury-toxicity, Cliff. His mercury reading is literally off the chart!"

"Oh? I'm not sure I understand, Lisa, why you are calling me about this?"

I drew a breath, and dared to propose the link.

"A lot of people—physicians, even—Cliff, are beginning to realize, you see, that the preservative used in the immunizations is mercury-based, and the amount of mercury in even one shot, never mind dozens, is well in excess of safety guidelines."[8]

Cliff was silent, considering. There had been a steep rise in vaccine injury cases, beginning in the 1990's and parallel to the increased mercury load in baby shots. Mine was not the only call he had received from a parent about this issue. Already, Cliff had begun to wonder if these things could be connected.[9]

"What I want is a recall of these shots, Cliff, before more children have to suffer the way Wesley has. It seems to me that litigation would be one of the best routes to both publicizing the problem and stopping it."

"Well, that depends, Lisa. I have a lot of questions."

"Surely. I can appreciate that. But would you be willing to investigate what I'm saying? Wesley's treating physician is Dr. Mary Megson, right here in Richmond. I'm sure she'd be willing to speak with you."

"Okay, Lisa. I know the best vaccine experts in the field. Let me begin by consulting them, and see what they have to say. That seems like the next step to me."

I did not know that the vaccine experts with whom Cliff would consult would be Dr. Mark Geier and his son David. Mark, a physician, geneticist and vaccine researcher, had led the fight to replace the whole cell pertussis vaccine (DTP) with the safer acellular form of the pertussis vaccine (DTaP), a change which saved thousands of children from permanent brain damage.[10]

"Thanks, Cliff." I breathed a sigh of relief. "Oh, one more thing. I'm sending a letter out to notify some of the federal officials whom I hope will help. It will have a copy of Wesley's lab with the mercury result. Can I copy you on it?"

"Sure. I'd like to see it. Thanks."

I was pleased. Cliff had not shared my sense of urgency, but of course, he was not yet convinced. What was important is that he seemed genuinely interested and open-minded.

When I got off the phone, I pulled up the letter I had just finished composing on my computer. I didn't want to send it to the Centers for Disease Control and Prevention (CDC), nor to the Food and Drug Administration (FDA), since I credited them with approving products that caused my son's disorder. Having learned that the Occupational Safety and Health Administration (OSHA) was exceedingly strict on exposure issues, I chose to write them instead and only copy the CDC and FDA. So, to a copy list which included these agencies, my senators, congressmen, and governor, as well as the American Medical Association, I now added one more name: Mr. Cliff Shoemaker. I printed the letters, and had them in the mail that afternoon. With them, and Wesley's toxicology lab, I enclosed my hopes that someone would help us.

CHAPTER THREE

CHELATION

"Industrial poisoning with mercury and its derivatives is quite frequently reported in the literature (Giglioli 1909; Hamilton 1949; Hunter 1940). It is as old as the Roman Civilization when mercurialism was known as the 'disease of slaves' because it was a common incident among slaves working in the Spanish mines of Almaden. The poisoning was so terrible that only criminal slaves were made to work in these mines."

Mercury and Calcium Excretion in Chronic Poisoning
with Organic Mercury Compounds,
Suad Al-Kassab M.Sc., Ph.D., and Najat Saigh, B. Sc.,
Journal of the Faculty of Medicine, Baghdad (1962)
Vol. 4 (N.S.), No. 3

Early Winter 2001

It was perfectly white as far as the eye could see. Wesley, whom I held in my arms, sensed he stood at the brink. There at the edge, where identifiable outlines and hues disappeared, he clung to me with his arms about my neck and his legs wrapped about my waist. His physical proximity, his closeness, his touch, was so unusual in these days. When I did experience them, it was because Wesley was experiencing great fear. Too, he was cold. He was cold because he was naked. And he did not understand how his mother could be so cruel.

There were tears on my cheeks. Just when I thought I'd become accustomed to them, the torrent seared my face again. I had always planned to be so happy, and such a good mother. And now, I knew, in these moments, I only terrified my child. Truth be told, I terrified myself also. I tried too hard to comprehend the enormity of my life, lived its length, with Wesley's autism. I tried to comprehend the daily struggle to remain sane while my child suffered sporadic and indescribable agony. Autism instructed my soul in desperation. In those moments, I failed to be the sum of my strengths and fought not to become less than the total of my weaknesses. There were times I wondered if my spirit and mind could withstand the strain. There were times that Wesley's panicked reactions convinced me that neither of us could. This was one of those moments.

I chastised myself for this dark reverie, and returned to the matter at hand. I reached up and pried Wesley's arms from around my neck. He made no sound, but desperately fought to sustain his grip. I could not remove his legs from around my waist, for every time I did, his arms lurched back around my neck, but I was determined to get him off of me. I had to get him to let go. It had to be done. And quaking, I resolved that it would be done.

His panic, like so many other things, was an enigma. I was oblivious to the oblivion he perceived. I knew only that I had one immutable goal in mind, for this cataclysmic moment, and that was to give my autistic son a bath. After Seth and I finally succeeded in wrestling our son into the tub, we sat upon the ceramic tile, restraining Wesley by the shoulders to keep him in the water, and stared at each other, exhausted. How could it be that giving our son a bath had become so impossible? We did not yet understand the terror now in Wesley's soul because we had not yet grasped the havoc that mercury had wrought in his brain.

"Children can heal from things that adults can't. This is scientific fact." Seeking to capture the gaze in Wesley's distant blue eyes, I remembered these words. I learned about the astounding ability of children to heal from injury when a pediatric oncologist lectured to me and my fellow chaplain interns during my residency at St. Luke's Episcopal Hospital in Houston, Texas, in 1988.

"If you remove a part of a child's lung," I recalled the specialist saying, "It will regenerate. If you do the same with an adult, it won't." Always,

I had marveled at that revelation. I never expected, however, that this medical lesson would become my source of hope as I sought, years later, for reassurance against my own son's catastrophic diagnosis.

I wondered to myself, "And what about the brain? If you damage the brain with poison, can it regenerate?"

Once Mary made her diagnosis, once she boldly decided to risk her standing and her medical career to speak the truth to me, the course of treatment before us was clear. Wesley's body had been injected with poison. It would remain in his body, wreaking havoc, unless Seth and I chose to treat him, and pull it out with chemical compounds designed to bind to the mercury. The process of extracting it was called chelation.

Seth and I gained courage by researching the history of lead poisoning that resulted from paint only decades earlier. The agent used to detoxify a child of lead was the same agent used to detoxify a child of mercury: DMSA or meso 2,3-dimercaptosuccinic acid.[1] It was a white viscous liquid packaged in a capped measuring syringe. Wesley would have to take one syringeful of the foul-smelling slime every four hours by mouth and around the clock, for three days at a time. The goal of this dosing schedule was to keep the chelating agent level in the blood, so that the mercury, once captured by the DMSA, did not have any opportunity to retreat and hide once again in the tissues until the cycle was complete.

For three days we would dose Wesley with DMSA and then for four days we would let him and his weary body rest, while replenishing his stores of zinc, iron, magnesium and the other good metals, with supplements. Every month we would check his mineral levels and run a complete blood count and liver enzymes to make sure we were chelating him safely.

The coordination of schedules and dosing was made more precarious by the fact that the medicine had to be kept cool. Our friends and family began to expect us to place a zip-lock bag with a measuring syringe, filled with a white suspension, in their refrigerators when we came for long visits. Seth and I were continually checking with each other to make sure each dose had been delivered and confer on where the next one would be stored.

As we began the treatment, I watched my son intently for any sign, any reassurance, that what we were undertaking might improve his condition.

The sign for which I eagerly waited appeared quite quickly. It was Wesley's third round of DMSA. I was in Wesley's bedroom helping him get dressed one morning shortly after we had begun the treatment.

"Seth, come here now!" I shouted to my husband. When Seth arrived in Wesley's bedroom, he found me kneeling behind our little boy, my fingers feeling the backs of his knees.

"What is it?" Seth asked me.

"See for yourself," I answered, eager for his opinion, before prejudicing him with my own.

"Huh," replied Seth, "What is that?"

"I need to go back through my articles, Seth. If I remember correctly, in some children, this is a sign of metal coming out," I replied.

I referred to the red rash that had appeared vividly on the backs of Wesley's knees. Tiny raised red bumps, about a millimeter across. Thirty to forty had appeared on the back of his right knee, and a lesser number on the left. Wesley was in the second day of a three-day cycle of DMSA, and I was certain that the chelation and the rash must be related.

"Seth, would you go to the kitchen and get me one of the kits for urinary heavy metals?"

Seth fetched the kit. We looked at each other apprehensively while catching Wesley's urine sample in a white plastic container. I rushed to complete the paper work and called FedEx to transport it to Illinois, where it would be analyzed by a laboratory called Doctor's Data International (DDI). We would wait more than two weeks for the result, which, I prayed, would be life-changing for me and life-saving for Wesley.

More mercury. The results from DDI showed a high level of mercury in Wesley's urine. This time the line did not run off the page, but it still extended past the reference range, and the elevated range, into the final column indicating the need for alarm. I felt compelled to document Wesley, his treatment and his results, now more than ever. I did not yet know how important this would be. Fortuitously, among pediatric patients being chelated for mercury, this blue-eyed child, whose gaze still stole hearts even through the haze of autism, was uniquely consistent. Every time the DMSA pulled a significant quantity of mercury from his tissues, the rash would appear on the backs of his knees. Every time the rash would appear, I would catch a urine sample from my son and send it for toxicology testing. Consistently, these samples showed high levels of mercury. So, unlike so many other parents, who did not know when their children were dumping mercury because they had no outward sign, I always knew when Wesley was. Because of Wesley's rash, the luxury of good insurance, and an amazingly supportive spouse, I amassed a comprehensive clinical record on Wesley's poisoning.

For fourteen straight months, I would watch the soft underneath of Wesley's knees, taking urine samples whenever the red rash appeared. By the end of this stretch, Wesley would become, perhaps, the best documented subject in the nation. He was verifiable proof that at least some children diagnosed with autism were actually suffering from mercury poisoning.

"Mary," I asked, seeking insight I did not have, "why the knees? Why is the rash on the back of the knees?"

"Your joints, Lisa, are full of metallithionine, the substance in the body that naturally binds metals. Wesley probably had a huge concentration of mercury in his knees."

And with the revelation that mercury had been concentrated in Wesley's knees, I became enlightened. I now theorized that Wesley had stopped jumping by his third birthday not because his brain had malfunctioned in some inane neurological mystery, but because his knees were full of mercury. Likely, the pain in his knees was more than arthritic for Wesley.

In the brightness of memory, I could still see my new son in his "Johnny Jump-up," a cloth seat secured by a spring to the frame of my living room door. Wesley's toes barely touched the ground, and when they did, he would leap back up, his knees would bend and his legs would lift and this enchanting little boy thought that he could soar. His light-filled eyes laughed and a smile burst across his face time and time again.

Now, Wesley's knees didn't work. He could no longer jump, and didn't even seem to remember how. Ordinary representatives of the medical community had previously informed me that this regression was neurological in origin, and ultimately "genetic." They never told me whether this degeneration could be due to the deterioration of synapses, or the demyelination of neural connections, or the inability of the central nervous system to carry a signal, or the breakdown of the muscles themselves—all the effects of mercury being deposited in my son's joints. They did not tell me, because they had no idea why Wesley could not jump, and I did not challenge them. Only now did I begin to understand, as ignorance gave way to understanding and understanding to hope, with each dump of mercury from Wesley's brain and body.

Words failed me as I took my five-year-old by the hand and helped him onto an exercise trampoline—hoping with all my heart just to see those knees bend in play, as they had so often before, when this child was well. With prompting, Wesley jumped, but only as a perfunctory and mechanical exercise. He would eventually regain both the innate ability to jump and the joy in experiencing it, but only after many hours in the day, many days in the week, many weeks in the year, and precious years from his childhood, spent in occupational and behavioral therapy.

Spring 2001

"What's that smell?" said the smartly dressed mother as she entered into the preschool class to pick up her child. The noon bell had rung, and parents and toddlers were everywhere. Preschool had begun for the spring.

"I don't know, but it really is disgusting, isn't it?" replied another women, a child on her hip.

They both looked around the room for the source of the piercing and acrimonious odor but could find no suspicious offender, no potent and rancid object, to credit the smell. They shrugged their shoulders and left the room.

Amazing that this room, some thirty feet long and eighteen feet wide, was filled so utterly with this stench, and yet no one, except the preschool teacher and I, knew from where it came.

"Lisa, it really is quite pungent," Denise said in her always quiet, always calm voice. She had been Wesley's shadow for two years of preschool inclusion. Thankfully, Seth and I had registered him, prior to knowing anything was catastrophically wrong with our son's neurological development, at Sabot School, a Montessori preschool in Richmond's West End. In fact, this treasure-trove of learning was actually located on the first floor of my church. Had Wesley been registered at any other school, and had the school been notified of his diagnosis just before the fall session began, he would have certainly been turned away.

Not so at Sabot. With a teaching staff that sported Masters Degrees in Childhood Education and Special Education, and a director, Dr. Irene Carney, who had done her Ph.D. in Early Childhood Development, Sabot was absolutely equipped to welcome my child with autism. From the start, all the Sabot staff were extremely supportive, and Denise, most of all.

"It's a dream come true, really, being able to work with Wesley in this setting," she told me. I thought at times that Denise, the mother of three daughters, had found a long-lost son in Wesley, and I was eternally grateful. Denise's special education training and her gentle, intuitive ways enabled Wesley to cope with Sabot School and Sabot School to cope with Wesley.

When Wesley had tantrums, falling on the floor and screaming and biting, Denise would calmly wrap Wesley in a blanket and softly, repetitively, rub his back. When he was obsessively preoccupied with sand, she would introduce other children into the sandbox so that his entranced-mind might be liberated, if only momentarily, by the intruding fingers of another five-year-old intent upon building a castle. Denise seemed to know how to cope with every circumstance, except perhaps this: how to explain the odor that emanated from Wesley's diapers.

And that smell was not caused by his eating cream cheese or onions the night before. It had nothing to do with what he digested during the day, but what had been injected into him in his infancy. All that mercury. As others wondered about the putrid metallic odor aloud, I silently came to realize that my precious child was an industrial disaster. His small body had been infused with so much mercury before and after birth that, as Seth and I treated him with medications to pull it out, he smelled like a power plant on a polluted river. Simply the odor of the urine in his diaper, from a three-hour morning at preschool, made bystanders choke. I might have found the smell simply repugnant, as did the other parents, if I had not known from where it was coming. Realizing it was pouring out of my child, however, I found it sickened me to the center of my soul. In the intensity of that odor, I could measure the strength of the toxin that assailed my son's body and spirit.

There was no doubt, this particular cycle of chelation, this dumping of metals, especially mercury, was worse than most. There was the odor, of course. But this time, the odor not only nauseated others, but also incapacitated Wesley. For three days in May, he stayed home from school and lay either on his bed or on the floor, not wanting to eat or move. The odor was as strong as I had ever known it to be. I gently ran my hand over his forehead, brought him water, and gave him children's Tylenol. He whined and whimpered and slept. I took off work, as I had so often, and stayed by his side.

After three days, the cycle ended. After one full day without medication, Wesley's head finally lifted from its pillow and a hint of his sweet smile showed about the corners of his lips. The return of that enchanting smile caused tears to gather in the corners of my eyes. With my help, Wesley got up slowly and came down the stairs. It was then I knew something had changed.

Instead of two-footing the stairs, allowing one foot to catch up with the other before advancing another step, my son was alternating his feet upon the stairs, one step at a time. Suddenly, my child was descending the stairs as I did, and as he never had before. He was certain of his feet, and poised with his balance, and I was dumbfounded by the change.

This first revelation was followed by a second, while Wesley and I sat on the front porch relaxing after our ordeal. Wesley loved to sit out on the rocker in the breeze, whatever the season, and so I took him there, hoping the caress of spring would soothe him. When Wesley sat down, this autistic child, who had always had a bewildered look on his face, seemed to gaze with clarity at the world around him and at me. I puzzled and puzzled over what had changed, unable to discern at first what was so markedly different and yet ironically, too, so subtle. It was then that I realized: Wesley's pupils had contracted in the bright sunlight. All of the months and years in which he had carried such a horrific amount of mercury, his eyes had registered his toxification by their dilation, a clinical symptom of mercury-poisoning. Mercury had kept the pupils from shutting down, so that Wesley's eyes could not limit the amount of light that entered on a bright sunny day. Is it any wonder that he would sometimes fall to the ground and scream when moving from inside to outside? At times like that, I had been powerless to stop the light from momentarily and painfully blinding Wesley.

But now, in the softness of full daylight, Wesley did not construe the sun as his enemy any longer. Instead, the light gave impetus for his eyes to react as they always should have, and only now could, because a substantial amount of mercury had been pulled during those three long days. Rapidly, as I revisited the changes in Wesley's pupils and his newfound ability to descend the stairs normally, and realized that my son was better able to see, I became convinced that a significant amount of mercury had settled in the optic center of Wesley's brain. I guessed, and Mary would later confirm, what Wesley had regained was his depth perception. How long had it been since the world made any visual sense to my son? Did the mercury from the Rho(D) shot lodge in his brain before birth, corrupting his vision in infancy? Or did the immunizations, with their additional and excessive loads, overcome his ability to see normally while he was a toddler? Unable to answer these questions, I set my jaw, and clenched my fists in an anger that, like the mercury, was quiet yet catastrophic.

It had never occurred to me that my son was effectively blind. After all, his eyes moved intentionally. In fact, they seemed perpetually and futilely to search and seek for something indefinable. But the information they captured, when sent to the brain, was received by tissues tormented by the mercury. Depth perception had disappeared from Wesley's field of vision. Though his eyes might see, his brain could not perceive his surroundings with any accuracy at all. The world was, for Wesley, a maniacal fun house. Worse than a hall of mirrors, what Wesley saw in his field of vision as he took each step up to this point in his illness, was precipice and abyss and blizzard. His inability to see normally, and the terrifying nature of what he did perceive, caused him to bump into walls and stumble down stairs.

I chastised myself for not understanding how my child had struggled to process the outside world until this dramatic change. As the exiting mercury vacated some of the visual areas of Wesley's brain, I could perceive that they began to function once again. The change in Wesley's pupils and his new ability to transition into the sunshine, walk down stairs, and suddenly match a picture to its corresponding 3D object during therapy, might have seemed dramatic, in and of themselves, had it not been for the bath.

Had I only understood that Wesley had no depth perception from the time of his diagnosis to this point, I would have known why he hugged the faucet once Seth and I finally succeeded at wrestling him into the tub. It was the only violation of the white, the only beacon in the storm. Shiny and gray, the stainless steel faucet protruded in stark contrast to the white abyss of the fiberglass shower. In order to have this only point of reference to secure him, Wesley had to be within two inches of it. Therefore, he would plaster his back against the tub directly beside the faucet, and refuse to move anywhere. To wash his hair, I had had to lean across the tub and wedge my hand between his head and the white tub wall. I had no idea that for Wesley, the spigot was a flag in the blizzard and a meager promise of return from a world of white infinity. That faucet was Wesley's only hope of ever finding his way back to a place where there were shapes and colors, however odd they might seem to him.

At last, I knew why this naked child clung to me as if he would die, should I let go of him, whenever I stubbornly tried to place him in the bath water. My precious child, my second son, thought his mother was about to pitch him into a chasm when I, instead, was only trying to get him in the tub. He thought I was seeking to physically cast him off, and away, and out, and down, into a white void that had no end. For me to hold Wesley by the side of the white fiberglass tub, I now realized, was for me to dangle him over the sheerest cliff on Mt. Everest. Wesley feared for his life, convinced that if he let go of me, he would fall for an eternity through the nearly seamless and smooth whiteness. And in the face of such terror, he could utter not one single cry, nor explain to us the horror that gripped him, just as he gripped me.

Now, after an unusually large dump of mercury in Wesley's urine, Seth and I watched in amazement as our little boy sat gleefully in the tub and splashed in the water as he once had before, in infancy, before mercury fully invaded his brain.

CHAPTER FOUR

AN UNEXPECTED INVITATION

"We said this before you got here, and I think we said this yesterday, the point of no return, the line we will not cross in public policy is to pull the vaccine, change the schedule. We could say it is time to revisit this, but we would never recommend that level. Even recommending research is recommendations for policy. We wouldn't say compensate, we wouldn't say pull the vaccine, we wouldn't say stop the program."

(IOM Transcript, p. 74)

—Kathleen Stratton, Ph.D., Study Director,
Immunization Safety Review Committee,
and Member of the Institute of Medicine Staff

"…we are not ever going to come down that it is a true side effect…"

(IOM Transcript, p. 97)

—Marie McCormick, M.D.,
Committee Chair of the Immunization Safety Review Committee and
Sumner and Esther Feldberg Professor of Maternal and Child Health
at the Harvard School of Public Health

(Drs. Stratton and McCormick speaking to the committee members
whose mission was to evaluate the possibility of a link between
mercury and autism.)

January 12, 2001, Vol. 4 (N.S.), No. 3

APRIL 2001

FROM AN ENVELOPE, EMBOSSED WITH THE LOGO OF THE DEPARTMENT OF HEALTH and Human Services and stamped with the words, "To Protect the Public Health," I pulled Dr. Kathryn Zoon's reply. Dr. Zoon, Director for the Center for Biologics Evaluation and Research for the FDA, whose responsibilities included vaccine safety, had been given the mundane task of writing to a mother who contacted OSHA claiming her son had been poisoned by mercury in his medicines.

"What's wrong?" Seth and I had been married for twelve years. He could always tell when I was upset.

"Listen to this! Here is what Zoon says: 'All vaccines licensed in the United States by the Food and Drug Administration have been demonstrated to be safe and effective.'"[1] My voice grew louder, "But on the next page, get this: '...there are no existing guidelines for safe exposure to ethylmercury, the metabolite of thimerosal.'"

I exclaimed to Seth. "Even though she admits they have no idea how much ethylmercury is safe, the vaccine which contains it is! If no guidelines even exist for safe exposure, Seth, how can she say a vaccine containing it is safe?! It's as if the toxicity of ethylmercury suddenly vanishes just because you put it in a vaccine! I don't think so!"

Seth momentarily wondered if he should try to assuage me, and then thought better of it. The more I read, the more furious I became.

"Seth, Dr. Zoon does not declare mercury safe here. What she says instead is that 'we believe that the data are not sufficient to support the causal relationship between ethylmercury exposure and autism.' I think 'belief' is my area of expertise. She's supposed to have science, quantifications, and safety tests, for Pete's sake! Now, do you think just because someone is unable to show how a substance is causing harm, that this proves it's safe to inject into our son and millions of other children?"

Quickly, I identified a strategy that I disdained even more than outright denial, a strategy I would confront time and time again as federal officials sought to protect the vaccine program over the children to whom these vaccines were administered. Unable to declare a known poison, neurotoxin and carcinogen safe for injection into pregnant women and children, they would instead protest that "there was no evidence of harm." I hadn't asked for evidence of harm; I had proof of that incarnated in my son. What I had asked for was proof of safety.

I fired off a rebuttal to Dr. Kathryn Zoon that was comprised of the most articulate, carefully expressed anger I had ever summoned and constrained by ink to a page:

"You suggest there is a ten-fold safety factor built into EPA standards for exposure to mercury. How misguided that we have violated those very standards 30 to 100 fold with our newborn infants. My masters degree is in divinity, and yet I can see the folly of injecting such a large amount of neurotoxin into children who have not developed fully formed blood-brain barriers. It is a fact that a certain percentage of the population is mercury sensitive. Shall we just write this percentage of children off in the face of an unsound and antiquated medical practice that has the favor of the pharmaceutical industry? ...The only ones I pity more than these children devastated in infancy are those on whose watch this indescribable tragedy has occurred. Yours Sincerely..."

SUMMER 2001

"Lisa, this is Dr. Megson's office. We just got a call from the Food and Drug Administration wanting to know about Mary's work."

I breathed in deeply and hesitated, almost unable to breathe out. I knew immediately—the educated anger in my letter had been felt by someone federal.

The office manager continued on, striving to be as matter-of-fact as possible. "Mary's wondering who did you write, and what did you say?"

I gulped. "I'll bring the letter to you first thing tomorrow."

Before Mary's practice received patients the next morning, I entered the office, a copy of my letter in hand.

"Come on back," Mary said characteristically, summoning me from the waiting room back into her office. "Did you bring me the letter?"

Mary grinned, but there was a hint of misgiving in her eyes.

"Here it is, Mary," I responded, waiting nervously to see how she would react. Without Mary, I would never have known what to say to the authorities. But what I had now divulged to them in my correspondence, regarding

Wesley's diagnosis and lab results, implicated Mary as a physician who questioned the safety of the vaccines. It also identified her as a doctor who was labeling innocuous "autistic" children as "mercury-toxic," and as such, this physician and the children she had begun treating threatened the legitimacy and authority of the Food and Drug Administration. Identifying Wesley and his injury to the FDA meant identifying Mary as well—the cod liver oil, the chelation, Wesley's improvements. Because I knew that my advocacy could imperil Mary professionally, I had striven to protect this woman of keen intellect and courage by the carefully chosen words and sentences of my letter.

Sitting at her desk, Mary's eyes moved back and forth across each line with haste. She read about one half of the first page in silence, then looked up and said, "Who did you send this to?"

I responded, "CDC, FDA, Health and Human Services, American Medical Association, American Academy of Pediatrics..."

"Oh my God..." was all Mary could say. At least, at first.

"Mary?" I was desperate to hear more and fearful that I had been too strident. "O Mary, I hope I haven't created problems for you with this!"

I waited tensely for Mary to summon her next words.

"You know, it's been hard, Lisa. Day after day, I keep seeing the kids we've hurt with the shots come into the office, and I'm only seeing such a small percentage. And they just keep coming. And, you know, we're getting them better."

Mary became energized. She was speaking more and more quickly.

"Yes, Mary, I know."

"No one from the government has paid any attention before. But now, they've called because they want to know about my research. Lisa, I want you to come with me to the Institute of Medicine on July 16 in Boston."

From being panicked to perplexed, I was now the one who was stunned. I had no idea what the Institute of Medicine (IOM) was.

"It's a part of the National Academy of Sciences, Lisa. As a committee, the Institute of Medicine is the highest federally-recognized advisor to the nation on matters of medicine. The Institute of Medicine is examining Thimerosal safety at its next meeting. You have to come. You will travel with me. I want you to tell them about what we're doing to make the kids better."

I felt completely out of my depth, but nodded anyway, relieved that Mary felt victorious rather than vilified. Mary continued on while I just stood there, dumbfounded.

"Hey, how's Wesley?"

JULY 15-18, 2001

Sunday night, after arriving in Boston and checking into our room, Mary and I unfurled Wesley's chelation chart. Upon this banner-sized chart was a graph recording the amounts of mercury Wesley had excreted throughout nine months of chelation. With points plotted originally in pencil, and connected with a line I had drawn, the information on my homemade graph was not professionally presented, but it could not have been more powerful. The reference line, denoting "safe" exposure levels for adults, ran parallel to the horizontal axis on the graph, and was only two inches above the graph's bottom line. The peaks which were overlaid upon this graph, denoting laboratory results for Wesley's urinary mercury excretion levels, formed a series of hills and valleys, some nearly extending off the top of the chart.

"It doesn't stand out enough, Lisa. Here—here's my yellow highlighter," said Mary. Together, we traced the mercury line in fluorescent yellow ink.

Mary had given me a greater charge than this. I was to speak tomorrow during the public comment section of the meeting. Mary had entrusted to me the responsibility of describing her Vitamin A protocol and presenting the evidence that Wesley was part of a subpopulation, vulnerable to the mercury in his vaccines.

"There, that's better!" Mary declared. "Hey, you need to eat! Something with lots of protein!"

I laughed. I knew Mary was referring to my pregnancy. My third baby was due in December. Had it not been for Mary and her reassurance, I would never have attempted so daring a feat as to believe I could have a healthy child after autism had beset Wesley. Because of what Mary had taught me, however, I had the blessing of knowing I could protect my unborn child from the mercury that had stricken Wesley. I knew to do this, but on this night before the IOM meeting, I wondered how many others did not?

That night we dined with Lyn Redwood and Sallie Bernard of the Coalition for SafeMinds, the parent-led Sensible Action For Ending Mercury Induced Neurological Disorders.[2] Lyn and Sallie were two mothers in the first generation of parents who identified their children, diagnosed with autism, as mercury-toxic. By their conversation, I knew both were steeped in an extensive knowledge of vaccines and Thimerosal. As we chatted over dinner, we spoke of disability, recovery, and the need to end "mercurial" medicine in order to protect children who, unlike ours, had not yet been injured by mercury.

The next morning, the gathering in the ballroom of the Charles Hotel in Boston seemed historic. The placard at the door read:

NATIONAL ACADEMY OF SCIENCES

INSTITUTE OF MEDICINE

IMMUNIZATION SAFETY REVIEW COMMITTEE

THIMEROSAL-CONTAINING VACCINES AND

NEURODEVELOPMENTAL OUTCOMES

PUBLIC MEETING

MONDAY, JULY 16, 2001

THE CHARLES HOTEL

ONE BENNETT STREET

CAMBRIDGE, MASSACHUSETTS.

The room was full to capacity and many stood along the wall. Among those in attendance were federal officials, including Dr. Robert Chen, Director of Vaccine Safety, from the Centers for Disease Control and Prevention, as well as doctors, lawyers, parents and some media. Despite the formality of the meeting, the room was electric. This session of the Institute of Medicine was called to order by its chair, Dr. Marie McCormick, the Sumner and Esther Feldberg Professor of Maternal and Child Health at the Harvard School of Public Health. Acknowledgements were made, and the presentations began.

Although I had a degree in theology, not toxicology, I could follow a high percentage of what was being said. Each time a presenter stated, "I think the level of mercury is possibly too high for this particular population," meaning pregnant women, neonates, infants and children, Mary's eyes and mine would confer in anticipated victory. We glanced at each other with frequency as the day progressed.

In the early afternoon, Dr. Thomas Verstraeten presented his research findings. As soon as he began speaking, I instinctively disliked the man.

At first, I did not know why. But the longer he talked, the more reasoned my aversion to him became. This scientist, it seemed, had designed a study purportedly to discern any correlations between mercury exposure through vaccines and neurodevelopmental disorders, especially autism, in children. At the beginning of his presentation, Verstraeten announced, "First, I should mention that as of eight a.m. European time I have been employed by a vaccine manufacturer. That means since two a.m. American time. Of course I did not make this presentation between two a.m. this morning and now, so this presentation is work that I did while I was at the CDC as an Epidemic Intelligence Service officer, and it was solely funded by the CDC."[3]

As he spoke, I felt stunned. The author of the CDC's primary study on the issue had transited through the revolving door between government and industry even before he addressed the Institute of Medicine. The conflict-of-interest implied by his hours-old departure to the pharmaceutical industry suggested the conclusions he was about to present would not offend his now current employer.

Amid databases and statistics that apparently fluctuated like the tide, Verstraeten reported, "In Phase One of our analysis, we found several significant associations between Thimerosal and neurodevelopmental disorders. However, in an analysis in a smaller and independent dataset, we could not confirm those associations..."

I rolled my eyes. Regardless of how many children might be at risk, I thought, Verstraeten seemed a man ultimately and publicly beholden to the industry which had now given him shelter. Not yet fully understanding the significance of this observation, I awaited further presenters and their messages.

The first was the federal toxicologist, Dr. George Lucier, from the National Institutes of Health, who did several calculations of the mercury content in vaccines, and then added to that the estimated environmental mercury exposures children were receiving. Coming to the crux of the issue with a directness that few dared, Dr. Lucier announced his uncomfortable conclusion to the already restless committee members, as well as the assembled gathering: "Ethyl mercury exposure from vaccines added to dietary exposures to methyl mercury probably cause neurotoxic responses which are likely subtle in some children."

Mary and I looked at each other in euphoria. This was the leading federal toxicologist. Surely, if he understood this to be true, everyone else would as well.

I sensed the weight of the day's testimony argued, undoubtedly, for the case against mercury, made by researchers and parents. I felt bold. I had to, for quickly it became my turn to address those gathered.

As I approached the mic, both the moment and I were pregnant. When Dr. McCormick called my name on July 16, 2001, she had no idea what this clergywoman from Richmond would say, or why I was even in attendance at a medical conference such as this. I arose from my seat beside Mary and moved to the microphone located at the back of the ballroom. I must have seemed slight and unassuming, tall and slender as I was, except for my silhouette that clearly revealed me to be early in my second trimester.

"Madam Chair," I said as I addressed Dr. McCormick. Fourteen years of church council meetings had taught me Robert's Rules as well as boldness. "I ask for permission to speak from the front of the room. I have something I'd like for people to be able to see."

Why, I wondered, did the Institute of Medicine arrange and designate their microphones so that parents and advocates had to speak from the back of the room? Our words were disembodied and weakened before the committee by this poor process. Intuition told me that these committee members didn't want to have to look us parents in the eye.

Still, Dr. McCormick could not have been more hospitable. As I took my place at the front of the assembled gathering, Dr. McCormick sent one of the staffers for a portable microphone. A husband and wife, parents like me attending the meeting and seated nearby, accompanied me forward at my request. Behind me, they unfurled Wesley's chelation chart, revealing the bright yellow zig-zag that represented Wesley's mercury dumps to the entire assembly.

I drew a deep breath and began.

"Members of the Institute of Medicine panel, physicians, researchers, parents and guests, I am Reverend Lisa Sykes. I am pastor of Christ United Methodist Church in Richmond, Virginia. I am also proudly the mother of Wesley, age five. Wesley was diagnosed with autism at two and a quarter years of age. His diagnosis is now billed as multiple metal toxicity." I drew a deeper breath still.

As the committee members seated on the front row—only feet away— looked toward the chart, they realized what I was asserting and immediately understood the implications. Most responded by redirecting their eyes elsewhere. One was so bold as to place his hand over his brow and never look up again. Others fidgeted and grimaced; some even glanced at this unexpected speaker, but no one wanted to look at the unmistakable yellow line that threatened to surpass the upper edge of Wesley's chelation graph.

Not the committee members, but I, a minister and mother, should have been the one fidgeting nervously during this presentation. But I was not. My second son had been felled by mercury, but the one who now turned in my womb would be protected. I would make sure of that. Wesley had paid a high price so that I would know to keep this third son safe. The movement which I felt from my unborn child, and the hope it gave me, was all the courage I needed. This was little different, I thought as I continued to pursue the evading glances of the committee, from preaching on Sunday.

"Dr. Robert Chen of the CDC, who is here today, in his article, *Safety of Acellular Pertussis Vaccine Follow-up Studies*, has openly stated that rare or adverse reactions to the vaccines among subpopulations can only be detected —and I quote here—'can only be detected after product licensing and general use'. My son has the tragic misfortune to be in such a subpopulation, I believe. He carries a benign G-alpha-I protein defect. Dr. Mary Megson has discovered that when this defect is compounded by the pertussis toxin, cells no longer can bind dangerous metals. The metallothionine that some of you have mentioned is disabled. Having disabled this mechanism in a perfectly healthy child, our medical protocols then load these innocent children with thirty times the EPA standard... The result in my son is clear. He absorbed the Thimerosal.

"I seek to get my child back, and I see improvements. As a parent of a child who still has no voice at five, I really must beseech the government with all my heart and my soul, my belief and ethical conviction, to apprentice itself to researchers who are already beginning to bring these young children back, instead of debating whether or not Thimerosal is an issue. These kids are recovering because it is an issue.

"As a religious leader, I beseech the medical establishment quickly, to join the fight in a search and rescue operation for these young children who can be helped and who very possibly may be saved. I feel like the funding needs to go first to studying the biological treatments already in place and effective, rather than statistical studies. I feel that the biological treatments and improvements are more insightful.

"As one trained in medical ethics, I also think we need to look at the separation of the profit from a product from its liability, as is the case with vaccines. Surely this bifurcation that we have allowed has contributed to the disaster we now face when we look into the eyes of our autistic children that do not see.

"I assert to you that any effort which fails to address these goals is insufficient and morally unacceptable. Thank you very much."

"You did great!" Mary mouthed to me, as I returned to my seat. Once again, Mary's words brought relief to me.

Dr. McCormick called the last person listed for public comment. "Thank you. The last speaker will be Beth Clay."

Beth responded very professionally, as one who had long been involved in federal government, and more recently, in an investigation of Thimerosal conducted by the Government Reform Committee under Congressman Dan Burton. Her comment took the form of a question formulated with great discernment.

"My name is Beth Clay and I am with the Government Reform Committee. I actually have a question for Dr. Halsey that I wasn't able to ask during your presentation. As a long-time and well-respected advisor to the government on vaccines, you mentioned that during the approval process, you all were not presented data in an appropriate fashion to explain the level of mercury in the vaccines. Had this data been presented to you in a fashion as we now understand it, would you have supported the approval of vaccines that contained Thimerosal?"

"Mary, where is he from?" I whispered.

"Johns Hopkins."

Dr. Halsey drew a deep breath, and then began with a stammer: "...the package labeling contained the concentration of Thimerosal, and we did not —I did not and others did not—go through the calculations... that showed how much mercury was there. I do not approve the vaccines. I do believe that if the labeling had included the dose in micrograms, someone would have picked this up earlier than it was picked up. There is no doubt in my mind about that. I feel badly that I didn't pick it up..."

I needed no scientific degree to recognize regret. My pastoral experience identified that quickly enough. There, before the entire assembled body of the Institute of Medicine, with more federal officials per square foot than any building in Washington, Dr. Neal Halsey began his public apology. Perhaps, I thought, it was not regret—it seemed more like remorse. In any case, there could be no doubt, Dr. Halsey was officially acknowledging the failure of his Committee on Infectious Diseases, which he chaired for the American Academy of Pediatrics (AAP), to assess the amount of mercury in the new immunization schedule and the danger it might pose to children.

Beth was generous. She did not comment that the mathematical calculation to convert .01% to 25 micrograms of mercury per dose of vaccine was merely eighth grade math.

As Mary and I walked out of the Charles Hotel on July 16, 2001 to begin our trip back to Virginia, we felt we had won the most important debate of our lives. Mary lifted her hands in the air and I followed suit. We reached up and grabbed fistfuls of nothing and shouted, "YES!"

With pleasure and a sense that everything would soon be fine, we giggled.

"You know, Lisa," Mary said, "Before you walked in that door, everyone knew who you were."

I looked at Mary, stunned. "What do you mean?"

"I didn't want to make you nervous. But you know the letter you wrote to Zoon? Every federal employee in that room knew your name before you ever came here because of that letter."

My words had not failed me before the revered Institute of Medicine, but now I stood speechless.

CHAPTER FIVE

A REAL AND PRESENT DANGER

"One of the things that I think we need to consider is, as a couple of the speakers have said, that the cat is out of the bag, the horse out of the barn, and that Thimerosal is going to be out of the vaccines."

—Dr. Ben Schwartz, M.D., National Immunization Program
At The National Vaccine Advisory Committee
Sponsored Workshop on Thimerosal Vaccines
Bethesda, Maryland
Day Two – Volume I August 12, 1999
(Transcript, p. 237)

SEPTEMBER 2001

IT WAS PERFECTLY BLUE. ON THAT DAY, THE SKY HAD BEEN AS BRILLIANT A HUE AS I had ever seen, and the Virginia foliage was beginning to hint at its hidden treasure of gold and bronze and copper. Why was it then, that I found looking heavenward so oppressive? I gazed at the vast expanse above me, searching with my eyes—straining, squinting, for a tale-tell sign the world had not gone mad. I was searching for a tail—a narrow but unending contrail of vapor cloud that traced the path of a jet in the sky. There were always planes in the sky above Richmond. But not on this day, or in the days that followed immediately afterward.

On September 11, 2001, not only the aircraft of the nation were grounded, but so too was its soul. Members of my church, stranded around the country on business trips, called Richmond wanting to speak to their pastor. They could not get home because the white lines that usually crossed the sky had been erased, as if from a blackboard, and the sky was eerily blank. Everyone was scared. The two buildings in New York City that had most scraped the sky were now rubble upon the ground. Shoes that people had been wearing at 10,000 feet were scattered everywhere, but their bodies could not be found. Portions of the Pentagon had burned, and in a field in Pennsylvania, a plane load of brave people died upon impact after overcoming terrorists. For two days, I did not think of autism. Autism seemed so minor, with 3,000 people dead and ash obscuring the New York City skyline. Autism, it seemed to me, was not so dire after all.

OCTOBER 2001

Just as I had come to realize the inability of the government to secure the borders of the nation on September 11, I also came to realize its inability to safeguard the children within its borders on this October morning.

Summoning the newly announced IOM conclusions on my computer, I read the words of the Institute of Medicine Immunization Safety Review Committee, announced by Dr. Marie McCormick, with disgust: "...where only supplies containing the preservative are available, the vaccines should be administered rather than foregoing immunization. While the health effects of Thimerosal are uncertain, we know for sure that these vaccines protect against real, proven threats to unvaccinated infants, children, and pregnant women."

Yet, the very next paragraph in the press release acknowledged: "A connection between exposure to certain forms of mercury and nervous system abnormalities has long been recognized." [1]

"Damn it."

At last, the highest scientific advisory board in the land had issued its conclusion—one so tepid that I, uncharacteristically, cursed out loud. The association between mercury in vaccines and autism, its members ruled, was "biologically plausible." Plausible. Not probable. Not terrifying. Just plausible. No need to take any action, not yet. The expectation of an urgent recall and ban that Mary and I had seized upon in our naiveté as we left Boston seemed stolen from our grasp.

News reports that covered the IOM report on television emphasized that it was just a "little bit" of mercury in the vaccines.

"A little bit of mercury?" I repeated aloud. "A little? What about 'a little bit' makes the second most toxic element on the face of the earth benign?"

A little bit of mercury—the size of a single speck of salt—could poison a lake, but it wouldn't damage your child's brain? Could federal scientists and regulators not successfully quantify the toxicity of mercury when mere micrograms of mercury could kill? I felt sick to my stomach.

DECEMBER 2001

What courage I had summoned to conceive this last Sykes son, even after all Seth and I had gone through with Wesley. Had I known that national tragedy would be added to personal tragedy, I might not have been this bold. But I didn't know. Instead, I held onto hope that I could exit my years as the mother of young children in joy instead of sorrow. I resolved that this third son would be a child to heal our hearts.

"You are the kind of parents who need to have more kids!" Mary had proclaimed to me one day in her office, with her usual exuberance. Without her, I might never have dared to consider having another child after losing one to autism. "You know you can keep this one safe!" Mary reassured me. "We'll just be very careful with the shots—no mercury—and you are going to breastfeed this baby for a year!" Though I consulted so carefully with Mary about this third child, I only teased Seth about the idea. Even though he had every confidence in the physician who treated Wesley with such insight, autism still terrified Seth. Had it not been for my intrepidness, Seth would never have imagined Joshua.

Our third son, an eight pound, thirteen ounce infant whom we named Joshua Stuart, was born on December 4, 2001, after twenty furious minutes of labor. As my precious and hungry newborn nursed upon delivery, I summoned enough cognizance to remind my new obstetrician, "Remember to use my Bay Rho."

"Shhh, Lisa. I know. Don't worry. This is it."

For weeks, not knowing when I'd go into labor, I had carried a Bay-Rho injection around with me on ice. Because my blood type was B- and Joshua's was B+, I would need a shot to prevent problems if there had been any mixing of our blood during the delivery, just as I had been required to have one at twenty-eight weeks of pregnancy. I was probably unique among the Rh- pregnant patients that year because I was keenly aware of what most doctors did not even know: the standard Rho(D) shot carried a startling thirty-five micrograms of mercury, ten times the safe limit for an adult, never mind a newborn infant.[2] Given to a pregnant woman at delivery, it would taint her breast milk and purvey poison to her newborn infant when the child nursed.[3] As my previous Rho(D), given during this pregnancy at twenty-eight weeks gestation, had been mercury-free, so I was determined, would this one be also.

"Oh, dear sweet Wesley!" I cringed to think Wesley had received mercury in the Rho(D) during my pregnancy with him and again after his birth through my milk. "Not that nightmare! Not again! No one is going to poison my child or my milk this time!"

Reassured by my obstetrician, I lapsed back into exhaustion, my eyes closed, my child enfolded.

My obstetrician had only recently become a student of neurotoxicity, as I was a new patient of hers. Like many OB's, she had not been taught anything about heavy metal poisoning in medical school. But during eight of the nine months of my third pregnancy, I educated her on the dangers of mercury, showing her labs from Wesley's chelation, and soliciting a sacred promise from this doctor that neither my child nor I would be injected with any Thimerosal-containing product. Not willing to rely only on that promise alone, I went so far as to list both myself and my baby, as yet unborn, as "allergic" to Thimerosal when I pre-registered at the hospital for labor and delivery.

The obstetrician had to wait for the baby to finish nursing before I would surrender him to her. Then, she conveyed this newest son first to his father, and next, to the waiting and impatient nurse. A parade of people, all following the clear hospital bassinette in which Joshua was wheeled, exited my room en route to the hospital nursery, and momentarily, I was blissfully alone and grateful for the quiet and the dim lights.

"Lisa?" I heard the OB's voice interrupt the silence from outside in the hallway.

"Yes?" I replied, curious as to why she was returning so soon.

"I need to tell you something." she said.

"Yes?" I asked, wondering what comment could be so important that it had brought my doctor back to my bedside.

"I wanted you to know..." There was a long pause. "Until you told me," she uttered the words slowly, as if they were painful to pronounce. "Until you told me," she began again, as if getting up momentum enough to finish her sentence, "I had no idea there was mercury in the Rho(D) shots..."

Weary, I received my doctor's admission, and replied in a soft and solemn voice, "I didn't either—not until Wesley got sick."

JUNE 2002

While I spent the early months of 2002 consumed with my newborn son, Joshua, a father-son team of researchers, Dr. Mark Geier and David Geier, were bringing new discovery to birth. At the age of merely twenty-one, David began structuring a study to identify relationships between the particular vaccines given to children and any medical problems or "adverse outcomes," as they were called clinically, that resulted from them. It was summer 2002, and after reviewing and comparing a myriad of vaccines and their components, David selected as the subject of his new study an old friend, DTaP vaccine. Introduced into the American market as a result of his father's efforts, the DTaP vaccine came in two forms: a Thimerosal-containing vaccine and a Thimerosal-free one.

Long before I knew vaccine safety issues ever existed, and long before the mercury content of the immunization schedule increased drastically in the 1990's, Mark had already won one war to protect children from unsafe vaccines. His battle started when, as an expert before the National Vaccine Injury Compensation Program and civil litigation, Mark noticed a high rate of adverse reactions due to the whole cell DTP vaccine. In the late 1980's, Mark, together with two of his fellow scientists, decided to challenge the makers of whole cell DTP and force the profit-driven pharmaceutical industry to distribute the DTaP, or acellular vaccine. With his expertise in vaccines and an unflinching commitment to safety, Mark and his colleagues successfully challenged the vaccine manufacturing industry, occasioning a slow switch over to the safer DTaP vaccine.

Had it not been for an ongoing conversation with attorney Cliff Shoemaker, David would have considered differences in the DTaP vaccines to be superfluous. Now, however, he focused upon the difference in mercury content. Always thorough, David also noted other differences between the shots he had selected to study, including aluminum content and antigen levels. Having been apprenticed in vaccine study by his father, he would carefully take each difference into account. Ultimately, he would be able to determine if reports of "adverse outcomes," particularly autism and other related neurodevelopmental disorders, were different between groups of children who were exposed to more mercury versus those who were exposed to less, based on which DTaP vaccine they had received.

After constructing data sets and running programs, the results were printed. Now, it was up to David to analyze the results—to search for patterns—to form comparisons. David's father, Mark, worked alongside him, eager to contribute his experience and mathematical expertise to the effort. After an afternoon of computations, the Geiers had a preliminary result.

"No, we've screwed up!" David said to his father in frustration. "This can't be right!"

"Why do you say that? What is the result?" Mark demanded, knowing he had scrutinized each step of the analysis.

"This shows that there is a six-fold increased risk for autism following thimerosal-containing DTaP vaccines in comparison to thimerosal-free DTaP vaccines. The kids who got the Thimerosal-containing vaccines were six times more likely to develop autism! That can't be right, can it?" David's voice rose in pitch and volume.

"David, that's a huge effect! Why, if that's true, then..." Mark looked up, and he and David froze.

"Let's recheck the calculations."

Anne did not see her husband or son emerge from their study that evening. Chronic night-owls already, Mark and David did not sleep that night, but repeated the entire study, from the construction of the datasets, right through the final analysis of the results.

"There it is, again!" Mark exclaimed, horrified by the six-fold difference in his results.

"There's got to be an error in the database!" David suggested to his father.

"Well, David, check that by comparing these results to those for another diagnosis. Let's see if you get a higher effect for, oh, say, speech disorders. Or mental retardation."

The sleep-deprived researchers continued, unwilling to accept their initial findings or relinquish their urgent pursuit. Using the same datasets, in order to test their reliability, David directed his program to assess the number of children reported to have either mental retardation or speech disorders following administration of Thimerosal-containing and Thimerosal-free DTaPs. The results of these subsequent analyses were just as unnerving as the first. David found that there was a 6.1-fold statistically significant increased risk for mental retardation following administration of a thimerosal-containing DTaP vaccines and a 2.2-fold increased risk for speech disorders in comparison to thimerosal-free DTaP vaccines!

It was almost dawn when Mark and David ceased, temporarily, from their work. David could only discount it. "Something's wrong. The effect must be due to some variable I've overlooked." Seeking reassurance, he turned at his father. "You and I both know vaccines are safe, after all." Mark made no reply. He simply looked solemnly back at David.

David slept a few hours, and then continued to search diligently for another explanation to discredit his original findings. In order to think rationally, David could only assume himself and his results to be wrong. He made a concerted effort to recall the mantra he had heard all his life and had accepted, despite the demonstrated problem with the whole cell Pertussis vaccine, which had now been replaced. "Vaccines are medical sciences' greatest contribution to the world. They are safe and effective. Any risk is theoretical..." David had no desire to espouse scientific reform. Instead, he sought abstract and academic absolution for his doubt.

"My initial conclusion must be wrong. I need to verify that it is wrong. It has to be wrong!" David's thoughts were becoming rapid and disturbing. How could he account for the undeniable difference in autism rates between the two groups of children? After ransacking his mind, David thought of one possible explanation to account for the huge discrepancy in adverse outcomes between the two groups of children: one receiving Thimerosal-containing DTaP and one receiving Thimerosal-free DTaP vaccines in his dataset.

Like many others who tried to dismiss the mercury as a contributing factor to neurological disorders, David, at a loss for any other identifiable explanation, began to scrutinize the parents. Perhaps, he reasoned, parents of the children who had received Thimerosal-containing DTaP vaccines were more acutely aware of thimerosal-associated problems as a result of the media. Perhaps they were over-reporting adverse outcomes in general, and the higher rate of neurodevelopmental disorders among their children was merely one illustration of their heightened state of anxiety. If this were true, David reasoned, parents frightened by news stories in the media simply reported more adverse events in general following immunization. If so, then not only autism and neurological diagnoses, but others as well, should be over-reported in the sample.

Once again, David assembled a list of adverse event outcomes that he did not believe could be linked biologically to Thimerosal, including: deaths, vasculitis, seizures, visits to the emergency room, and gastroenteritis. To his astonishment, David found that these outcomes were comparable among the two groups he was examining in the database. In essence, these results demonstrated that the parents of children receiving the Thimerosal-containing DTaP were no more likely to report these outcomes than those receiving the Thimerosal-free DTaP vaccines. No, he could not blame unfounded hysteria nor parental paranoia for the six-fold increase in autism after Thimerosal-containing vaccines.

At issue then, was the fact that neurological disorders were much more common among the set of children receiving Thimerosal-containing vaccines. This and this alone separated the two groups, and now, unless David could find another reason to account for the discrepancy between these two groups and vaccine types, he had no choice but to face his finding. Neither David nor Mark would shun the truth, even if it were scientific sacrilege.

Cognizant that an Exposure to Thimerosal study might hold immense implications for both the medical community and their own careers, the Geiers prepared their manuscript for submission to *Experimental Biology and Medicine*, one of the top peer-reviewed scientific publications in the world. In the article they submitted, Mark and David dared to suggest an association between Thimerosal exposure through vaccines and neurodevelopmental disorders. They did not, however, comprehend how shocking their conclusion would be, as they assumed the number of children affected negatively by mercury must be very small. In addition, they continued to search for an unidentified variable that could have confounded their results and produced the six-fold difference in neurological outcomes.

Therefore, they worded their paper very cautiously to reflect their reservations regarding this newly identified "Thimerosal-effect." In the manuscript Mark and David submitted to *Experimental Biology and Medicine*, they carefully sought to select and arrange their words, so as not to blaspheme vaccines:

> "The hypothesis that exposure to thimerosal-containing vaccines could be associated with neurodevelopmental disorders is not established and rests on indirect and incomplete information, primarily from analogies with methylmercury and levels of maximum exposure from vaccines given to children. The hypothesis is biologically plausible, but the possible relationship between thimerosal from vaccines and the neurodevelopmental disorders of autism, attention deficit/hyperactivity disorder (ADHD), and speech or language delay remains seriously suspect. As of the present there are no peer-reviewed epidemiological studies in the scientific literature examining the potential association between thimerosal-containing vaccines and neurodevelopmental disorders. Here, we show the first epidemiologic evidence, based upon tens of millions of doses of vaccine administered in the United States, that associates increasing thimerosal from vaccines with neurodevelopmental disorders."[4]

After the manuscript was accepted for publication, David retired his worries over the Thimerosal for more immediate considerations. He and his father had a number of articles about to be published, and they were occupied submitting and correcting the galley proofs for manuscripts. At the time, these endeavors seemed to be much more pressing.

It was with these thoughts consuming his energies, that David joined his parents for vacation in West Palm Beach, Florida in November. The father-son team forgot their preoccupations while playing tennis and simply enjoyed the warmth of the Florida sun. They were in mid-match, when a clerk from the hotel shouted for "Geier."

"Strange," Mark thought. "What could be this urgent, that a hotel employee has come to track us down?"

"Sir," said the clerk as Mark identified himself, "You need to call home immediately. Your assistant said something about Congress calling."

DECEMBER 2002

By now, I had held my infant son, Joshua, in my arms for a year; I had chelated Wesley for two. Between Joshua's nursing and Wesley's fitful nights, I relegated sleep to those who had normal lives and normal children.

On this night, I was grateful it was Joshua and not Wesley who cried for me. When he would stir, Wesley took hours to get back to sleep, often relenting from wakefulness only close to dawn. He would be agitated and irritable until the fragile state called sleep overwhelmed him more than the fierce injury called autism. But this night it was simply a ravenous Joshua, eager to eat and then babble a midnight reverie to his mommy, who woke me. I lifted the crying infant from his crib, and quietly descended the stairs to the den. I illumined the darkness by plugging in the Christmas tree. Though I was not happy to be wakened, Joshua was delighted to have his mother's undivided attention, and his obvious affection and the petite colored lights on the tree made a wakeful midnight magical, instead of maddening.

"No, my dear, you sure don't have autism..." I told a weighty Joshua as he greedily consumed his meal and his mother's touch. "Let him drink me dry!" I laughed to myself with a profound thankfulness in my soul: no doubt about it—this little boy was perfectly normal, and having been vigilantly protected from mercury exposure, he would remain so.

Content to cuddle my baby close, I turned on the television, to see what bizarre B-flicks or late night Christmas specials it had to offer. What were the odds... I would later wonder... what were the odds that I would wake in time to hear C-SPAN re-broadcasting one of the many Mercury in Medicine congressional investigative hearings conducted by the Government Reform Committee under Congressman Dan Burton?

At first glance, I did not recognize this senior Republican congressman from Indiana, whose accent was Midwestern and whose face was lined with honesty. This tenacious man, seated on an impressive leather chair behind a cumbersome desk which bespoke federal authority, had just finished showing a movie clip of a child in immense distress: screaming, crying, and beating his head into a wall. After only a minute of watching this excruciating visual depiction of a child with autism, Congressman Burton, a catch in his throat, began to speak, not only as an elected official, but also as the grandfather of a child with autism:[5]

"…Our government has to 'fess up about this… Now, my grandson and thousands of children across this country were normal kids, and they got vaccinated with multiple vaccines. Mercury in the brain has a cumulative effect. All scientists will tell you that. It doesn't wash out easily. It gets in the fatty tissues and it stays there. And so, it has a cumulative effect. And yet, we continue to get reports that say there's no scientific evidence that mercury causes autism. They don't say it doesn't. They say, we can't conclusively prove that mercury causes autism. They don't say it doesn't… So we can't let the pharmaceutical companies and our government cover this mess up today because it ain't going to go away. And it's going to cost the taxpayers trillions more if we wait around on it…

"So, I've said enough… Our first panel is Dr. Baskin, Dr. Geier, and Dr. Spitzer. We'd appreciate it if you'd approach the witness table and stand to be sworn. Please raise your right hand. Do you swear to tell the whole truth and nothing but the truth, so help you God?"

I never imagined, as I watched Dr. Mark Geier take his seat before the Congressional committee, that he and his son would make a breakthrough discovery in the treatment of autism, nor that my son would be the first child to receive it. Nor did I know, at this time, that Mark had interrupted his family's vacation in Florida to fly home unexpectedly and testify on "Vaccines and Neurodevelopmental Delays." Nor did I know that Mark had arrived home with only twelve hours to submit preliminary information to Congressmen Burton and Weldon, and less than a day to prepare his congressional testimony.

As his testimony began, my pulse quickened: "We analyzed the incident rates of neurodevelopmental delays reported to the VAERS* data base following thimerosal-containing diptheria, tetanus and acellular pertussis, called DTaP, in comparison to thimerosal-free DTaP vaccines… This slide

---

*Vaccine Adverse Event Reporting System

shows that autism and mental retardation were approximately six times more statistically significant, and speech disorders were two times more statistically significantly following thimerosal-containing DTaP vaccines in comparison to thimerosal-free DTaP vaccines."

I made a concerted effort not to let my excitement at Mark's initial remarks cause me to disturb Joshua, who by now had fallen asleep in my arms. I had difficulty keeping still and quiet, though, as Mark easily dispatched the flawed defense made by the Institute of Medicine on administering mercury to children:

> "...The IOM analyzed the mercury dose children received at six months of life and averaged it over every day in a child's life, that is, one hundred eighty days, showing that the dose received by the child was only in slight excess of the EPA limits. This type of averaging makes no scientific sense. As an example, if I were given a lethal dose of mercury and my dose was averaged over more than fifty years of life, I would not have received a dose exceeding the limits, despite the fact that I would be dead. Realistically, children are receiving large doses of mercury at intervals that far exceed all the federal agency guidelines and not by fivefold, but by over a hundredfold."

Congressman Burton looked grim as he asked Mark his opinion regarding recent studies supported by the government, purporting to show the safety of mercury exposure from Thimerosal-containing vaccines, based on the fact that mercury levels measured in infants' blood after vaccination were low.

Mark answered, "I've been asked to comment on the *Lancet* article which measured mercury in blood, urine and stool... in infants three to twenty-eight days following thimerosal-containing vaccines in comparison to infants receiving thimerosal-free vaccines. The findings of low-level mercury in the blood is only indicative of measuring too late. If they wanted to see it, they should measure three to twenty-four hours after the shot, and it does nothing to assure that these children were not exposed to potentially damaging levels of mercury... So why is it supposed to be reassuring that they measured later, and it's not in the blood; that means it could be in the brain. So that study to me, has no validity."

"YES!" I almost shouted, waking my baby boy from sleep. "Shhhhh... go back to sleep, Joshua. Momma's sorry. Shhhhhh..." I kissed his head gently, as the slate blue eyes of my third son inquired of me what had happened.

I didn't answer but instead began gently rocking him. Since coming to realize Wesley was mercury-poisoned, I had heard so few like Mary who were willing to discover and speak the truth. For me, Mark's testimony was affirmation and inspiration combined. Though he didn't know Wesley or me, Mark was telling our darkest truths. He had spoken about Wesley being poisoned directly, and now he spoke about it happening indirectly, through me:

"RhoGAM, a product containing thimerosal, given during pregnancy to Rh-negative women, appears to cause or contribute significantly to the recent dramatic increase in the rate of autism seen in the United States. As far as RhoGAM goes, I practice as an obstetrical geneticist. I do amniocentesis. I give RhoGAM. I was not aware that RhoGAM contained Thimerosal. It no longer does, but it did for a number of years."

I looked at Joshua as his eyes closed again and remembered Wesley. I found myself stifling the tears that were my unspoken testimony. Mark ended his comments as a classicist, commenting on something I had observed in my study of the humanities:

"History has written that the fall of Rome may well have been related to lead poisoning from newly invented lead pipes. Let it not be written that our great society poisons itself with mercury preservatives."

"He knows," I confided in my infant as he drifted off to slumber. "He knows what I know and so much more, Joshua."

My third-born son had fallen asleep in my arms. Seated in my den, I looked down at Joshua. Though I wished it with every waking moment, I could not retrieve Wesley's infancy, nor with it my lost opportunity to protect him from mercury. Unable to turn back time, unable to protect Wesley from the damage mercury had already done to his brain, and yet unable to cease from desiring this impossibility, I had incarnated my longing to keep my wounded child safe in this newborn baby son.

CHAPTER SIX

SIMPSONWOOD

"Personally, I have three hypotheses. My first hypothesis is it is parental bias. The children that are more likely to be vaccinated are more likely to be picked up and diagnosed. Second hypothesis, I don't know. There is a bias that I have not yet recognized, and nobody has yet told me about it. Third hypothesis. It's true, it's thimerosal. Those are my hypotheses."

—Thomas Verstraeten, MD, MSc
Epidemic Intelligence Service, National Immunization Program, CDC
(Simpsonwood Transcript, p. 161)

DECEMBER 2002, SILVER SPRING, MARYLAND

THE BROWN CARDBOARD BOX THAT SAT UPON THE COFFEE TABLE HAD BEEN GATHERING dust. The contents inside were a stack of papers a foot deep without index or title. No wonder Mark and David had hesitated to wade through them. But on this day in late December, snows had hushed the busy suburbs of Maryland and the obstetrical genetics practice of Dr. Mark Geier. He could still think of so much else that urgently needed doing, but his wife, Anne, had tired of this box and its intrusion upon her living room.

"Dave, will you come here!" The fatherly tone in his voice made it clear this was not a request but a command. Mark reasoned, "If I have to go through this stuff, the least Dave can do is help me."

"Yeah, what do you want?" Dave said impatiently. This brown cardboard box wasn't on his list of priorities either.

"Your mother wants this out of here now! We need to sort through it, and I nominate you to help!" said Mark, who enjoyed conscripting David to this amorphous task, as Anne had conscripted him.

"Oh, not that! What's in there anyhow?"

On December 10, 2002, David and his father had been exiting Congressman Burton's Hearing on Mercury in Medicine when appreciative parents and eager journalists assailed them in a volley of thanks and questions. Into this bedlam waded Lyn Redwood of SafeMinds, who had stood outside the meeting room as if in wait, a heavy brown box in her hand.

"Mark, David, here! I've brought these for you to look at," declared Lyn, foisting the package into David's arms.

"What is this?" David replied, wanting a bit more clarity about why he should lug a box containing several pounds of white paper through the Congressional offices he was scheduled to visit.

"These are more documents SafeMinds obtained from the federal government through the Freedom of Information Act. They are all from the CDC. Promise me you'll have a look at them!" Lyn's soft Southern tone did not mask the insistence in her voice.

Amid the clamor, and somewhat befuddled, Mark and David politely assented as Lyn quickly retreated from the crowd.

"Here, you carry it..."

"No, I'm not going to carry it—you carry it!"

Anyone who knew the Geiers recognized the comic banter of this father-and-son pair of researchers. For the rest of the day, Mark, David, and this cumbersome brown box were shown into the offices of the congressmen and senators most concerned that the nation might be poisoning its own children.

"So, today's the lucky day, is it Dad?" David teased his father, who had already pulled several inches of unidentified documents from the box.

As the snow continued to fall outside, Mark and David grudgingly undertook a task they considered only a tedious distraction from the real work at hand: their research.

Mark had lost count of how many pages he had turned. Many of the printed pages documented CDC studies, but there were also letters of correspondence and various initial findings from sundry epidemiological samples within the Vaccine Safety Datalink (VSD), a government project created in 1990 to study the adverse side effects of vaccines. Mark and David found these mildly interesting, especially after Burton's hearing. All of the documents begged the question already in their minds—how could one study the possible association between Thimerosal, administered as part of the standard childhood immunization schedule, and neurological outcomes?

Mark glanced at yet one more document, located two-thirds of the way down the box's depth. He sighed in resignation, picking it up and thumbing through the first few pages.

A typical transcript, the participant's names were all listed at the front, as was the date and title of the conference whose proceedings were here recorded. The date indicated was June 7–8, 2000. The subject of the conference: *A Study of Thimerosal In Vaccines*. Preparatory remarks recorded at its beginning indicated the topic of discussion at this meeting was an epidemiological study, done in its entirety using the Vaccine Safety Datalink of the CDC, to determine whether an association existed between mercury exposure, through Thimerosal in vaccines, and the epidemic of neurological disorders being identified among the nation's children.

"Odd," Mark thought. "No one testifying before Congress on behalf of the CDC or FDA mentioned that there was any completed study on this issue."

At the center of the discussion, recorded in the black and white of the transcript, was a study done by Dr. Thomas Verstraeten, a Belgian officer of the Epidemic Intelligence Service, serving the CDC as a resident expert.

As Mark scanned the pages, his eyes came to rest on a peculiar comment at the bottom of page thirty-one, wherein Dr. Verstraeten confessed his initial reluctance to pursue the very study this transcript recorded him presenting to a panel of CDC officials and representatives from... Mark leafed back to the first pages.... industry! The pharmaceutical industry!

Mark had to take the incredulousness he was now feeling, and put it into words—urgent words. "David! David, you gotta see this!" Mark waved the transcript in the air. "It's... it's a transcript. It records a meeting about the mercury. Now, listen to this—here's the author of a study on mercury in the VSD speaking—someone named Verstraeten." Mark flipped back to page thirty-one.

"It is sort of interesting that when I first came to the CDC as a EIS officer a year ago only, I didn't really know what I wanted to do, but one of the things I knew I didn't want to do was studies that had to do with toxicology or environmental health. Because I thought it was too much confounding and it's very hard to prove anything in those studies. Now it turns out that other people also thought that this study was not the right thing to do, so what I will present to you is the study that nobody thought we should do."[1]

"A study *nobody* thinks should be done? Nobody at the CDC, I guess!" David joked.

As Mark and David delved further and further into the document, however, they ceased to laugh. When they reached page forty, they barely remembered to breathe.

"Oh my God! Look at that!" David exclaimed, reading aloud one of the first clear statements of findings which Dr. Thomas Verstraeten presented to this gathering of federal officials and pharmaceutical industry executives on the association between mercury and neurodevelopmental disorders:

"...we have found statistically significant relationships between the exposures and outcomes for these different exposures and outcomes. First, for two months of age, an unspecified developmental delay, which has its own specific ICD-9 code. Exposure at three months of age, Tics. Exposure at six months of age, an attention deficit disorder. Exposure at one, three and six months of age, language and speech delays which are two separate ICD-9 codes. Exposure at one, three and six months of age, the entire category of neurodevelopmental delays, which includes all of these plus a number of other disorders."[2]

David ran his fingers repeatedly back and forth across his forehead, as if he were struggling with a migraine. Mark was grim. He sat stone silent for several minutes, his mind conjecturing a chronology of events that might have culminated in this presentation.

"2000, Dave! Let me see that," said Mark, reaching again to possess the document. "This damn conference occurred on June... June...." Mark was so angry that he had trouble flipping the pages back to the coversheet. "... seventh and eighth! June 7 and 8, of the year 2000. They have known since 2000 that the mercury was causal."

Mark grasped the paper tightly, as his temper began to burn hotly on this cold winter day. He scanned the page again: "...developmental delay, tics, ADD, language and speech delays, and the entire category of neurodevelopmental disorders!"

"They were right all along. The parents of the autistic kids.... They were right!" David gasped, still scanning the transcript in his father's hands.

Mark's mind was following a different line of inquiry than David's. "Dave, where was this conference held? It says here at the beginning..."

As the pages resumed their undisturbed alignment, David read the place name at the bottom of the first page. "Somewhere called Simpsonwood— never heard of it..."

"Don't you see?" Mark's question was urgent. "Pharmaceutical reps, government officials, off-site, reviewing a study that Burton knows nothing about. I didn't hear any of those CDC officials even hint at anything like this!" Mark declared, as his voice, and the paper he held in his hand, rose simultaneously, "but here it is, a complete study showing causation and biological plausibility! They're hiding it! They know the mercury isn't safe —they know it's doing damage—and they're going off-site to have a secret meeting about the problem..."

JUNE 2000, NORCROSS, GEORGIA

When officials from the Centers for Disease Control and Prevention and the executives from the pharmaceutical industry arrived at Simpsonwood United Methodist Retreat Center on June 7, they just missed grasping the hand of Christ as they entered.

Carved in the imposing mahogany wood doors is an astonishing life-sized figure of Jesus Christ. By design, this Jesus stands ready in a pleated alb and sandals reminiscent of Native American dress to offer welcome to any who will receive it. His arms open in such a broad expanse that his left outstretched hand is poised precipitously close to the door's heavy worn knob— so close, in fact, that thousands preparing to enter have instinctively grasped Christ's hand instead of the doorknob.

Inspired by a love for people and a desire for generations to find peace in this place, Anna Louise Simpson, as she was christened in 1887, donated 239 acres of rolling woodland to the United Methodist Church in 1971.

Her generous 2.3 million dollar gift set her mind at ease because she had lived all her life knowing her homeplace was historically tragic. It was from these 239 acres and the surrounding woodlands, in accordance with the Indian Removal Act of 1830, that tens of thousands of Cherokee Indians had been wrested from their homes and land by the United States Army and forced to walk westward, being given blankets infected with small pox.[3]

In donating this land to the church,"Ludie," as this Gwinnett County teacher was known to her family and friends, was able to give one of the Trail of Tears sites a new beginning. For this reason, the church had intentionally placed the Christ Doors prominently at its main entrance, to give gracious welcome in a place of historic displacement. Knowing that Simpsonwood, in its tranquil setting along the Chattahooche River, would be dedicated to the love of God and the service of all people, "Ludie" Simpson found comfort in 1971 as she lay dying, at the age of eighty-four.

The staff at Simpsonwood, whose literal mission was to offer a ministry of Christian hospitality, had no idea why this meeting had been convened off-site from CDC headquarters at 1600 Clifton Avenue in Atlanta. Their duty was simply to attend to the needs of their fifty-two distinguished guests, one of whom was Dr. William Weil with the Committee on Environmental Health of the American Academy of Pediatrics. He stood to speak on June 7, 2000, and summarized his understanding of Verstraeten's findings:

> "I think that what you are saying is in term of chronic exposure. I think that the alternative scenario is that this is repeated acute exposures, and like many repeated acute exposures, if you consider a dose of 25 micrograms on one day, then you are above threshold. At least we think you are, and then you do that over and over to a series of neurons where the toxic effect may be the same set of neurons or the same set of neurologic processes, it is conceivable that the more mercury you get, the more effect you are going to get."[4]

None of the fifty-two Simpsonwood attendees were there by chance. A small, confidential circle of bureaucrats from the Centers for Disease Control and Prevention had "tapped" an exclusive list of experts to be their guests at the Simpsonwood Retreat Center. Though the committee would seek to guide and direct federal officials as the issue of Thimerosal came frighteningly into focus, no federal guidelines or regulations would be observed, no public notice or open access would be granted to this meeting held on June 7 and 8 at Simpsonwood, interestingly enough, one week before a congressional investigative hearing would expose the conflicts of interest between pharmaceutical companies and the Federal government health agencies.

Among those in attendance at Simpsonwood were William Egan, Acting Director for the Office of Vaccine Research and Review at the FDA, and Vito Caserta, Chief Medical Officer for the Vaccine Injury Compensation Program. Though their presence at this meeting, and their positions, indicated a keen interest in the subject matter, the transcriptionist would document their presence only as names in a list of attendees. These prominent civil servants would sit silently, listening to every word uttered at Simpsonwood, and say nothing.

As the conference convened, Thomas Verstraeten presented his report. The gathered audience must have listened with intense interest. Comments upon the Verstraeten presentation were recorded for historical witness and posterity:

"25 micrograms": this was the standard amount of mercury contained in a single dose of many, if not most, currently marketed vaccines.

"Toxic effect": this was to cause the neural cells in the brain to wither and die in the presence of a poison.

"...More mercury.... more effect...."

Dr. Robert Chen, or "Bob" as he liked to be called, the Chief of Vaccine Safety and Development for the National Immunization Program of the CDC, responded:

"One of the reasons that led me personally to not be so quick to dismiss the findings was that on his own Tom independently picked three different outcomes that he did not think could be associated with mercury (conjunctivitis, diarrhea and injury) and three out of three had a different pattern across different exposure levels as compared to the ones that again on a priority basis we picked as biologically plausible to be due to mercury exposure."[5]

Here, in the sheltering shadows of Simpsonwood, Bob Chen was evaluating the unexpected consistencies which indicated Verstraeten's findings were not a fluke. Ordinary ailments, that should not have any linkage to mercury exposure, were level across the cohorts and time periods Verstraeten had examined. Pink eye had not spiked in its frequency as the total mercury burden in the immunization schedule had increased, but autism had.

The federal employees, on whose watch children had been injected with a hundred times the EPA safe level of mercury for an adult, would be assured of this, at least: the pharmaceutical giants were now as nervous as they had become. Did Chen desperately hope that these powerful corporations with powerful lobbies would realize that the course of action in their best interest was the same course of action in the best interest of the highest ranking officers in the CDC? Would a common fear of being exposed create a common cause and a shared alliance, for the good of all involved and the protection of current public health policies? The members of the pharmaceutical industry sat quietly, saying virtually nothing out loud during the entire event. At last, Dr. Robert Brent, Developmental Biologist and a pediatrician from Thomas Jefferson University and the DuPont Hospital for Children, posed the $64,000 question:

"If it is true, which or what mechanisms would you explain the finding with?" [6]

Dr. Verstraeten responded clearly, "You are asking for biological plausibility?" [7]

"Well, yes," said Brent.

The truth is, Merck had known, in a concrete way, the danger mercury in vaccines posed since at least 1991. In that year, Scandinavia first refused to buy Thimerosal-containing vaccines. As a result, one of Merck's own employees, Dr. Maurice Hilleman, who served on the Vaccine Task Force, had been asked explicitly to examine the Thimerosal preservative in vaccines, identify the problems, present an analysis, and offer suggestions for resolution. Hilleman concluded:

"The 25 micrograms of mercury in a single 0.5 mL dose... extrapolated to a 6 lb baby would be 25X the adjusted Swedish daily allowance of 1.0 micrograms for a baby of that size... If 8 doses of thimerosal-containing vaccine were given in the first 6 months of life (3 DPT, 2 HIB, and 3 Hepatitis B) the 200 micrograms of mercury given, say to an average size of 12 lbs., would be about 87X the Swedish daily allowance of 2.3 micrograms of mercury for a baby of that size. When viewed in this way, the mercury load appears rather large."[8]

So what if Scandinavia refused Thimerosal in 1991? After all, the Scandinavian countries did not vaccinate as aggressively as the United States, nor did they have a comparable population. Scandinavia could refuse mercury in its shots, and this would necessitate only minor changes in production. It would be a nuisance to manufacturers—but not a disaster.

But if the United States made any such statement, the crisis for the pharmaceutical industry would be grave. The United States, with its increasingly aggressive immunization schedule, beginning with the Hepatitis B vaccine on the first day of life to protect day-old newborns from a disease spread by promiscuous sex and dirty needles, could not be altered. To restrict sales of such mercury-containing vaccines in the United States could mean an economic crisis for the billion-dollar industry and vaccine manufacturers around the world.

At the time, Merck seemed unconcerned by the flighty behavior of the Scandinavian health officials, for unlike these regulators, "the U.S. Food and Drug Administration... does not have this concern for Thimerosal," the memo stated. [9]

Did those employed by the pharmaceutical giants wish to be back at their desks, under a mountain of paper work, or anywhere else, but here at Simpsonwood? Had the inviting surroundings and hospitable atmosphere become suddenly oppressively stagnant?

Whatever their frantic wishes, as Dr. Verstraeten responded, he didn't lie:

"When I saw this, and I went back through the literature, I was actually stunned by what I saw because I thought it is plausible."[10]

Plausible? Plausible that the epidemic of autism had been manufactured and legislated into existence? Plausible that demand for stimulants like Ritalin and psychotropics like risperadol and antidepressants like Zoloft had increased with the increasing frequency of diagnoses like autism and ADD and ADHD? Plausible that children with autism and ADD and ADHD constituted a huge sector of pharmaceutical consumers?

Dr. Richard Johnston, Immunologist and Pediatrician at the University of Colorado School of Medicine and at the National Jewish Center for Immunology and Respiratory Medicine, interrupted the ongoing cerebral assessments of Thimerosal. What prompted his comment was not his review of Verstraeten's findings on Thimerosal, nor his wish to respond to any particular opinion that had been expressed, but instead, his poignant desire to protect one specific child from such a toxic fate—his newborn grandson. In a rare and passionate aside, recorded in the transcript, Dr. Johnston stated:

> "This association leads me to favor a recommendation that infants up to two years old not be immunized with Thimerosal containing vaccines if suitable alternative preparations are available... My gut feeling? It worries me enough. Forgive this personal comment, but I got called out at eight o'clock for an emergency call and my daughter-in-law delivered a son by C-Section. Our first male in the line of the next generation, and I do not want that grandson to get a Thimerosal containing vaccine until we know better what is going on. It will probably take a long time. In the meantime, and I know there are probably implications for this internationally, but in the meantime I think I want that grandson to only be given Thimerosal-free vaccines."[11]

Dr. Johnston was wrong: his conviction that his grandson should receive only Thimerosal-free vaccines would have no international implications. The public would remain unaware of the VSD study. With no one willing to advocate for their protection, the hundreds of thousands of mercury-sensitive infants born in the years and at the peak of the catastrophic mercury load were tragically less fortunate than Dr. Johnston's grandson.

The tension that hung in the room must have been unmistakable as Dr. Weil began evaluating the doses of mercury and the specific outcomes these various levels of exposure created:

> "The number of dose related relationships are linear and statistically significant. You can play with this all you want. They are linear. They are statistically significant... I think you can't accept that this is out of the ordinary. It isn't out of the ordinary... The increased incidence of neurobehavioral problems in children in the past few

decades is probably real... I work in the school system where my effort is entirely in special education and I have to say that the number of kids getting help in special education is growing nationally and state by state at a rate we have not seen before."[12]

In obvious contrast to the official and frequent conjecture by the CDC that the increase in autism was merely due to better diagnosis and an ever-expanding medical definition of autistic disorders, Dr. Weil realized this study only confirmed what he, and millions of others involved in education around the nation, already knew by observation. The special education classrooms had waiting lists, handicapped school buses were in short supply, and state educational budgets were unable to cope with the demands. It had not always been so.

While a child with autism might spend twelve years of life futilely trying to read his own name, Dr. Brent had no trouble reading the writing on the wall—and he pronounced the message that he, and everyone else at Simpsonwood, saw with great clarity:

> "The medical legal findings in this study... are horrendous... So we are in a bad position from the standpoint of defending any lawsuits if they were initiated and I am concerned."[13]

Now, for a few, had the tragic irony become obvious? The pharmaceutical industry employed mercury, in the form of Thimerosal, as a preservative and antimicrobial, because it was cheap. It had disregarded proven issues of toxicity, and falsely asserted that Thimerosal was safe for injection into humans. Now that it was clear that Thimerosal was unsafe, and that at least one member of this committee wanted not one iota of it injected into the baby he loved, the fear of numerous lawsuits caused by the cheap preservative for catastrophically expensive lifelong injuries inclined this committee to count the cost, at last. Instead of numbering lost human lives, those at Simpsonwood seemed to calculate the lost dollars from anticipated lawsuits and settlements if this information ever became public.

Dr. John Clements, from the Expanded Program on Immunization of the World Health Organization, wished aloud that the study had never occurred.

"I am really concerned that we have taken off like a boat going down one arm of the mangrove swamp at high speed, when in fact there was not enough discussion really early on about which way the boat should go at all....

"And I really want to risk offending everyone in the room by saying that perhaps this study should not have been done at all, because the outcome of it could have, to some extent, been predicted, and we have all reached this point now where we are left hanging..."[14]

Though local physicians continued to inject mercury into babies in blissful ignorance, under the false tutelage of the federal agencies and pharmaceutical companies represented among the participants at Simpsonwood, Dr. Clements himself, and the others in this room who had received a full presentation on the Verstraeten study by its author, could no longer claim such absolution. Limits had been exceeded, both in the levels of mercury injected into infants and pregnant women, and in the levels of facts which could be denied.

The challenge that those at Simpsonwood now identified before themselves was not the issuance of public warnings about dangerous levels of mercury in the drug supply, especially in regard to vulnerable populations, but instead the avoidance of acting so as to occasion controversy and incrimination.

Dr. Clements now sought to delineate adequate boundaries for the information under discussion:

"I know how we handle it from here is extremely problematic. The ACIP* is going to depend on comments from this group in order to move forward into policy, and I have been advised that whatever I say should not move into the policy area because that is not the point of this meeting."

While the attendees needed to avoid the appearance of setting public health policy, Dr. Clements also seemed interested in avoiding the appearance of something else: guilt. How to be successful at this endeavor was still ambiguous. Why he and this body needed to be successful, however, was perfectly clear: the findings of this study, if they were released, would be akin to the explosive power of an atom bomb.

---

*Advisory Committee on Immunization Practices

Disseminating the knowledge that one in every 150 infants had become autistic due to massive amounts of mercury, hidden in vaccines injected into their bodies as required by law, would shake the soul of the nation. Furthermore, the realization that one in every six children was now affected by a developmental and/or behavioral disorder as a result of this same exposure would shatter public confidence in the vaccination program.

Let angry parents, and grandparents, and godparents and aunts and uncles and cousins and kin begin to add up the toll they had paid in heartache and savings and hope and vocation, and the sum would be so great as to occasion revolt. Those whose young had been maimed, if galvanized by this truth, might bring the nation to melt-down, or at least the federal health agencies, no matter what this committee finally said:

> "But nonetheless, we know from many experiences in history that the pure scientist has done research because of pure science. But that pure science has resulted in splitting the atom or some other process which is completely beyond the power of the scientists who did the research to control it. And what we have here is people who have, for every best reason in the world, pursued a direction of research. But there is now the point at which the research results have to be handled, and even if this committee decides that there is no association and that information gets out, the work that has been done and through the freedom of information that will be taken by others and will be used in ways beyond the control of this group. And I am very concerned about that as I suspect it is already too late to do anything regardless of any professional body and what they say."

Though Dr. Clements, confronting the Verstraeten study, assessed the situation created by Thimerosal with an image of global catastrophe, he seemed unable to foreswear an indoctrinated and unquestioning faith in vaccines. To be at Simpsonwood, afterall, was to have been called as a defender of this institutionalized faith, a staunch adherent to its bureaucratic beliefs at a critical point in history. Conscience was demonstrated not by doubt but by absolute assent. As if praying the rosary, those who believed in it recited a hollow litany of intercession for humankind: vaccination is the greatest good and gift of modern medicine... its benefits are proven... its dangers, only theoretical... the toxicity of a poison becomes negligible upon its inclusion as a component in a vaccine... to question vaccination is to harm public confidence... to harm public confidence is to reduce uptake... to reduce uptake is to place the vulnerable at risk... one cannot place the vulnerable at risk, so vaccination is never to be questioned...

Amid crisis, instead of recanting his faith in that which had just been demonstrated to inflict incalculable injury, pain and suffering on newborn children around the world for two decades, Dr. Clements of the World Health Organization appeared to steady himself and his professional position by unswervingly affirming his commitment to ongoing mass vaccination programs with Thimerosal. Refusing to abandon his belief, Dr. Clements declared:

> "My mandate as I sit here in this group is to make sure at the end of the day that 100,000,000 are immunized with DTP, Hepatitis B and if possible Hib, this year, next year and for many years to come, and that will have to be with Thimerosal containing vaccines unless a miracle occurs and an alternative is found quickly and is tried and found to be safe..."

Could this official of the World Health Organization in its Expanded Program on Immunization be unaware of 2-phenoxyethanol? Though safe and alternative preservatives were already used in production, Dr. Clements did not mention this fact to the assembled authorities. While his adherence to the practice of a vaccination faith was unwavering, Dr. Clements' closing remarks were tepid:

> "So I leave you with the challenge that I am very concerned that this has gotten this far, and that having got this far, how you present in a concerted voice the information to the ACIP in a way they will be able to handle it and not get exposed to the traps which are out there in public relations... I thank you for that moment to speak, Mr. Chairman, and I am sorry if I have offended you. I have the deepest respect for the work that has been done and the deepest respect for the analysis that has been done, but I wonder how on earth you are going to handle it from here..."

Dr. Roger Bernier, Associate Director for Science at the National

Immunization Program of the CDC, was as pedestrian about this matter as any other. Despite his detachment, even Dr. Bernier seemed to realize this meeting had dangerous implications for everyone in attendance:

> "We have asked you to keep this information confidential... So we are asking people who have done a great job protecting this information up until now, to continue to do that until the time of the ACIP (Advisory Committee on Immunization Practices) meeting... That would help all of us to use the machinery that we have in place for considering these data and for arriving at policy recommendations."[15]

Had the room caught on fire, someone would have shouted for help; had one of the staff suffered a heart attack, the physicians in attendance at Simpsonwood would have performed CPR; but were the nation's children in real and imminent danger of being poisoned by their unwitting pediatricians, which was indeed the case, this gathering of experts from government and industry most certainly planned to say nothing.

No one in the room asked, *"When exactly did the vaccine become more important than the child to whom it is administered?"*

Those with oversight for vaccination programs had arms that could reach around the globe. It was theirs to decide what vaccines and what vaccine components would be injected into the bodies of children around the world. Their power was absolute, for their product, it was thought, purveyed health and life and protection. With such reach and such power, there could be no mistrust, not about the infallibility of those who mandated the vaccines, nor about the contribution made by the vaccines themselves to society. To order the piercing of the skin with a sterile needle, the depressing of the plunger by benevolent hands, and the esteeming of a vaccinated infant's sacred cry as an initiation into a critical rite promising health and strength, those who sought to maintain plausible deniability, those who practiced cognitive dissonance, upheld the faith that worshipped vaccines and the power of those who manufactured and approved them.

Like one who fashions an amulet or charm, so did they fashion vaccines into household gods and idols, ignoring the base metal components. With this idolatry, unavoidably, came the profanity. False gods always exact their tribute. The most forbidden and most ancient prohibition in all the world religions—the most barbaric—returned to humankind cloaked in beneficence. Under the auspices of government, inculcated by corruption, and sanctioned by a compromised scientific community, child sacrifice was once again practiced when the poison was knowingly protected rather than the child. Yet, did those at Simpsonwood ever consider this faith misguided, or ponder that unswerving assent might be profane?

By accepting the sacrifice of children in the modern day, as in ancient times, adherents of an absolute faith in vaccines believe themselves to be protecting their nation, securing health for its people, and forestalling cataclysm and plague. Now as then, it is faith misplaced and corrupted. The sacrificial lambs today are chosen not on the basis of their birth order or their physical traits or obvious weaknesses as they were in the past, but on the basis of a genetically-determined susceptibility and sensitivity to poison.

At the end of the Simpsonwood Conference, the critical safety issues Verstraeten's study raised seemed awash in a tide of denial. Granted, there needed to be more studies. Granted, there may have been confounders obscuring an absolute clarity in his conclusions. Nonetheless, Verstraeten had specifically identified statistical correlations between mercury exposure and developmental delays, tics, ADD, language and speech delays, and neurodevelopmental delays that were "*statistically significant.*" Had no one in the room heard him when he said that?

The study, along with the comments and opinions of all the participants, were to be considered by eleven carefully chosen experts who remained behind at the Simpsonwood Retreat Center on June 9. Verstraeten, along with the other forty attendees, awaited the conclusions on the stark issue he had presented so forthrightly.

On Friday, the Simpsonwood Eleven, as they referred to themselves, were charged with gauging the evidence offered in regard to an association between Thimerosal and adverse outcomes. Should they deem it necessary, the Simpsonwood Eleven were also to suggest further areas of study. After careful review of all the information and opinions, they would render their verdict on the validity of Verstraeten's controversial work and conclusions.

Within twenty-four hours, the Simpsonwood Eleven's report and entire meeting transcript were prepared and distributed. The header said, "National Immunization Program, Office of the Director, Centers for Disease Control and Prevention." The subject line read "Transcription of consultant notes".

The cover sheet showed that Gayle Hickman had faxed them to Roger Bernier on Saturday, June 10, with the note: "Roger, I am faxing this to you per our conversation."[16]

The next page was entitled "Scientific Review of the Vaccine Safety Datalink Information, June 7-8, 2000, Simpsonwood Retreat Center." The panel had responded to three questions:

1.   Do you think the observations made to date in the Vaccine Safety Datalink Project about a potential relationship between vaccines and some specific neurologic developmental disorders (speech delay, attention deficit hyperactivity disorder, and developmental delay) warrant further investigation?

2.   If you think the observations on some specific neurologic development disorders to be valid, how strong or weak do you consider the data to be at this time; i.e. how much does the evidence support a causal relationship? (Scale: 1-6, with one being very weak and six being very strong), and

3.   If you think the observations on some specific neurologic developmental disorders constitute a signal, what do you think the next steps should be to further investigate a potential relationship?

To the first question, nine of the eleven had answered "Yes" indeed, further investigation was clearly merited. However, the reasons the Simpsonwood Eleven gave did not focus solely on increasing medical knowledge. Recorded among the consultant's comments were these:

"Concerns have been expressed, the data from this study exist and will become known, and there is a need to understand them better."[17]

And this:

"... the possibility that the association could be causal has major significance for public and professional acceptance of Thimerosal-containing vaccines. Finally, lack of further urgent study would be horrendous grist for the anti-vaccination mill."[18]

A third statement argued:

"You had a prior concern; you obtained mostly negative findings, but some positive results. If you do not treat this as a signal, other much less responsible parties will do so, and follow-up will be out of your control..."[19]

To the second question, four experts would assign a "1": "very weak" evidence supporting causation; six would assign a "2": "weak" evidence supporting causation; and one, Dr. Weil, who had troubled the conference with his remarks, even as the conference had troubled him with its cursory treatment of Verstraeten's findings, once again became the iconoclast, assigning a "4": "medium" evidence supporting causation.

Weil stated in his written comments: "A number of dose-related relationships are linear and statistically significant..." and, "The increased incidence of neuro-behavioral problems in children in the past few decades is too rapid to have been genetic..." and, "...the difficulties in interpretation... are not great enough to reject completely such a causal relationship..."[20] Dr. Weil was the only one of the eleven who seemed willing to admit that he had been convinced by visiting Epidemic Intelligence Service Officer Verstraeten.

Another one of the Simpsonwood Eleven added a note to his proposed outline for further study, it read: "All these suggestions may be moot since it appears the vaccine manufacturers seem to be already in the process of developing alternatives—thimerosal-free vaccines. Plus, it may be that ACIP, AAP, ACFP, etc., may feel compelled to act in the near term to avoid perceived (whether theoretical or real) risks to vaccine recipients. Thus, these combined actions may render these questions (and possible avenues to address them) of only academic interest." [21]

Apparently, two generations of children suffering development and behavioral disorders were collateral damage, to be considered unfortunate but justifiable. Statistics cited millions of persons, most of them children, diagnosed with autism in the United States.

For each child with a life-long developmental disability, requiring millions of dollars of care over a lifetime and exacting an even higher emotional cost from his caregivers, there were two parents, likely heartbroken. An ongoing epidemic of autism, if revealed to be the manufactured plague of the pharmaceutical industry, *even if it was a plague in decline due to the culpably slow withdrawal of Thimerosal from the market*, would not be deemed a subject "of only academic interest" by anyone but a fool. Instead, this issue had the potential to cause national and international political, economical, and social upheaval. Esteemed solely a public relations issue by this Simpsonwood Eleven member, the damage inflicted on newborn life was to be spun so as not to engender any decline in confidence in the National

Immunization Program which, it seemed, was guilty of poisoning the public en masse, in utero, in infancy, and even, in ignorance.

Responding to their deliberations, Verstraeten wrote an e-mail to Walt Orenstein, Jose Cordero, Roger Bernier, Bob Chen and select others of the National Immunization Program within the CDC. At 3:55 p.m., on Monday, June 12, 2000, Verstraeten pressed the send button. The e-mail message he sent read:

"Subject: Notes on the External expert meeting on thimerosal.

"First I'd like to give my thanks to the organizers of the meeting. I thoroughly enjoyed the opportunity to present my findings to such a select audience. As many of you have told me before, it's not usual for a EIS officer to work at this level. I am fully aware of this and the more grateful for it.
"I was however surprised by some of the statements made by some participants on the biological plausibility..."[22]

Verstraeten went on to list five important considerations, seemingly absent from the transcript's comments and the consultants' deliberations, needing consideration and review if biological plausibility were to be correctly judged. He concluded:

"As I remember, the biological plausibility played an important role in the assessment of the causal relationship as made by the Simpson 11. I hope the arguments made here demonstrate that a more balanced presentation and discussion would have been desirable."

When Bob Chen received a carbon copy of Verstraeten's email, he sent it on to Roger Bernier, with the question, "What do you think about circulating Tom's notes below to the consultants?"[23]

Bernier's electronic response when it finally came, was decisive: "I do not favor circulating this to the consultants."[24]

Verstraeten then e-mailed a fellow researcher and toxicologist, Philippe Grandjean, who was removed from this debacle by nationality and employment. Verstraeten complained to him in frustration:

"Dear Dr. Grandjean,
...I apologize for dragging you into this nitty gritty discussion, which

in Flemish we would call 'muggezziften.' ...Unfortunately, I have witnessed how many experts, looking at this thimerosal issue, do not seem bothered to compare apples to pears and insist that if nothing is happening in these studies then nothing should be feared of thimerosal. I do not wish to be the advocate of the anti-vaccine lobby and should like being convinced that thimerosal is or was harmful, but at least I feel we should use sound scientific argumentation and not let our standards be dictated by our desire to disprove an unpleasant theory.

Sincerely,

Tom Verstraeten"[25]

Sitting in their living room in suburban Maryland on that snowy February afternoon, Mark and David knew nothing of the Simpsonwood Eleven, and they knew nothing of the many revisions that were to come of the Verstraeten study, in which all findings of a causal association to neurodevelopmental disorders would be eliminated prior to its official publication in November 2003. They knew only that what happened at Simpsonwood, based on the transcript in their hands, was a violation of science, morality and the public trust.

The care and restraint they had exercised in first raising the possibility of a link between mercury exposure, from Thimerosal, and neurodevelopmental disorders, now seem misplaced. Almost by accident, they had stumbled upon statistical traces of gross negligence that the CDC had already analyzed and acknowledged within the secretive circle of Simpsonwood! Sickened by the failure of scientists, corporate executives and government officials to stop the injection of excessive levels of the poison mercury into children, they resolved that afternoon to break the shameful silence shrouding the CDC. Assiduously turning the pages of the transcript over in their hands, Mark and David began to outline the design of an extensive follow-up study to the original one they had already completed on Thimerosal.

These two men, who were so very rational and reasoned, could not adequately describe the haunting urgency that compelled them to conduct this research. That which they had first found unbelievable now seemed undeniable, though some had obviously tried. Armed with new evidence, contained in the Simpsonwood transcript and reviewed by the CDC, Mark and David were emboldened; their confidence, buoyed, and their resolve, immense. Convinced now, of the correctness of their previous findings, they would begin a study to attempt to examine all aspects of the relationship between Thimerosal and neurodevelopmental disorders. They would also begin to ponder how they could gain access to the Vaccine Safety Datalink, the statistical body of information from which Verstraeten's substantiating and now silenced analysis had come.

Ironic, Mark thought, that quietly, in small circles, and controlled environments, those charged with protecting the public health were betraying it. Ironic, that this unmistakable, statistical and crushing truth contained in the Vaccine Safety Datalink could be obscured by bureaucratic deceit, just as completely and quickly, as the greenery outside the window had been obscured from view by the whiteness. As the Geiers continued to struggle with the import of the Simpsonwood transcript, the snow continued to fall now in utter darkness.

CHAPTER SEVEN

PICKING UP THE PIECES

""The most dangerous thing you can do is to take any one impulse of your own nature and set it up as the thing you ought to follow at all costs. There is not one of them which will not make us into devils if we set it up as an absolute guide. You might think love of humanity in general was safe, but it is not. If you leave out justice you will find yourself breaking agreements and faking evidence in trials 'for the sake of humanity', and become in the end a cruel and treacherous man."

—C. S. Lewis
Mere Christianity

JUST AS WESLEY SUFFERED FROM POISONING, SO THE NATION SUFFERED AMNESIA. The case histories of Mad Hatters Disease had been distilled into a two-dimensional cartoon from *Alice in Wonderland*. These days, no one thought that the Hatter was mad because he had absorbed mercury through his hands when he was forming felt into hats, a known occupational hazard in the early 1900's. Nor did they consider how many symptoms of his condition were reminiscent of ADHD.[1]

Nor did anyone remember the mercury-induced diseases of America's past: pink disease and acrodynia, the result of mercury used as an ingredient in teething powders, also at the turn of the last century.[2]

And no one in America seemed to have ever heard of Minamata Disease, the catastrophe that resulted when Japan's Chisso Corporation polluted Minamata Bay with mercury. For years afterward, the government asserted that those poisoned from eating the bay's mercury-contaminated fish were suffering from an "infectious" illness. Lawsuits and compensations to thousands of victims of mercury poisoning continue to this day.[3]

Isn't a hundred years of poisoning people with mercury enough?

The symbol used for autism is the puzzle piece, created in 1963 by the National Autistic Society. How appropriate I now considered this, as all I seemed to do these days was to try and put the pieces together. Whether tracing the history of mercury-induced illnesses during the last hundred years or discovering the countless biochemical imbalances affecting my own son, I was always trying to "piece" together that which had fallen apart.

I came to realize that Wesley had "fallen to pieces" physiologically, after receiving massive doses of mercury through my Rh- immunoglobulin in utero and through his vaccines after birth. I was like a jigsaw aficionado intent on assembling this puzzle, one with thousands of exquisite and intricate pieces: my son's malfunctioning, mercury-toxic brain. While I had no idea if all the pieces could ever be put back into place, I was resolved to try, correcting one metabolic imbalance at a time. I dreamed of restoring my son to the picture of health.

Had the treatments we pursued and the results they occasioned been less dramatic, I might have abandoned Wesley's regime of two dozen supplements, special diets and chelation. But for almost every intervention I tried, I could now name what piece of the puzzle I had regained.

With each round of chelation, as Wesley's body burden of mercury came down, so did his hands: from their usual station at eye level, where he flicked them in front of his face incessantly, his hands now were more relaxed and had on occasion rested quietly in his lap. A gluten-free, casein-free diet banished the bright red color from his ears and the deep purple rings from beneath his eyes. Antifungals and probiotics resulted in die-offs, bringing to a halt a year and a half of chronic diarrhea. Perhaps all of these things together had given me the greatest improvement of all: Wesley no longer dropped to the floor, writhing in pain and biting the small flap of skin between his index finger and his thumb until it bled.

Mary's treatments had done much to ameliorate the wrenching symptoms of "autism", but while many crises had calmed, my son still seemed lost and far from me. He was blank. Empty. No longer in excruciating pain, he was still unable to register joy at his own birthday or affection at my embrace. Though I desired to fill him with my love if he could summon none of his own, his eyes telegraphed only a vacancy within his soul that constantly haunted mine. No matter what I did, no matter how I tried, I could not discern anything but autism's cavernous darkness, encompassed by the tragically beautiful blue of his eyes. What piece had I missed? What substance might still be absent from my son's mind and body?

JANUARY 2003

I breathed deep and pulled out the first pre-filled syringe from the transparent pharmacy-orange container. Methyl B-12.

"First A..." I thought back to the fat soluble vitamin A in the cod liver oil. What Mary recommended made such a difference in Wesley's ability to see and hear.

"Now B..." I encouraged myself. I already had "C" covered with the calcium supplement, I laughed! Wesley's alphabet, I told myself, is all biomedical. He is learning the ABC's of recovery, and I am learning the basics of how to give a shot. My hands trembled as I removed the cap to reveal a tiny silver needle.

"You sure you don't want to do it?" I whined to Seth.

"Oh, no," he protested with ultimate resolve. "You can't ask me to do that."

This was to be my job.

Mary wanted to see what effect additional methyl groups, delivered in the form of methyl B-12, would have upon Wesley's cognition and biochemistry. Dr. Richard Deth, a neuropharmacologist and professor of pharmacology at Northeastern University, just published an article explaining how mercury causes oxidative stress and how that stress deprives the brain of needed methyl groups.[4] That which mercury had stolen from Wesley, I had every intention of giving back—even if it meant learning how to inject the ruby red solution in the syringe into my son. What piece of the puzzle, what part of my son's mind, I wondered, might I regain this time?

The answer came quickly, within days.

"Seth, do you see that?" I studied Wesley in detail with every glance.

"See what?"

"The dimple?"

Seth first looked at me as if I were crazy.

"Look!"

A laughing child, with eyes that had suddenly been re-inhabited by tiny dancing sparks of light, smiled so broadly that I could see my son had a dimple, one dormant and obscured by autism until I put back this piece of his puzzle. Wesley's features were suddenly animated; his expressions defined and readable; his dimple, outed!

"Lisa, he looks great!" said the mother of another autistic child whom I met at the grocery store. "What are you doing? There's such a big change in him..."

Not only had the pallor diminished, but the rose was back in Wesley's cheeks. He began to look healthy again, and his emotions were etched more deeply into the contours of his face, by the will of his spirit, than I had seen since he was an infant. Methyl B-12, for Wesley, was a piece of his psyche, put back.

"Thank you, God," I offered, as a beaming seven year-old boy grinned up at me.

That one piece would have been enough, but this time I gained two. Seth and I had taken our sons, Adam, Wesley and Joshua, to the mall one night. Walking along the upper level, along glassy banisters that showcased the storefronts, I giggled as Seth reached down to tickle the boys.

Laughing with a joy that had so recently been extinct, Wesley took off at a run. Previously, his darting away from us had been no cause for concern, because his gait when he ran was almost semi-circular. It slowed him down. I knew, every time anyone saw my son run, they immediately realized he was disabled.

Yet, this time was different. Wesley took off in a full sprint, along the curve of the glassy corridor, and I could see every stride—straight, long, perfect.

I just stared, astounded. Then, the realization that with Joshua in my arms, I was not at liberty to give chase, dawned on me.

"Seth," I suddenly shouted, coming to my senses, "Go after him!"

By the time Seth caught up, Wesley had run thirty yards with the grace of a gazelle.

"Did you see that?" I said stupidly, catching up to Seth, Joshua in my arms and Adam by my side.

"Now," said Seth, taking several rapid breaths, "Just who do you think was chasing him?"

Wesley grinned up at us both, in mischief and delight.

As soon as I got in the door to my home, I dropped the packages and left Seth to oversee the boys. He already knew where I was headed: www. google.com, I typed. The server could not respond fast enough for my curiosity. At last, the search box appeared: "Vitamin B-12 deficiency symptoms." I clicked. I waited. I read.

"Seth!" I shouted up the stairs.

"What?" he asked, slightly annoyed that he was left to get the boys in their pajamas.

I felt too triumphant to pay any attention to his frustration. Instead, I telegraphed my new discovery up the stairs much more loudly than the hour or the distance demanded. "An abnormal gait is a sign of a B-12 deficiency"

"How many pieces," I asked myself, "How many more pieces are there?"

The internet became the late night town hall where parents of autistic children gathered, unhindered by the need to find respite care for their disabled children. The internet was the first to inform parents that the Homeland Security Bill—ballooned from an original thirty-five to 484 pages packed with pork—had passed with a rider to shield Eli Lilly from lawsuits due to its product Thimerosal.

"You've got to be kidding!" I shouted at the computer screen as I read that an unidentified senator added a rider to the Homeland Security Bill, not to protect the nation from terrorists, but Eli Lilly from lawsuits due to Thimerosal. The rider, hidden in the expanse of the epic bill at the last possible moment, was passed unknowingly by the U.S. House of Representatives.

"Of course, Thimerosal is perfectly safe! That's why we need federal legislation, added covertly, at the stroke of midnight, to a bill of epic proportions, in order to protect the makers of the poison manufactured for injection into our children! Of course, it's perfectly safe!" I was rarely so caustic or sarcastic.

Seth looked up at me. He was not sure which he needed to address more: the injustice of the rider which had now passed into law, depriving his son of legal redress, or the outrage of his wife which had now passed into orbit, depriving his home of any quiet he might have hoped to enjoy that evening.

"Lisa, you knew they would try something like this..."

"Yes, yes, that's true! But how despicable! No debate! No identification of the rider at all! Whoever did this is a coward! A corrupt coward! He can't even stand and fight! He has to trick the nation into betraying its own children—AGAIN! You know what I found out on the net? Congressmen Burton and Weldon, our strongest supporters, voted for this ludicrous thing because even they didn't know it was there! Apparently, once Congressman Burton became aware of it, he went to the Senate, which had yet to vote on the bill, and spent hours, asking various senators to remove it, but they all declined. The pressure to get the Department of Homeland Security up and running was so intense, that no one wanted to begin again with an amended bill in the House."

My husband knew me too well: "So what are you going to do, Lisa?"

"I don't know," I answered, "but we've got to do something!"

For the parents, "something," as it turned out, was a rally: "Know the Cause, Find the Cure," in Upper Senate Park in Washington, D.C., on January 8, 2003. The action alert went out by e-mail from Laura Bono, President of the National Autism Association, NAA, to the ever-increasing list of parents who realized they had mercury-poisoned children and, subsequently, searched the internet for help.[5] Laura, an enterprising and very purposeful autism mom from North Carolina, had realized the need for an open and public non-profit organization to connect the parents of autistic children. Thankfully, NAA was in place as the bugle for an internet army of parents when the covert Homeland Security Rider became law. Laura became the strategic communication hub for much of the mercury-cognizant autism community. She had never heard of Lisa Sykes from Richmond, Virginia, before I responded to her action alert.

Through the NAA alert, Laura Bono conscripted me to my first public demonstration. I took the day off work, brought my nursing son, Joshua, to stay with his aunt and uncle in my home town of Vienna, Virginia, just outside D.C., and joined in my first public protest. In keeping with Laura's recommendations, I arranged to meet with my congressman's health aide, Colleen Maloney, that afternoon.

This appointment would serve as my follow-up with my congressman. I had already assembled six mothers of autistic children to meet with Congressman Eric Cantor at his home office in Richmond, Virginia, a few months earlier. Armed with before-and-after photos of our children, chelation reports documenting off-the-chart mercury readings, and the fury that only the mothers of unnecessarily injured children can feel, we meet with Cantor in September 2002, newspaper and local television reporters in tow. During the course of our first meeting, Cantor likened the Thimerosal debacle at the CDC to the financial scandal of Enron, promising, "I am going to use my power as a Congressman to look into the CDC..." Foolishly, I believed him.

As the day of the rally neared, Jo Pike, one of the moms in NAA working to organize the event, e-mailed me with a request. "Could you do an invocation at the start of the rally?" Beneath her message was an automatic tag-line that appeared on all of her e-mails; this message captivated me because it was scripture, and certainly because it was encouragement:

> "But thus says the Lord: Even the captives of the mighty shall be taken, and the prey of the tyrant be rescued; for I will contend with those who contend with you, and your children I will save."
>   —Isaiah 49:25

I learned that Jo, and many other parents like her, were characterized by a profound and deep faith. It was this faith that helped them fight, rather than succumb, to the overwhelming demands of autism. I was thrilled to accept Jo's request. It would be a small contribution from my vocation to this just cause. If ever anything I had done was in accord with Christ's call to welcome the children, this was!

The day of the rally was cold! The wind whisked by the small assembly of parents—no more than thirty had found the information and opportunity to attend. The care and cost of an autistic child left many isolated in their homes with only outraged hearts for company. And so NAA invited parents to dedicate empty chairs, upon which their children's pictures would be placed. As I arrived at Upper Senate Park, my first task was to help unload the chairs and tape to each one the picture of a poisoned child. I was given instruction by a lovely red-head whose curly hair cascaded well down her back.

"Lisa? Is that you? I'm Jo."

I looked up, and embraced this friend and ally whom I had never met. Jo was not my only internet acquaintance to be incarnated that day. A very organized, petite brunette, with a wry sense of humor and obvious efficiency, also approached. I had already guessed: "Laura?" Laura was a dynamo, with focused eyes and sequential, neatly delineated goals. The hour before the rally was a who's who of internet names that now became faces I could recognize and companions whom I could embrace.

As the rally began, the speakers were arranged in order of appearance: there was the 9–11 widow and mother of an autistic child whose rights had been taken away by a bill meant to honor her dead husband; Congressman Dan Burton; and Dr. Edward Yazbak, former Pediatric Director of the Child Development Study, an Assistant Member of the Institute of Health Sciences at Brown University, and an early pioneer in the biological approach to autism. I was amazed to find myself, a Democratic leaning pastor, standing right beside the Republican congressman who had surprisingly come to be one of my great heroes.

I waited for Jo to finish her introductory remarks, and call me forward for the invocation. I began:

"Let us pray:
  To You,
  Who knows what they see with their kalidescope eyes
  Who hears what they cannot say
  Who feels the hurt they cannot hide
  Who promises them justice one day…"

Offering this prayer was such a simple responsibility to fulfill. I did not know, but by its end, Jo had tears in her eyes. The prayer said, I turned to assume my previous spot on the grey stone ellipse as Congressman Burton approached the podium. Instead of passing me, he slowed and stopped, and so I responded in kind. To my surprise, the Midwestern congressman leaned over and kissed me on the cheek in thanks. I thought to myself, "He must be a Methodist!"

The Homeland Security Rider, which was repealed with the start of the next legislative session, backfired on those who had schemed to pass it in stealth. It catalyzed the parents into organized groups, now keenly attuned to political maneuvering at the federal level. It gave impetus for three Republican congressmen, who threatened to switch parties if the rider was not repealed with the start of the next legislative session, to argue forcefully against the contention that Thimerosal was safe. And finally, it provoked so much publicity in national papers that a reporter for *The New York Times*, David Kirby, began to examine the issue for his future book, *Evidence of Harm: Mercury in Vaccines and the Autism Epidemic, A Medical Controversy*, which would debut on the *New York Times* bestseller list in 2005.

Chapter Eight

A Providential Circle

"If there is a problem somewhere… this is what happens. Three
people will try to do something concrete to settle the issue. Ten
people will give a lecture analyzing what the three are doing.
One hundred people will commend or condemn the ten for their
lecture. One thousand people will argue about the problem. And
one person—only one—will involve himself so deeply in the true
solution that he is too busy to listen to any of it."

—Elias Chacour, *Blood Brothers*

June 2003

A Kansas mother of three autistic children, Kelly Kerns was the first
parent to contact the Geiers. As she called, she was so intent on choosing
exactly the right words for each of her sentences, that she did not immediately grasp the significance of the lovely tinkling sound that gently beck-
oned her. On the phone, engrossed in conversation with Mark and David,
Kelly did not initially comprehend the full import of soft random pitches that
serenaded her like the gentle cascade of a wind chime.

"Everyone is so mad about the rider! It's a confession of guilt! Tell me,
how many years 'til this thing comes down?" she asked the Geiers.

In the second immediately after Mark replied, "Ten years!" Kelly lost her
breath twice. The first time because, as she expressed in her reply, "I don't
have ten years."

The second time because, as she spoke, the musical cadence of crystal-like sound finally reached its crescendo, and now, it was too late for Kelly to do anything about it.

Mark and David let words of encouragement forming upon their tongues die upon their lips as they were silenced by the sound of a tremendous crash reverberating over the phone line.

"Oh my God, Andrew!" Kelly screamed.

Utterly unable to be of any assistance, all Mark and David could do for the next several minutes was listen to a frantic mother screaming at her son. Andrew, the second of Kelly's three children and a twin boy, knew as well as any other child that the best time to get into trouble was when mom was on the phone. He surmised this, even though he had autism. The three year-old, in one of his manic moments, had leapt from the staircase of the family's impressive Kansas home and onto the crystal chandelier.

The musical clarity of that chiming, which Kelly had heard but not understood, was the momentum of her son as his body swayed and the chandelier swung, from one side to another. Now, the child was grounded, shouting not in fear at how far he had plummeted or even at what his mother might say, but only in protest of being confined by a mountain of crystal and brass. "Mom, get off! Mom, get off! Mom, get off!" he screamed, eager to be up and moving once again.

Kelly freed her son, only to see him resume his incessant motion about the house, completely oblivious to the chaos he had just created. Kelly at last remembered the receiver, still lying where it dropped from her hand onto the floor. Tears streaming down her face, a hitch in her breathing, she barely dared to pick it up again. Testing the line, dreading to imagine what these two scientists must be thinking, if they were still listening, she whispered, "Hello?"

"Yeah, we're here. Is everyone okay?" David was almost afraid to ask.

"I'm so sorry..." was all Kelly could choke out, before sobs overtook her.

Mark and David, who were together on speakerphone in their basement office, looked at one another, bewildered. This was the first call they had ever received from a parent of an autistic child. Knowing nothing about this woman named Kelly, whom they could hear crying a thousand miles away, Mark and David tried to offer consolation. The child was all right, obviously.

They were pleased Kelly had called. Hey, could she tell them a little about her child and his or her descent and diagnosis? This was the question that seemed at last to quiet her crying.

David felt outrage as Kelly recounted the story of, not one, but three perfectly healthy babies born without incident, developing normally, until well into the standard regimen of mandated childhood immunizations. Mark interrupted the conversation, wanting to lighten the emotions weighing on the Kansas mom he had never met. "Kelly, did we tell you we have a new article recently published in the *Journal of American Surgeons and Physicians* about all this?" [1]

Kelly, whose intellect was as strong as her emotions, yearned to know more. She had waited a long time to find champions for her children.

"You mean about Thimerosal?" asked Kelly, praying the answer would be yes. It was.

"Kelly," Mark began to explain, "The first thing we have done here is to add up the amount of mercury children are getting. You know, we've heard the other side say, 'The mercury exposure from vaccines is slightly in excess...' Kelly, do you want to know how much in excess?"

Though unsure, Kelly answered affirmatively.

"125-fold!" Mark proclaimed. As Mark detailed his calculations, he could not see that Kelly's jaw was on the floor. "The EPA guideline is 0.1 micrograms of mercury per Kilogram bodyweight per day. Now, let's say your child weighed about eleven pounds. Convert that and you get about five kilograms. So your child is allowed 0.5 micrograms of mercury exposure. Now at two months, your eleven pound child was immunized with Hepatitis B vaccine which contained 12.5 micrograms of mercury, and a Haemophilus influenzae type B vaccine, which contained 25 micrograms of mercury, and a DTP vaccine, which also carried 25 micrograms of mercury. Kelly, that means your child got 125 times the EPA Safe Limit!"

Kelly gasped.

David continued, "We just returned from presenting our new paper to the Attorney Generals at their conference in Oklahoma."

Kelly caught her breath for just a split second. "Attorney Generals?" she asked, confused.

"Well, the AG's are the chief lawyers for the states. One of their responsibilities is to bring suits in cases where the citizens of their state have been harmed. On behalf of the state they can seek damages—say the cost of the care a patient required as the result of consuming a dangerous product. Tobacco is the most obvious example. This is how the states got settlements for the medical care needed by those who came down with lung cancer and other smoking-related diseases."

"But I thought, for a vaccine, the pharmaceuticals were protected by the National Vaccine Injury Compensation Program, so you could not sue them...?"

David relayed the new learning he had gained at the conference: "Individuals can't sue, but the states can. They are free and clear to go after the pharmaceuticals, if an Attorney General will file. Here, tell me what state do you live in, Kelly?"

"Kansas."

David continued, hypothetically. "Well, say, if the Kansas Attorney General made up his mind tomorrow that the pharmaceutical companies had distributed a defective vaccine in his state that contained unsafe levels of mercury, and this vaccine had injured tens of thousands, then the Kansas AG could sue the pharmaceuticals without any obstacle."

Kelly's face widened with wonder, and then for the first time in months, a tenuous smile on her lips attempted to overtake the sadness that had, for so long, extinguished the joy in her eyes.

"The drug companies are not impervious? There is a public official at the state level who can bring a halt to all this?" Kelly's mind now outpaced David's helpful explanation. This is what she needed: a purpose, a direction, a chance to save someone else's child from the fate of her own three.

"David! What incredible news! I had no idea! I didn't know the states could sue for medical costs for their citizens..."

"Well, apparently, it's not just medical costs. The AG can file a suit to recover the costs for social services and educational services and the long-term care costs incurred by the states."

"Millions. You're talking about millions of dollars, David!"

"Yeah, I know." David's matter-of-fact acknowledgement was lost in the excitement of Kelly's sudden epiphany.

"This is great! Absolutely great! If Pharma gets hit by huge lawsuits from every state, they will have to stop putting the mercury in the vaccines! The kids will be safe!"

"That'd be the idea, Kelly," said David with a gentle laugh. He was impressed with this mother's tenacity.

"What if I go to the Kansas Attorney General?" Kelly suddenly asked. "What if I call him up and get an appointment? Would you all like me to do that? Would you come with me? I'd need you to explain your work, so they don't think I'm just some crazy mother!"

"Why, sure. I don't see why not." said Mark. Kelly could not see him shrugging his shoulders at David.

"Yeah, you get it set up, and we'll be glad to come."

David rolled his eyes. Did this woman honestly think she was going to gain entrée with the Attorney General for Kansas on the subject of mercury in vaccines and other drugs?

"We've got to go now," interrupted David, aware that his father had patients to see later that morning. After they hung up, the two men looked at each other.

"It'll never happen."

"Yeah. No chance."

JULY 2003

Preoccupied with tennis, Mark and David had nearly forgotten about the phone call from the mother of three autistic children in Kansas. Weeks had passed, and this particular afternoon, they were finishing a match on the private tennis court behind their house when the phone rang.

"Hello?"

"Mr. Geier?"

"Yes," answered David, wondering to whom this vaguely familiar voice belonged.

"Mr. Geier, this is Kelly Kerns, the mom in Kansas..."

Not again, David thought. Not right now. He had a score to settle with his father on the tennis court. But that was not what he said.

"Hello, Kelly. How are things?"

"Things are great, Mr. Geier! Everything is set. We have a meeting with Attorney General Phil Kline next Thursday at 10 o'clock."

It was the second time the Geiers had been surprised on the tennis court.

"What!" was all that David could say.

"The Attorney General has agreed to meet with us. You all can fly into Kansas City, and then we will need to drive about two and a half hours to Topeka."

David's hand went to his forehead as he sought to process what Kelly was saying. He knew her words should be making sense, but they weren't, at least not to him.

"Kelly, hang on a minute. Let me give you my father…"

David rejoined his father on the court, handing him the indigo cell phone which was always in his pocket. "Here, you talk to her."

"To whom?"

"To Kelly, the mom from Kansas. She wants us to come out there!"

"Hello, Kelly, this is Mark Geier."

"Dr. Geier! I can't wait to meet you. The meeting is all set up. Did David tell you?"

"Tell me what?"

"The Attorney General here in Kansas, Phil Kline, has given us a meeting next Thursday. I will pick you all up at the airport. Just let me know once you have made your reservations…"

Kelly continued to speak, but Mark, like David, missed much of what she was saying.

"Kelly, could you repeat that again…"

"Get your tickets, and just let me know when you will be getting in. I can't wait to meet you. You don't know how much I appreciate this."

Mark said farewell, and stared at David. David stared back.

"Well, I guess we were wrong."

"Well, I guess we were," Mark said curtly.

News of the Geiers' Kansas meeting spread rapidly. On September 29, 2003, at 6:45 a.m., before her son got out of bed, Jo Pike sent out an e-mail to a very large parent distribution list. Its header was "Parent Power!" and it sought to do the inconceivable in six pages: invite parents to participate in a national effort to meet with their state Attorney Generals, brief them on legal precedent and argument, provide them with the latest research to bolster the case against mercury, and finally encourage them, once securing an appointment with their Attorney General, to enlist the Geiers as participants and presenters.

The novel strategy would now enlist the most motivated and politically astute autism parents around the nation. As this information was electronically disseminated across the country, Mark and David had no idea that their political involvement with the Kansas Attorney General, and their names, were being commended to a nation of eager autism parents who, like Kelly, would be calling to recruit their expertise and help.

Reading each word of Jo's message, I grew more and more excited. I felt both a pastoral call and a parental responsibility to respond, and my resolve was only deepened by the fact that I lived in a state capital, some twenty minutes away from Attorney General Jerry Kilgore's office. A morning trip to downtown Richmond in an effort to protect all the children of the Commonwealth, and to saber-rattle before the pharmaceutical companies, was a worthwhile investment of my time and energy! My email reply back to Jo was simple: "I call Virginia!"

So I composed yet another letter to entreat an elected official to help end the administration of mercury to pregnant women, babies, and children; only because this letter was addressed to Richmond, rather than Washington, did I believe it might have some hope of success. Success came more quickly than I expected. The Assistant Attorney General, for Health, Social Services and Education in the Commonwealth, responded on December 1, 2003:

> "The Attorney General is greatly concerned about the issues you raise and has asked that I meet with you to discuss the matter in more detail... Please contact my secretary... to arrange the meeting. The Attorney General appreciates the time you took to bring this matter to his attention and I look forward to meeting with you."

The strategy that Jo had disseminated was sound and the argument clear. And in stark contrast to the federal bureaucracy, the state government seemed accessible. Immediately, I reached for the phone to call Mary.

"Hey, Mary, remember me writing the FDA? Well, this time it's the Virginia Attorney General. You can't stay low profile forever, you know!"

"What have you been up to this time?" Mary laughed cautiously, expecting some form of invitation at the end of our discussion.

I told Mary of the newly identified strategy and my need for medical experts to present at a meeting with Deputy Attorney General. Without hesitation, Mary indicated her willingness not only to attend but also to contact

Dr. Elizabeth Mumper, a research physician from Lynchburg who, like Mary, had come to understand how vaccines were disabling a certain subpopulation of children. The appointment was set for early in the New Year after I had traversed my pastoral responsibilities for the Christmas Season.

There were other preparations to make as well. I e-mailed Jo: "Can you send me the Geier's phone number? I need to see if they can make the AG meeting here in Virginia! Thanks, L."

Jo responded quickly by phone, but to no avail. "My computer crashed last week. I've lost their contact information."

I sighed. Well, that was that. I had no idea how to find Mark and David Geier, but I did have two phenomenal women physicians in the field of the biological treatment of autism, as well as Wesley's off-the-chart mercury lab, and my own outspoken passion to present to the Deputy Attorney General. What more could it take to convince a reasonable person to prosecute companies who marketed undisclosed poison for injection into babies?

I spent the next week assembling various studies and reference articles to deliver to the Assistant Attorney General. Most were on disc, so I took it to a copy shop to have the files printed and bound. One evening, shortly before our appointment with the Attorney General, Seth stopped on his way home from work to pick up the materials.

"Lisa, I got them!" he yelled as he came in the door. He knew the last couple days before one of these big meetings were hard for me to endure.

"Oh, you are such a dear," I said, kissing Seth for a substantial time longer than the usual two-seconds we typically had before our three boys demanded their daddy's attention.

As the boys circled in, I rescued the box from Seth's arms, and eagerly poured over its pages, checking to see that the order had been completed as I wanted. The first article was by the Geiers.

"Seth, look at this!" I shouted.

"I can't right now, I've got one boy on this leg and another boy on that one, and the third one in my arms."

"Oh, never mind looking! Guess what?"

Seth was none too interested in a game of twenty questions, as our children mistook him for an indoor climber.

"Would you just tell me," he said with an impatient laugh.

"Here at the bottom of the article on the first page—it's the Geiers' location. You can see it now that the article has been printed. For heaven's sakes, Seth, they're just in Silver Spring, Maryland!"

I left dinner waiting on the stove, and grabbed the phone.

"Directory Assistance. What city and state please?"

I assumed that the Geiers' phone number would be unlisted but was intent on trying to secure it anyway. Slowly the connection was made. I waited. The automated voice on the other end of the line began to spit out numbers.

"Yes!" I shouted as I scribbled down the ten digits. "I've got it. I've got the Geiers' phone number!"

Seth knew dinner was going to be late.

I frantically wondered what to say, as the beep of an answering machine sounded in the other end of the phone.

"Hello, Dr. Geier, this is Reverend Lisa Sykes of Richmond, Virginia. I have a meeting with the Attorney General's office here the day after tomorrow. I'm afraid I just found your phone number and wanted to know if I might give the Attorney General your contact information in case he has any questions. My number is..."

I slumped into a kitchen chair as Seth entered the room, still being pursued by Sykes boys. I was cautiously hopeful that the Geiers might respond. Seth, by contrast, had other hopes at the moment.

"So, can we eat now?"

The next morning, I was in a graduate seminar at the Virginia Institute of Pastoral Care, when my cell phone went off. Everyone in my small class knew how important this call was to me, as I had told them of the previous day's discovery, just as I had told them of my advocacy and exploits over the last semester. The professor smiled, already aware that I planned to slip out of the lecture if an urgent call came through. It had.

"Hello, I'm calling a Reverend Lisa Sykes?" said a deep and rather perplexed voice on the other end of the line.

"Yes, Dr. Geier, this is she. Thank you so much for calling me back!" My hands were shaking.

"You have a meeting with the Office of the Attorney General there in Virginia?"

"Yes, the Assistant AG. It will be tomorrow at 10 o'clock. I was wondering if I could give your name."

"Tomorrow at 10?" the voice interrupted. I could hear one voice interacting with another in the background. I was not even sure with which of the Geiers I was speaking, though I would learn in time it was David. "You don't know how rare this is! I think we can actually make it to the meeting tomorrow."

I never imagined that Mark and David Geier would travel to Richmond on virtually no notice to attend this meeting along with Mary and Liz and me! I was thrilled and nervous.

The Geiers were surprised the next morning by the provincialism of Virginia. Most of the state Attorney General Offices to which they had traveled were located in the state capitol building. These buildings were enormous, sometimes rivaling the size of the federal capitol in dimension, if not power. The State House in Virginia, however, had been designed by a native son, an architect by the name of Thomas Jefferson. In reverence for the legacy of this founding father, the state of Virginia had resolutely refused to alter the brick and column of its Palladian edifice with its characteristic rotunda, a symbolic receptacle for Jefferson of wisdom and learning.

Instead of diminishing the ensconced presence of Jefferson by expanding and altering his architecture, the state of Virginia uncharacteristically chose to locate its state officials in large office buildings in the nearby commercial downtown area. Thus, Mark and David found themselves entering a nondescript shiny grey high rise with inconspicuous entrances and guards posted just inside the door. They also found themselves in the company of three Virginian women. Mary, and I were graduates of the University of Virginia, home of another untouched architectural rotunda by Jefferson.

The Geiers recognized Mary immediately. Epidemiologically, Mark and David had traversed the same wilderness that Mary had clinically, arriving in the same place literally and metaphorically as she had, only three years later.

"Take the elevators to the seventh floor. Someone will be waiting there to meet you," instructed the uniformed guard, hastily.

Mark, David, Mary, Liz, and I all entered the elevator, chit-chatting nonchalantly. For Mark and David, this was just one more in a series of meetings with state officials. For Mary, Liz and me, this was a new and bold adventure. It was, I thought to myself, a variation on a theme of states rights which had played out in the south once before. Strangely, in the Civil War, it was the state of Virginia, along with other southern states, that had violated the rights of the individual, and the federal government which sought to redress the injustice. Now, it was the federal government that was violating individual rights, especially the right of informed consent, and the states which must seek redress. I prayed that the Deputy Attorney General might understand both the opportunity and the responsibility which my companions and I had come to place before them.

The elevator beeped. "Seventh Floor," announced an automated voice. We five stepped out of the elevator to be greeted by a woman in a blue blazer and a flowing floral skirt. "Hello. Welcome to the Office of the Attorney General. Before we go to the conference room, do any of you need to use the restroom?"

We looked at each other, a bit surprised to be surveyed on the current state of our bladders. The aide thought perhaps she had been a bit too expedient in her inquiry, and hastened to explain, "Once the meeting begins, no one will be allowed to exit the room." Again, we looked at each other, and we ladies, assuming prudence to be the best course of action, excused ourselves to the ladies room, just down the hallway.

Mary, with her usual spunk, piped up from behind a closed door, "Just how powerful is this guy that we have to pee before we see him?"

Liz and I burst out laughing. This protocol was absolutely comic. A great contrast, I thought, to the seriousness of the meeting about to take place. We women rendezvoused with the men, and were shown into a conference room, surrounded by windowless hallways. David commented to his father, "Reminds me of a Habitrail, Dad."

The conference room was empty except for a large table, encircled by some twenty chairs, a projection screen, already in place at my request, and the flags of the United States and the Commonwealth of Virginia on either side of the screen. The meeting was set to begin at 10 a.m., and last for one hour. I had asked for two, but the scheduler was most begrudging of the Deputy Attorney General's time. Mark and David readied their power point presentation with an ease and confidence that came from giving it numerous times before. Mary, Liz and I stood chatting, unsure what to expect.

The door opened suddenly, and in walked a man of average stature, blonde hair, and boyish face. The Deputy Attorney General stopped at the head of the table, in preparation to shake the hands of his guests. Surveying those standing before him, he focused on me, and pointing at me without explanation said, "Bradley."

I, who had been rehearsing in my mind what I would say in greeting, was completely surprised.

Tilting my head to the side, I said, "Excuse me?"

"Bradley!" said the Deputy Attorney General once again.

"Has he confused me with someone else?" I wondered silently.

"Childbirth classes!" he finally blurted out.

A sudden wave of recognition swept across my mind.

It had been ten years. I was pastoring my first church, and this man was a young lawyer. His wife was expecting, as was I in 1993, and we and our respective spouses had enrolled in a course to prepare expectant parents to meet the challenges of natural childbirth. Bradley classes were not for the faint of heart. They were for those who realized medical intervention could reduce the likelihood of having a healthy child. I had known to safeguard my child from medical intervention during labor. If only, I thought to myself, I had known to protect him from mercury, before and after birth.

"I know you," he declared with satisfaction, "You and I were in the same Bradley class when we were expecting our first children."

Mark, David, Mary and Liz all looked at me. What were the odds? This meeting was beginning quite well, after all. I then made the introductions.

The meeting began. The Geiers, experienced with presentations to Attorneys General, sought to specify the importance and scope of the issue by showing the Detroit WXYZ television series of investigative reports by Steve Wilson. [2]

Wilson's hard-hitting nightly television segments had so embarrassed the CDC and FDA that he was told he would lose his job over them. Pharmaceutical patrons were threatening to boycott his news show by withdrawing their advertising dollars. Trouble was, after it aired, the series won Wilson an Emmy for investigative journalism, and when that occurred, the station could hardly fire him.

Segment by segment, Steve Wilson reported on Thimerosal's lack of safety data, the misrepresentation of vaccines as Thimerosal-free by health officials, and finally the federal conspiracy and collusion typified by the meeting held at Simpsonwood Retreat Center in Norcross, Georgia. As the tape played, Steve Wilson alluded to the secret meeting between CDC officials and pharmaceutical executives behind closed doors. Then, the screen was illuminated by footage of a stone gate with a large sign, saying "Simpsonwood United Methodist Retreat Center" and beside these words was emblazoned the trademarked "cross and flame", the emblem of my denomination. My jaw dropped, and as I closed my mouth, I hoped no one had seen.

"How dare they!" I shouted silently. "It was at a United Methodist Retreat Center where they plotted to continue poisoning the world's children instead of working to protect them."

I could feel my chest filling with air and then falling, heavily, and I realized that I no longer heard what was being stated by the recorded voice-over on the tape. "Isn't it bad enough they poisoned my child?" I shouted within my soul. "Did they have to desecrate my denomination, too?" The day would come, I knew, when this issue would gain enough notoriety and respect that I could bring it to the leaders and the Bishops of the United Methodist Church. But that day was not yet. I seethed as I sat, furious at those who would practice profanity as they abided in a sacred space and "practice medicine" as they injected poison into children.

Mary had watched the clip, and then glanced over at me. She bit the end of her pen gently, imagining with great accuracy what was going through my mind. She understood the two pronged assault I felt as a Methodist minister and the mother of an industrially toxic child. Mary not only knew her mute patients in great depth, she also knew their parents in great detail.

As the clip finished, Liz was the first to chime in. She gave a brief account of her realization that children were unknowingly being poisoned by their pediatricians with Thimerosal. It was a personal one. After stating her credentials and professional experience, Liz recounted, "I had a pediatric practice and I knew every child in it. I knew every one by name. As I sat in a seminar, and came to realize the information being presented on the toxicity of Thimerosal was accurate, the name and the face of every child in my practice diagnosed with autism, each child I had administered vaccines to, flashed through my head. And I knew. I knew I was the one who had given them the poison. I went to the ladies room, and I threw up."

"You don't have to convince me," said the Deputy Attorney General. "I know the FDA and CDC are corrupt. I hate them. They license RU486 so college girls can die in their dorm rooms. I'd love to get them. I have no trouble believing you at all."

I quietly breathed a prayer of thanksgiving for physicians like Mary and Liz and researchers like Mark and David who could bring public officials to such a daring declaration. How rare and precious they all were.

Mary began to further the evidence, speaking of Wesley's case history and the signs of mercury poisoning clearly evident in it. Pallor, vitamin deficiencies, mineral deficiencies, yeast overgrowths, sensory disturbances....

"You can treat these kids and get them better!" Mary asserted with a tone as strong as her conviction. She wanted the Deputy Attorney General's political support for researching treatments for affected children, as well as his legal involvement in prosecuting the pharmaceutical companies.

Mark and David chimed in again. "Since we published our first study in *Experimental Biology and Medicine*, there has been epidemiological evidence that Thimerosal is causing neurodevelopmental disorders. Since the Simpsonwood transcript was obtained by SafeMinds, we have had criminal evidence that there was a cover-up. But now, we can also present to you what we were before unable to present to anyone: the first published clinical evidence that mercury is causal."

Mary, Liz and I looked at one another in turn. What was this? A brand new study? No one could tell if the deputy AG or we women from Virginia were more mesmerized by what the Geiers had to say.

"Dr. Jeff Bradsteet and Dr. Jerold Kartzinel, physicians in Florida, Dr. James Adams of Arizona State University, and we have conducted a clinical study of 221 children and eighteen controls. We gave them DMSA, a standard drug used to pull heavy metals from body tissues, three times a day for three days. Then we did urine samples on each of the children, testing for cadmium, lead and mercury. The children with autism were found to have three times more mercury than controls. These higher levels of mercury are also being detected in hair and stool samples. It is painfully obvious that certain children, genetically, cannot successfully excrete heavy metals, mercury in particular. They have abnormally low levels of glutathione and cysteine."[3]

Mary and Liz had begun to furiously scribble notes on what the Geiers were saying. Mary smiled. The Geiers' new clinical study illustrated, in minute detail, what she was seeing in her practice and her patients every day.

"We've blocked the metabolic pathways." I heard Mary speaking in my memory. "We've created a metabolic syndrome in these children."

"This has to stop!" Liz argued to the Attorney General. "There aren't enough of us physicians who understand the injury to even begin treating all these children!"

The door to the conference room opened, and Carrie strode in authoritatively. She bent over and quietly stated, "Your next appointment is here."

"Cancel it, Carrie. Cancel all of my appointments until after lunch."

Mark and David smiled. They had predicted on the way here that this would happen. Appointments which were to follow their meetings with each Attorney General had been cancelled in every state capital they had visited so far.

The aide walked out, somewhat surprised but dutiful, nonetheless.

The Deputy Attorney General scanned the urgent expressions on those seated before him. "Outlawing a drug that the FDA says is perfectly safe will be problematic. Now, you want me to damage a product? I can do that."

The day waned on, as Mary and Liz took turns calling their offices by cell, and canceling the afternoon appointments which they had wrongly assumed they would be able to keep.

The Deputy Attorney General, as if upon a Bible, swore he would meet with those gathered around his conference table again, after the upcoming short session of the Virginia General Assembly concluded. Mark and David were thrilled. He clearly expressed his hatred of the FDA and CDC. For him, this debacle elicited a personal disdain for the national health agencies unique among the Attorney Generals with whom they met. Perhaps, Virginia could be a leader in litigation.

Mary, Liz and I were captivated by the Geier's synopsis of their most recent published clinical study.

As we exited the building, Mary wasted no time. "Mark, David, the study—what you are identifying—you know Lisa's son Wesley illustrates each of your points? I have never seen a child with any better documentation on the mercury toxicity clinically. She's been running urine toxicology tests for a year and a half now, and you really need to see her data."

Despite his promise and my calls and letters, the Deputy Attorney General did not respond with any further invitation to a meeting. The administration of which he was a part would resign from office in preparation for a run at the Governor's House, without ever taking any action publicly on Thimerosal. Nonetheless, this meeting was unparalleled in its success in this: it brought together our remarkable team, comprised of researchers, clinicians, and me, the minister-mom, who together would, in the coming years, occasion a heretofore unprecedented level of federal oversight, ecclesiastical concern, legal challenge and a new landmark clinical treatment for autism. And in time, my son, Wesley, would become the center of this providential circle.

Chapter Nine

Institutional Denial

Nothing is covered up that will not be uncovered, and nothing secret that will not become known. Therefore, whatever you have said in the dark will be heard in the light, and what you have whispered behind closed doors will be proclaimed from the housetops.

Luke 12:2-3

January 2004

It struck me like the bright morning sun out of the east as I drove on Interstate 64 to work. On my way to church in the blinding rays I found the words for which I had been searching:

> Surely, this nation does not make privileged the knowledge necessary to protect one's newborn from harm, yet with great sorrow, I must observe that it seems the CDC and the FDA do.

I had not needed to struggle so with the beginning of my letter; it had come quite easily:

Dear Deputy Inspector General Campbell,

I appeal to you for help, after having implored many other federal officials for assistance, to no avail. My letters of concern have gained the attention of Vice President Dick Cheney, Secretary of Health Tommy Thompson, my senators, my congressman, and Drs. Chen and Zoon of the Centers for Disease Control. Despite my ardent requests, none of these has acted so as to protect the lives of our most vulnerable citizens from a clear and present danger.

I had chosen language that often denoted a terrorist threat to communicate the terror of confronting, each day, the fact that my son's tragedy repeated itself, again and again, in countless children who otherwise would have lived normal lives. How many hundreds of thousands had we lost while parental pleas for a ban and recall of Thimerosal-containing drugs went unheeded? After realizing these agencies had colluded at a retreat center of my denomination, I abandoned the idea of engaging the officials at CDC or FDA on the issue of Thimerosal ever again.

As the CDC and FDA continued to defend and even threatened to expand the number of Thimerosal-containing vaccines in the immunization schedule, I regarded them as the institutional embodiment of an abuser. Thinking as a pastor, and judging their continuing actions to be immoral, I became convinced that to safeguard the nation's children from injected poison, I must not turn for help to the abusers, with their denials, but instead to another agency, a separate and healthy agency within the federal family.

I determined to address my pleas for help, not to scientific, but to oversight agencies. I no longer sought an investigation of scientific facts but instead an investigation of alleged unlawful conspiracy. What had happened at Simpsonwood was not just illegal, in my opinion—it was criminal. Industry and government officials conspiring to hide the toxicity of Thimerosal and the damage done to children at one of my denomination's own retreat facilities repulsed me. I would send this newest letter I was writing to the Office of Investigations within the Office of the Inspector General for Health and Human Services, praying that it would be the federal entity that came to the rescue of the little ones. But that was not enough.

Was it as a mother or as a minister that I resolved with premeditated purpose to attend the February 9, 2004 meeting of the Vaccine Safety Review, VSR, of the Institute of Medicine? It was the follow-up to the IOM meeting in Boston which I had attended with Mary in 2001.

"I am going to Washington," I had confided in Mary only weeks before the meeting date, "so that I can read the Simpsonwood transcript into the official IOM record. I am determined, Mary, that this review committee will know what happened at Simpsonwood and face recrimination, if it does not acknowledge the scandal in its conclusion. I have to read Verstraeten's outcomes publicly before the committee. There's no other way."

FEBRUARY 2004

The weeks had passed and my speech was ready. As I prepared to leave Richmond, I turned my cell phone on to hear it chime. Knowing that I would be driving up to D.C. the night before the VSR Meeting, Mary had called and left me a voice mail on my cell.

"Lisa, I won't be at the Institute of Medicine. I couldn't rearrange my patients after all the speaking engagements this month. You go and speak. Be bold, and have courage. Call me when you get back. Thanks."

I smiled. Too few people instructed one another in courage these days.

I didn't debate long about whether to approach Mark and David Geier when I saw them seated on the other side of the bubble-shaped auditorium in the National Academy of Sciences Building in Washington, D.C. Having met them in Richmond, I was eager to speak with them again and wish them well in their upcoming presentation before the IOM. I did not realize they were actively debating walking out in protest, to underscore their belief that this meeting of the IOM was rigged: its conclusion, predetermined.

As soon as we had finished exchanging polite greetings, however, an announcement was made over the auditorium's intercom that Congressman Dave Weldon would be a few minutes late due to Washington traffic gridlock. I made my way back to my seat. In anticipation of the congressman's near arrival, Dr. Marie McCormick began her initial comments to the assembled committee members, presenters and members of the media and public. Of the meticulous verbal preface she gave, one remark, and that one alone, would resound in my memory:

"I would like to remind everyone that this is an information-gathering session…. therefore, I ask everyone here today to be extremely mindful of the fact that the ki-i-tee…the committee," Dr. McCormick continued, correcting her verbal stumble, "has made no conclusions and that it would be a mistake for anyone to leave here thinking otherwise".[1] I prayed this statement was true; however, there already seemed to be some apprehension in the declaration that it was not. Why had she stumbled over her words, I wondered?

My reflections were interrupted by Congressman Weldon, a physician and Army veteran who had served Florida since 1994, ascending the steps at the front of the bubble-shaped auditorium and taking his place behind the podium. Weldon's expression was severe; his tone, immovable; his declaration, inflammatory:

"...The failure, however, to get answers to these questions on vaccine safety is beginning to undermine public confidence. I must begin by sharing my disappointment at the number of reports that I continue to receive from researchers regarding their difficulties in pursuing answers to these questions. It is past time that individuals are persecuted by asking questions about vaccine safety... I am repeatedly informed by researchers who encounter apathy from government officials charged with investigating these matters, difficulty in getting their papers published, and the loss of research grants. Some report overt discouragement, intimidation, and threats, and have abandoned this field of research. Some have had their clinical privileges revoked and others have been hounded out of their institutions...

"...This atmosphere of intimidation and concern, to a certain degree, even surrounds today's hearing. I received numerous complaints that this event is not a further attempt to get at the facts, but rather a desire to sweep issues under the rug.

"...In 2001," Weldon recalled, reminding the IOM of its Boston meeting, "...you concluded that exposure to Thimerosal-containing vaccines could be associated with neurodevelopmental disorders. I urge you not to retract from this conclusion, but to build upon it. Your recommendation in 2001 that there be an immediate effort to end the administering of Thimerosal-containing vaccines to infants was wise. Unfortunately, almost three years later, infants are still receiving Thimerosal-containing vaccines. Furthermore, federal officials seem poised to recommend possibly administering thimerosal-containing flu vaccine to children six, seven, and twenty-three months old.... In fact, a review of the medical literature by me and my office shows information suggesting ethylmercury may be... harmful...

"...The CDC has a built-in conflict of interest that is likely to bias any views. CDC is tasked with promoting vaccination, ensuring high vaccination rates, and monitoring the safety of vaccines. They serve as their own watchdog—neither common nor desirable when seeking unbiased research. This has been a recipe for disaster with other agencies..." [2]

No one in the room moved. All of the parents in attendance must have felt their pulses quicken, as did I. Weldon was truth-telling, and such an event by a congressional representative in a federal forum was long-sought and elusive treasure.

"In the aftermath of the Space Shuttle Columbia accident," argued Weldon, powerfully, "the Gehman Commission found that a critical problem in the Shuttle program was that the same individuals who were responsible for getting the space shuttle off on time were also responsible for flying it safely. The Gehman Commission recommended separating these functions. This same conflict is inherent in the CDC. Unfavorable safety reports lead to lower vaccination rates, and association between vaccines and autism would also force CDC officials to admit that their policies irreparably damaged thousands of children. Who among us would easily accept such a conclusion about ourselves? Yet this is what the CDC is asked to do."

Despite the very formal tone of the meeting, we parents were inwardly euphoric. Congressman Weldon has spoken magnificently for us. After paying appropriate platitudes to high government officials, Weldon concluded with a controlled but poignant observation, which some construed as a barely veiled accusation: "Also, the relationship between the CDC and vaccine manufacturers has become extremely close. If a conflict of interest does not exist here, then we certainly have the appearance of one."

As Dr. Marie McCormick, continuing as moderator of the meeting and Chair of the IOM, rose to thank the Congressman for his remarks, I observed just how intentionally she controlled her response in the rigid and careful way she positioned her lips. Dr. Marie McCormick announced the beginning of the scientific presentations; among them was one made by Dr. Mady Hornig.

A professor of epidemiology at the Mailman School of Public Health at Columbia University, Dr. Mady Hornig was unfamiliar to many of the parents. Though her academic position on the Thimerosal debate was yet unknown to me, by her walk and direct gaze, Mady gave me the impression of being one who reached conclusions only after long study and then, held those conclusions tenaciously. She was short, with curly dark hair that did not quite touch her shoulders. As she began her two-part presentation on epigenetics, the etiology of pathogenesis in autism, and the history of animal models, the assembled members and guests of the IOM understood that this woman was stunningly brilliant. She did not quibble over the fact that there was an ongoing autism epidemic in the nation, and she highlighted the reality that autism had physical symptoms, in contrast to its psychiatric classification.[3]

At last, Mady began to border on the provocative as she contrasted the response of an adult to a specific viral exposure with that of a neonate. Mady labored for forty-one of her fifty minute presentation to speak abstractly and prudently. Her erudite summations demanded neither affirmation nor opposition. They were merely scientifically descriptive. Perhaps, in being so intently academic, she gained the ear of the committee members for what she had not yet dared to utter early in her presentation.

When she at last declared it, even in carefully couched language during the last few minutes of her presentation, Mady's dramatic public confession was this: She had simulated the administration of Thimerosal, as it was contained in the immunization schedule of the 1990's, with mice. Mady began by describing what happened when infant mice got dosed with Thimerosal, proportionally, based on their weight, in the same way as the infants born in the 1990's. Of three strains of mice, two were apparently unaffected. The third strain, however, characterized by autoimmune sensitivities, was transformed. From typically developing infant mice, members of this susceptible strain became frenetic.

Mady observed, as she projected an image of the animal upon the screen at the auditorium's front, "...we have tail biters. About forty percent of the animals after six months become self-mutilatory."

My thoughts flashed to memories of Wesley who, before chelation with a massive load of mercury in his body, would bite his hand until it bled. Suddenly, realizing the grotesque parallels between Mady's poison-stricken mouse and my own stricken son, I was captivated by each terrifying detail this professor described. Mady continued undeterred but aware that the focus upon each of her words had now become intense. She reached down to her computer to start the video and animate the mouse's illuminated image upon the wall. Instead of a streaming image, however, only still frames appeared.

"Again, my movies are not playing in their entirety." Mady hid her frustration well. Despite the lack of moving pictures, the still image of the mouse, projected several feet tall on the front screen, was disconcerting enough.

Mady noted that, were her video to work, the audience would see the animal was frantically and excessively grooming herself, and even her companion. "What you would see here is that this animal, who wildly self-grooms, not only takes care of her partner...but she actually grooms its head until she injures her partner," Mady commented with unnerving academic dispassion.

I suddenly had to suppress my body's undeniable urge to vomit. At last, I asked myself, at last—had someone shown the basic scientific sensibility to test Thimerosal, in keeping with the quantity and administration schedule Wesley had received during the 1990's, on mice? After hundreds of thousands of American infants, and millions of children around the globe had been injected with astronomical amounts of a known neurotoxin, had someone finally done the same with lab mice? Had we decimated two generations of children, so as to forestall the sacrifice of one laboratory of rodents, only now offered up to Thimerosal by a private researcher? Where the hell was the FDA? I vanquished the tears that welled up in my eyes. The dark thoughts in my mind, however, could not be banished: "We experimented on millions of children first, to see if it was safe enough to give to a dozen mice." I railed silently, as my breathing accelerated. I tried to forestall every tear occasioned by my sheer anger— and almost succeeded.

Mady closed by discreetly and indirectly challenging the established faith which the government placed in the current vaccination policy, one that sanctioned the administration of Thimerosal. Stunningly, her confession turned into contention:

"In the period that Einstein was active as a professor, one of his students came to him and said, 'The questions on this year's exam are the same as last year's.' 'True,' Einstein said, 'But this year all the answers are different.' So it behooves us to keep our eyes open to the possibility of new answers." In a parabolic way, Mady informed the committee of her belief that Thimerosal was an unacceptable component of the nation's immunization program.

Mady's careful candor was followed by various academics and presenters. Among those was Dr. Elizabeth Miller, the Head of the Immunization Division at the Communicable Disease Surveillance Center in London, England. In a prim British accent, she chided Weldon for his remarks at the opening of the session: "I will take a little bit of exception to Congressman Wellun's assumption that if you are doing a study that is funded by government, you are there to prove that there isn't an association... I'm there to test hypotheses and form opinions based on the evidence, not to confirm a preexisting opinion..."[4]

Dr. Miller feigned indignation well. She demurely took offense at Weldon, whose name she did not pronounce correctly, despite concerns she had expressed in an e-mail on June 26, 2001, sent at 11:25 am, to Dr. Chen regarding the validity of her study. Prior to commencing her study, and upon realizing the mercury content of vaccine per dose which she was to study had been overestimated in her data, Dr. Miller had asked two significant questions of Dr. Chen:

"If this is true, then do we have sufficient exposure to ethyl Hg by 4-6 months of age to pick up an effect? Do I have to give my GPRD* grant money from WHO** back??? Liz" [5]

What Dr. Miller realized in 2001, as she recalculated the total exposure levels, was that the children in the British database had insufficient levels of exposure to thimerosal to cause a reliable rate of effect. Though Dr. Miller would characterize the British DTP immunization schedule as more "aggressive" than the American one, she would fail to mention to what degree the complete American immunization schedule regularly and repeatedly dwarfed that of the British one for cumulative mercury load.

Dr. Miller also failed to mention to the information-gathering body on February 9, 2004, that when Dr. Thomas Verstraeten, then of the CDC, reviewed her concerns in 2001, Verstraeten concluded: "I hate to say, but given these concerns, it may not be worth doing this [the study] afterall."

Miller's study, deemed epidemiologically insufficient in 2001, was presented to the IOM in 2004 as independent and scientifically sound.

Having scrutinized the recorded data on record for DTP vaccine in Britain, using the General Practice Research Database, Dr. Miller found not only that there was no causal association between Thimerosal exposure and Developmental Disorders or tics, but also that, in fact, exposure to Thimerosal, in the unadjusted odds ratios, actually showed a "protective effect" for neurodevelopmental disorders.

"Sure! A child is less likely to have a malfunctioning brain if you just

---

* General Practice Research Database
** World Health Organization

give it a 'little' neurotoxin!" I paraphrased to myself in quiet sarcastic rage. I could not help rolling my eyes. Was this woman with an academic position actually arguing that administering poison to a child was beneficial? Dr. Miller did temper the insanity of her initial observation, commenting, "So there is a suggestion of protection, although, as I say, I am not postulating that that is a real protective effect. But certainly there is no suggestion of an increased risk with increasing number of doses received by four months of age..." [6] While Dr. Miller finally admitted Thimerosal did not protect a child from autism, she was not about to admit that it caused it either, or that her study suffered from serious design flaws.

With a demeanor I found disingenuous, Dr. Miller sweepingly affirmed her commitment to Thimerosal-free vaccines; however, she conveniently noted that such vaccines, having little or no mercury, could not be produced in the short-term for the developing world. "Because of their poverty," I thought to myself. "While richer nations can afford disposable single-dose vials which did not require a preservative, Developing Nations will continue to receive the multi-dose vials withThimerosal used for a preservative."

Despite the study's obvious flaws, Dr. Miller seemed to be currying the scholastic favor of the IOM Committee with ease as the presentation progressed. Indeed, it was Dr. Miller, in her cold and condescending presentation, whose palatable message the committee members warmly received. This committee longed for the conclusion that mainstream medicine had not poisoned two generations of the world's children, no matter how aberrant the argument.

Dr. Robert Davis, from the University of Washington and Group Health Cooperative, was presenting at the IOM as proxy. From the time the Verstraeten study was first presented at Simpsonwood until it was heard by those at the IOM, it had been revised multiple times. Though the revised study had become the primary research on which the CDC relied to defend its use of Thimerosal, the study's chief author, Dr. Thomas Verstraeten, was artfully unavailable to comment upon it. Verstraeten departed U.S. soil for his native Belgium to work for the mammoth pharmaceutical and vaccine manufacturer, Glaxo-Smith-Kline, only hours after he had addressed the July 16 meeting of the 2001 IOM in Boston. Because he now lived in Belgium on an undisclosed pharmaceutical salary—from such a location, and with such patronage—

Verstraeten was immune to Congressional subpoenas and unavailable to anyone in the United States who might have questions regarding his research.

Therefore, in Dr. Verstraeten's place, Dr. Davis took the podium, preparing to defend Thimerosal as a part of an immunization schedule that, for
decades, had delivered high-dose mercury to infants and children. As he
walked onto the elevated stage at the National Academy of Sciences auditorium, I thought him to be a satisfied member of an unquestioned alliance.
Dr. Davis had come to present not only Dr. Verstraeten's study but himself,
as an unbiased intellectual import from academia. Sadly, he reminded me
more of the fraternity boys I met during college who had an uncanny ability
to be loyal, even when wisdom labeled such loyalty as illogical. As Dr. Davis
began to speak, I did not know that he was the recipient of millions of dollars
from vaccine manufacturers and the CDC, and I was not prepared for what
he was about to say.

Dr. Davis never disclosed these monies. Instead he presented his
credentials, acknowledging that he had worked for NIH, and had done some
funded work for the pharmaceutical industry. He had helped the CDC and
others with safety data. In all this work, Dr. Davis contended he had absolute
freedom to publish, and trumpeted his integrity and objectivity by citing his
role in removing the Rotavirus vaccine from the medical market. With this
declaration, he stated for the committee and all in attendance, "I'm an independent investigator." [7]

Having thus demonstrated his credentials, Dr. Davis almost stuttered as
he mentioned that the Verstraeten study had assessed the neurological and
renal toxicity of Thimerosal. Examining those case histories for a diagnosis
of autism, Dr. Davis declared there was no increased risk associated with
additional doses of Thimerosal. Having run the study with various exclusion criteria, there was no change, Dr. Davis declared, in the relative risk.
In fact, like his colleague Dr. Miller, Dr. Davis reported that at seven months
of age, looking at cumulative Thimerosal exposure, the relative risk suggested
a protective effect.

In contrast to the results presented at Simpsonwood, the final version of
the Verstraeten study now being publicly discussed, asserted that there was
"no evidence of an increased risk for autism..." with increasing thimerosal
exposure. While Dr. Davis noted that his data had been "adjusted" and that
individual records had been "excluded" from the original database, he failed

to mention that this transformation in the study's findings was achieved only after it had been revised many times or that, now, the original data had been "lost".

The initial findings, Dr. Davis admitted to the assembled IOM Committee and audience—referring to Simpsonwood without naming the meeting —"...were somewhat worrisome... Those initial findings, based on sixty-two cases, were that at three months of age, when an infant received 62.5 micrograms of mercury as opposed to 37.5 micrograms of mercury, the child was two and a half times more likely to develop a neurological outcome than one who did not." Dr. Davis acknowledged this was a "...cause for concern on my part and on others' parts, and internally... if this were a real finding, we wanted to know about it..."

For a fleeting second, Dr. Davis actually spoke the word "Simpsonwood," referencing an increased relative risk for children getting mercury exposure at three months of age. "The exclusion criteria have been modified at times..." he continued to explain happily; when they were modified, this concern statistically vanished.

"Just like Wesley's language!" I rebutted under my breath.

"The 2001 IOM found that an association between Thimerosal and neurodevelopmental disorders was 'biologically plausible'—is there an association between accumulated exposure from vaccine and the Rho(D) and is the timing of exposure to thimerosal related to autism?" Clearly, Dr. Davis' answer was no, there was not. Though his argument was unconvincing, Dr. Davis accomplished, in part, what he set out to do.

Mark Geier, already the veteran of one major battle for vaccine safety reform, intentionally set aside retirement to fight this second one. Science, for Mark, gave transcendent purpose and meaning to life. It was humanity's greatest pursuit; it was humanity's most profound hope of healing and understanding. It was not a commodity for sale, and yet Mark knew, by what had been said in this auditorium, science had been bought and sold.

I did not know it was over the quiet protests of his son, David, that Mark at last resolved to speak the conviction of his heart at this IOM meeting, in the span of twenty minutes. Twenty whole minutes, to document the fact that an entire society had forgotten that mercury was toxic, and to decry those who would promulgate such ignorance. Mark began with their disclosures: "We don't receive any funding from any vaccine companies or any other companies. We are consultants at times to petitioners before the Vaccine Compensation Act and in civil litigation..."[8] And then, David stated their position and conviction: "We are people that have been convinced at this point that there is a causal relationship between thimerosal and autism..."[9]

David led the presentation, reviewing their published papers and the history of scientific literature documenting Thimerosal's toxicity, emphasizing the fact that it had always been known to be toxic. The Geiers sought to compel the IOM to veracity with the preponderance of scientific evidence, epidemiological and biological, and literature supporting their position. It was perhaps too ambitious an undertaking in its scope, as the pace of the presentation was deliberately quick, and those who had already been warned-off of the Geiers' work were unwilling to give David and Mark their focused attention.

One point, which no one failed to notice, was David's indirect defense of the comparative DTaP study, using the vaccine formulated with and without Thimerosal. David was careful to note that he and his father examined three separate and completely independent databases, all of which supported their conclusion that Thimerosal was fueling the autism epidemic: the Vaccine Adverse Event Reporting System, the Vaccine Safety Datalink and the U.S. Department of Education.

"We present this in direct response to what was said." In a very polite way, David was trying to inform the gathered experts and public that Miller's and Davis' position was idiotic. Mark commented, "...any which way you want... Thimerosal is a major contributor to the current autism epidemic."

A disciplined scholar, David made his point: children with autism excrete less mercury than controls; testosterone seems to have a synergistic effect making mercury more toxic and most importantly, Thimerosal in the vaccine schedule has resulted in a significant number of children developing neurodevelopmental disorders because, in the gene pool, there are many mercury-susceptible individuals.

"It is not a genetic epidemic," added Mark quickly, wanting to make sure their audience understood this explanation to be an absurdity. "I'm a geneticist. An epidemic is a rapid change in human disease. The fastest known genetic shift is one percent per 100 years." Having educated the assembled committee on this brief point, which he was sure they already knew, Mark breathed in deeply, and then exhaled a righteous anger. Unlike Mady's acceptable scientific subtlety, Mark was forthrightly spoken and openly irate. To be credible, Mark knew, scientific discourse had to be upheld by truth. At least two of the presentations before this committee failed miserably to meet that requirement.

"And I must say that I am a little bit embarrassed to stand here and listen to Verstraeten's work being presented, after what they said at Simpson-wood... In my view, this is not a scientific issue. This is about as proven an issue as you are ever going to see."

Now it was all of us parents around the auditorium who sat bolt upright. Parents who supported and admired the Geiers, and joined with them in a concerted effort to protect the children by approaching the Attorneys General, now, after the father and son team had sacrificed so much, would uphold them, even while the federal establishment was literally and figuratively turning away from them.

As Mark's voice increased in volume, so did the applause of the parents:

"What's going on here is a cover-up under the guise of protecting the vaccine program — and I'm for the vaccine program, but if you keep covering it up, you're not going to have a vaccine program!"

Mark did what David willed him not to do. In contrast to David's measured and carefully constrained criticisms, Mark foretold coming judgment —judgment upon the vaccine program to which he had dedicated his life, judgment which resulted not from scientific error but human greed. To those unaware of the history of Thimerosal, the profitability of cheaply manufactured vaccines, the waiting lists for special education classes and the agony of these children who were spilling mercury in their urine in controlled case studies around the nation, this accusation may have sounded like the desperate fabrication of a minority position. But to those who had seen mercury's toxicity in their patients and in their own children and grandchildren, Mark Geier was speaking as a true prophet, a harbinger, who expected judgment to be swift and absolute, if there was not repentance at once.

No one from academia would be as outspoken as Mark Geier. Yet, throughout the rest of the session, in the dim light of the auditorium, scientific point after point was made about the extreme toxicity of Thimerosal. Point after point was metaphorically scored in a game whose goal was to defend children from "mercurial" medicine. Scholars and surgeons and physicians by the names of Dr. Vasken Aposhian, Professor of Molecular and Cellular Biology Depart-

ment at the University of Arizona, and Dr. David Baskin, Professor of Neurology and Anesthesiology at the Baylor College of Medicine, and Dr. Boyd
Haley, Chair of Chemistry at the University of Kentucky, and Dr. Jeff Bradstreet from the International Child Development Resource Center, would all
bring strength to the team.

"...it is this toxicologist's view that the link between thimerosal and neurodevelopmental disorders in children has become more plausible," stated
Dr. Aposhain.[10] And,

"... a subset of autistic children appear to be more sensitive than their unaffected siblings to thimerosal...I believe it is moving more toward the causal
link," stated Dr. Baskin.[11] And,

"So we have observed with neurons in culture, being exposed to nano-
molar levels of Thimerosal, female hormones, estradiol is protective, and
the male (hormone) testosterone enhances the toxicity," stated Dr. Haley,
explaining the statistic of boys being four times more likely to succumb to
autism than girls.[12] And,

"This is our study, a case-controlled study of mercury burden in children with autistic spectrum disorders... The relative increase was significant,
about six times more mercury on average in children with autism," stated
Dr. Bradstreet.[13]

"God bless you," I whispered, with aching gratitude, to each presenter
as they concluded.

At last, the opportunity for which I had traveled to Washington, D.C.
was nearly mine. The public comment period began. Of the names on the
list, only the first few would be permitted to speak, due to time constraints,
and of those who did speak, Dr. McCormick announced, there would be a
two-minute time limit. Diligently, those whose names were on the list stood
to speak. Most were parents, and as was the case in Boston, the IOM situ-
ated the microphones for them at the back of the auditorium, from where
the painstaking words of sorrowful parents could be heard, but their faces
would not be seen. As one parent after another spoke, the committee stared
forward, unflinchingly, at the empty podium in the front of the room. No one
from the committee deigned to gaze upon the grieving.

Not to be relegated to the dim lights of the auditorium's rear, I brought an eight foot banner of Wesley's graphed mercury dumps. Instead of being plotted by hand and highlighted in Mary's yellow marker as before, this chart was an Excel graph, enlarged and laminated. So that the mercury line was unmistakable, I graphed the line in brilliant lipstick red. Perhaps the IOM would not look at me, but they would gaze upon my son's mercury data, nonetheless.

Once again, Dr. McCormick called my name, as she had in Boston: "…Lisa Sykes." I wondered if she remembered me. This time, I would not speak as I had in Boston, reverently, scientifically. No, this time with my clerical collar about my neck, I had come to speak boldly; I was both a mother bereft and a preacher called to make a public lament, searing in its honesty. Those who were to hear my words would later tell me, I was not speaking, I was preaching—using metaphor and emotion as evocatively as I ever had.

I stood at the microphone, as Angela Medlin and Amy Carson, incredible mothers and anti-Thimerosal advocates from North Carolina, who together constituted "Moms Against Mercury," took my banner to the front of the auditorium. As they held it aloft, I began to speak, my heart pounding uncharacteristically in my chest:

"The Greeks tell a story about a young man named Icarus who, with his father, built a pair of wax wings. He soared so well and so high on these wings that he thought he could reach the sun. As he neared his goal, his wings melted and he plummeted to earth.

"I fear now we are realizing that we have been too daring and too proud in our vaccine policy and that we have soared too high. Poison delivered as a vaccine preservative, Thimerosal, is poison nonetheless."

I had intentionally strayed from the cleaner, more abstract term, neurotoxin. "Poison" was undeniably offensive to those who wished to consider this issue with an academic and abstract sensibility. As one committee member after another turned to face me, I would dare to offend them, not with epidemiology, but with ethic, the domain and jurisdiction of the faith community I represented.

"The article just referred to by Dr. Deth at the microphone talks about methionine synthase (MS)…The article also states that the potential for Thimerosal to cause adverse effects on MS activity at concentrations well below the level produced by one individual Thimerosal containing vaccine. I might add to you that after we got all this mercury out of my child, (I motioned toward the graph) who is now eight years old, we began methylcobalamin (vitamin B12) injections that I give him each day. He is finally starting to learn. We are addressing a serious deficit that was caused. He was not born with it.

"I wanted to ask this committee, as I have asked the office of investigations that has oversight over Health and Human Services, to look into Simpsonwood, a meeting that occurred there on June 7 in the year 2000. Verstraeten was there. The quotes in the transcript of Simpsonwood are damning. Verstraeten said, quote..."[14]

Dr. McCormick, interrupted loudly, "You are going over, there are other folks behind you."

The room seemed almost paralyzed.

"This quote is so important, Dr. McCormick, I would appreciate being allowed to share it with you. May I please finish?"

I spoke with respect that assumed the Chair of the committee was not cutting me off simply because she understood the unutterable thing I was about to speak.

Up front, a curly-haired red-headed mother of an autistic son, who was seated at the end of the aisle where McCormick was standing, pointed her finger at McCormick and said in a shrill and threatening voice, "You let her finish!"

McCormick paused and I continued not waiting for an answer:

"The quote is that 'we have found statistically significant relationships between exposures of Thimerosal and outcomes, first at two months of age, an unspecified developmental delay which has its own specific ICD-9 code, exposure at three months of age, exposure at six months of age, and attention deficit disorder, exposure at three, six months of age, language and speech delays, which are two separate ICD-9 codes, exposure at one, three, six and nine months of age, the entire category of neurodevelopmental delays, which includes all of these plus a number of other disorders...' I am alarmed that what has been said at Simpsonwood has not been brought here to this committee and I must ask why!"

My voice grew calmly contentious as I was speaking not to Dr. McCormick, but to the breadth of the entire medical institution as impassionedly as I ever had spoken to my congregation from the pulpit:

"We have gotten rid of infectious disease, we think, but I would posit to you that we really have exchanged it for lifelong and widespread developmental disorders that our children may never recover from."

The auditorium erupted in applause. Parents were crying. Researchers were applauding. Committee members had now swiveled 180 degrees at the waist, to see the face of the clergywoman at the back of the room who spoke with an authority they had not granted her. Into the controlled atmosphere of this federal meeting, into the measured protocols of academic research, did I now bring a homiletical whirlwind. Dr. McCormick, though visibly strained, made no attempt to stop me speaking now.

"We are decimating an entire branch of the genetic family tree, where infectious disease was random. We have targeted one branch, and many researchers think we are talking about our brightest kids, those who would be our prodigies, our engineers, our scientists for the next generation...

"I will close now, going back to the issue of the Greeks, which someone else here has raised. They practiced infant sacrifice. Unintentionally, I would assert to you as a theologian that we have also!"

While everything I said to this point had been well deliberated and practiced, now I began to speak extemporaneously, and like Mark Geier earlier in the day, I would not regret expressing my rage as well as my conviction.

"I have lost one son to autism. I have a healthy younger son. You can more easily put a gun to my head and pull the trigger than you could inject Thimerosal into that baby..."

My voice, though strong, quivered with the intensity of my emotion. Now, I would declare the urgency of the moral imperative incumbent upon this committee and its deliberations:

"Every day we wait, every day we study, every day we debate, we lose more children!" I loudly declared.

I should have thanked the committee for their undivided attention, but I could not. My breathing was too heavy, and my throat too tight. I not only delivered a speech, but the contents of my heart. In doing so, I had made the IOM committee members immensely uncomfortable. They had not expected to be addressed by a preacher, much less a minister who was the mother of a mercury-poisoned child, who could quote scientific studies in addition to chapter and verse.

As I was about to abandon the microphone in my exhaustion, Dr. McCormick, obviously flustered by my display, over which she had no control, quickly approached her mic at the front of the auditorium. Referencing the many documents, complaints and comments the IOM had received in writing before the meeting, Dr. McCormick defended herself from one of the first questions I had asked in my address. Perhaps recklessly, she sought to legitimize the omission of Simpsonwood transcripts in the agenda which she and her committee had set:

"Just as a matter of fact, the committee has seen the complete Simpsonwod transcript, and we also have all of the concerns and complaints documented in our briefing book in terms of addressing those issues. So the reason it didn't come up today is because the committee has been made well aware of it."[15]

I may have lost my voice, I thought to myself, but she's lost her mind! She is admitting having those transcripts—all the committee members having those transcripts—and yet not one of them ever questioned the veracity of the Verstraeten Study as it was presented here today? And she just said this for the record?

I swallowed hard, and found breath for six last words, spoken with unswerving directness:

"Madam Chair, those are damning documents," I replied, surrendering the microphone and returning to my seat on legs that shook.

My breathing was still that of a parent seeking to save a child from the path of an oncoming car, when I became aware of two things. Those sitting around me in the auditorium were hugging me and patting me on the back. I felt like I needed a tissue even more than their praise, but I was grateful they received my comments approvingly, no matter how provocative my words had been. As the parents who followed me spoke much more quietly, and the meeting resumed a more controlled tenor, I realized there were others moving in the auditorium. Crouching figures. Crouching figures from the very front of the auditorium all moving toward me.

"Oh, dear Lord, they're going to throw me out!" was all I could think.

Thankfully, as the creeping persons neared my seat, I realized they were not security guards but instead members of the press.

"Do you have a business card?" they each asked.

Laughingly, quietly, I gave them my business card. Somehow, I summoned the sense to ask them for their cards also. Of those cards I received in the waning hours of that day and the last minutes of that meeting, one would be strikingly important in the weeks ahead. I looked down at it: "Lisa Reagan, *Mothering Magazine.*"

Lisa Reagan and *Mothering Magazine* would become key allies, as parent-led efforts to force a criminal investigation into Thimerosal intensified. So, too, would another mother, whom I never met that day in Washington, though she, like me, attended the entire session of the IOM.

A week after the IOM, I turned on my computer, and downloaded my e-mail, to find this note:

"Lisa,

My name is Leslie Weed, I am the mother of three beautiful daughters, my youngest is mercury toxic, Lanier, she will turn six in April, she has never spoken her first word. I am from Ponte Vedra Beach, Florida, just below Jacksonville. My husband and I flew to Washington, DC to the IOM meeting. I prayed all day that the TRUTH would somehow emerge. I had legions of Bible study groups praying all day long for us. I had signed up to talk but knew I was probably too far down to talk. I sat and prayed that someone would emerge from the crowd who could really impact the panel.

My prayers were answered when you walked up to the mic... You were so eloquent and your passion struck me deeply, you were articulating so beautifully what so many in the auditorium were feeling and thinking. Every jaw in the room was on the floor in awe. Tears ran uncontrollably down my cheeks as you exemplified, love, compassion, knowledge and courage. I have thought of your words everyday since my return home. I went to Washington, DC with a confidence that truth would prevail. I sat through the meetings, my body shaking the whole time, adrenalin, anxiety (the enemy in the room), and finally, I shook with joy after your beautiful speech.

I am sure our paths will cross before this is all over. I just wanted to thank you on behalf of the families and children, your words were far more reaching than I think you probably realized. God has

gifted you in a special way, I am glad you embraced it, He is working through you and I know wonderful things are on the horizon...
May the peace of the Lord be with you!

Leslie Weed

PS I attached my daughter Lanier's picture... I will pray for your son."

We did not know it yet, but soon the red head in the front of the auditorium, the Geiers, Leslie, and I would be part of an extremely small and resourceful team of researchers and parents who would discover how to hold the FDA legally responsible for its gross violation of American law and of fundamental medical ethics.

CHAPTER TEN

THE OFFICE OF SPECIAL COUNSEL PROJECT

"Mercury-Containing Vaccines May Help, Not Harm Kids"

"There have been widespread concerns that mercury-based preservatives used in vaccines might impair the neurological development of children, but the opposite seems to be true. Immunizing infants with vaccines containing the preservative Thimerosal may actually be associated with improved behavior and mental performance, according to two British studies published in the medical journal *Pediatrics*... There appeared to be protective effects from Thimerosal-containing vaccine exposure for general developmental disorders, attention-deficit disorder, and unspecified developmental delay."

—Reuters Health Wire, September 17, 2004

MARCH 2004

WHEN I RECEIVED THE LETTER FROM MATT KOCHANSKI, DIRECTOR OF THE Investigative Branch for the Office of the Inspector General for Health and Human Services, I concluded that the federal bureaucracy had gone blind. It seemed to me utterly unable to see the harm mercury was inflicting upon American children or to focus on the urgent need to protect them, despite all my efforts to bring this issue directly before its eyes.

"Upon review of your correspondence, we have determined that this office cannot take any substantive actions to address your allegations and concerns. Our jurisdiction is limited to criminal, civil, and administrative investigations to reduce the incidence of fraud, waste, abuse, and mismanagement within the programs of the Department of Health and Human Services. The issues that you present here are regulatory in nature, and by statute, this office is precluded from being involved in such matters."[1]

The emblem in the upper left corner of the page showed one profile circumscribed by a second profile circumscribed by a third profile, at last encompassed by the profile of an eagle. The significance it denoted was clear, as the emblem corresponded to the department's motto: "Leading America to Better Health, Safety and Well-being." The incompatibility between this adage and the reality of knowingly injecting the American public with mercury dumbfounded me.

"Normally, we would refer your information to the CDER (Center for Drug Evaluation and Research of the FDA), however, our research into the current status of Thimerosal use in vaccines render this course of action moot."

My eyes and my breathing both stopped, and they were unable to resume their normal course for several seconds. I stared at the words on the page. How could the ongoing injection of a known neurotoxin possibly be a moot issue for all of those whose functional lives had been stolen from them in infancy?

Based on his words, it seemed to me that Mr. Kochanski did not understand the real damage mercury had already done, nor its continuing place in the drug supply: "Currently, all vaccines in the recommended childhood immunization schedule that are for use in the U.S. market contain no Thimerosal or only trace amounts."

"It's not all out! Why does everyone think it is out?" With no official recall, stockpiles of mercury-laden vaccines would remain in storage and circulation for years until they were used up by unwitting pediatricians. I had become so frustrated with the reassuring refrain that mercury was no longer an issue because it was no longer in vaccines, even though vials with twenty-five micrograms of mercury per dose, the 'preservative level' of Thimerosal, were still being given to children.

"You know," I complained, turning to Seth, "Even local doctors are telling parents 'it's all out.' And then, you tell them to go look at the package insert, and they are stunned to find out it's still there! Mercury needs to be out, but it's not!"

Ever calm, ever steady, Seth sought to remind me that this federal letter was simply the newest in an increasingly large collection of responses, all of which were characterized by a seeming inability to make a judgment independent of institutional inertia. Seth advised me wisely that Kochanski was only responding consistently, albeit disappointingly, as had every other federal bureaucrat with whom I had communicated.

"Lisa, it's no different than all of the other federal 'Dear John' letters you've received..." Seth offered, seeking to soothe my frustration, but he could not.

"Yes, it is," I countered. "This is oversight! This is the Office of Investigations! They're supposed to investigate, right? So, how can Kochanski fail to even acknowledge Simpsonwood after I specifically cited it? He doesn't even mention it!"

"No acknowledgement of Simpsonwood at all?" Seth replied. Even he was stunned.

"I'm calling Andrea." I resolved out loud, my determination greater than ever before.

"Yeah, that'll work," concurred Seth, nodding. With his usual economy of words, Seth's thoughtful voice registered how serious my advocacy was now becoming.

Being from a family of civil servants who, in my big brother's case, had married yet another federal employee, I inherited political resources that few other parents in the autism community had. The first time Andrea sat at my dining room table, Wesley had thrown his arms about her neck. Andrea had auburn hair that swung just above her shoulders with each tilt of her head and with each laugh that resounded from deep in her soul. She was strong —a fighter, with instincts instilled from active duty in the United States Air Force and passion innate from being a mother. Now, as a federal investigator, she had occasion to protect children professionally in the course of her duties and would help me protect them personally, by sharing the benefit of her federal training and expertise. For Wes, and for all those like him she did not know, Andrea would become a critical and unsung hero in the fight against mercury.

My brother, a Second Lieutenant who handled street operations, crime scenes, and investigations for the Fairfax County Police Department, was my 'big' brother. Dan stood six foot six, with broad shoulders and a bearing that was impressive. The only situations that I had ever seen immobilize my "cop" brother were the moments when I lay his newborn nephews in his arms. From the time I placed one of them there, until the time I retrieved the baby, Dan would sit, staring at the child, frozen, frightened to move for fear that the newborn might somehow "break."

From the time my big brother was young, his favorite restaurant had been Red Lobster. Now, for the sake of one of those nephews, whom he had gingerly cradled in his arms, Dan and Andrea joined me, Seth and Mom on Broad Street in Richmond at Dan's favorite restaurant. Around a table graced with cheddar biscuits and a feast of shrimp, my federal family held an uncanny and startling conversation. Only three years earlier, I tutored Dan and Andrea in their marriage vows. Now, they tutored me in their field of expertise, instructing me on how to charge criminal conspiracy and collusion at the highest levels of government, while simultaneously bringing these accusations to national media attention.

"It's a shitty letter, Lisa," said Andrea, as straight-spoken as her military training, handing me back Kochanski's response. "Really shitty. You need to go higher."

"Higher than Investigations, Andrea? We are already talking about the Inspector General's Office! Where do you want me to go?"

"OSC," she pronounced the acronym with ease.

"OSC?" I queried, perplexed. "What is OSC?"

"Office of Special Counsel. The Special Counsel is appointed by the President. You need to go to OSC."

For a brief moment, my fingers glided over my lips. Yet one more letter to write. Yet one more federal echelon to scale. And how many letters had I written? How many tiers of government had I already surmounted? And what good had come of all my attempts?

"Andrea, why do you think they will respond when the OI did not?" I asked.

Andrea smiled a wicked grin. "Because, Lisa, you will make them. You are going to copy every media contact, every state contact, every federal contact you have. I don't care if the letter is only two pages long, you better have fifteen pages of cc's. That is where the pressure to force them to act is going to come from."

Now, it was my big brother's turn to instruct me. As a police officer, Dan had handled a myriad of crime scenes involving the press and knew what I did not: how best to bring pressure to bear on a given individual or agency, as needed, for the sake of criminal investigations.

"Lisa, listen to me. You're going to force feed OSC this issue. It's all you can do. You need to write an airtight letter, with all your charges, all your allegations. Make it perfect. Then, like Andi said, you 'cc' every magazine and newspaper and politician known to man, and when you send them the OSC letter, you also put a cover letter on it, comparing this to the tobacco scandal. But make the points that, in contrast to cigarette smokers, we are talking about babies; we are talking about a known but undisclosed poison in the baby shots. You've got to make the point that these shots are required by law and the parents aren't being informed. Reference the years and years of scientific evidence proving this stuff is toxic... And then list all the vaccines out there by brand and type that still have the mercury in them. You do that, and OSC will have to deal with the issue. They won't be able to walk away from it like everyone else has."

Throughout dinner I took notes. Out of love for Wesley, Dan and Andrea taught me how to pursue the federal government and force its agencies—which should have already fulfilled their duty—to act. Except for Dan and Andrea, every employee of a federal agency from whom I had sought help had only fled before the immensity of the Thimerosal scandal.

I had already decided which circle of parents would be the group to conduct the OSC Project. I culled through my email files until I found an electronic listing of all the names and contact information for each parent who had, to date, met with their respective state Attorney General. I reasoned that to secure an appointment with one's own Attorney General, these parents had to be politically savvy, well organized, and very intelligent. They also represented the nation, coming from various states across the country. Most importantly, despite differences in geography and personal experience, they were united by one unbreakable bond: they each had discovered that their child or children had been poisoned with mercury.

With butterflies in my stomach, I wrote an email describing the OSC

Project and explaining its strategy to them. I concluded with an invitation to these "Attorney General Parents" to become members of this project and signers of the letter listing our allegations against the Centers for Disease Control, Food and Drug Administration, Health and Human Services, and the Institutes of Medicine. The first to respond to my invitation was Kelli Ann Davis, a fiery red-head with a son named Miles who, like Wesley, was diagnosed with autism.

"Hey Girl!" she said, calling as soon as she opened the e-mail. "This is Kelli Ann Davis. I live in Fayettville, North Carolina. Remember when you spoke at the IOM?" Her voice was intense. I would soon learn that everything about Kelli Ann Davis was intense. "I'm the one who told McCormick to put a sock in it when she tried to cut you off!" I laughed out loud. Kelli Ann was as blunt as she was bold.

"Now, Lisa, help me understand this project." Kelli and I spoke with words that were rapid and an excitement that fostered hope. Despite the pace of our conversation, we did not miss a single detail in all that we sought to convey to one another.

"I can see how to do this, Lisa," Kelli Ann exclaimed, tantalized by the thought of enlisting a presidential appointee to our side. "We can send out the requests for contact information in waves, via e-mail. Say, first we do state contacts, and I'll give everyone in the group two weeks to get me those. After a couple of weeks, I'll send out a call for all the federal contacts. Then, finally, we will get everyone's media contacts. With fifteen families spread across the country, we should have the fifteen pages of cc's your sister-in-law wants easy—no problem."

Kelli Ann's response was the first and most essential to the project. After Kelli Ann and her husband, Jim, joined the effort, one by one, each of the other families responded affirmatively to my invitation: Scott and Laura Bono from North Carolina, Bob and Lori Krakow from New York, Michael and Bobbie Manning from New York, Jo Pike from South Carolina, Brian and Marcia Hooker from Washington, Jeff and Karen Trelka from Washington, Lee and Dana Halvorson from Iowa, Linda and Kerry Weinmaster from Kansas, Alan and Lujene Clark from Missouri, Christian and Lori McIlwain from North Carolina, Michael Wagnitz from Wisconsin, Arnie and Rita Shreffler from Missouri, and Nancy Hokkanen from Minnesota.

This would be one of the most focused parent-advocate collaborations yet to take place on the issue of Thimerosal. I quickly realized Kelli Ann was gifted in the compilation and organization of a massive amount of information. I teased her that God had meant for her to be an information specialist instead of the mother of an autistic child. As a result of her diligent efforts, the "cc" pages became richer in information and greater in scope with each passing day. The state list included Attorneys General from around the nation as well as governors and public health officials. Media sheets included local news reporters as well as national broadcast journalists. The group also listed intrepid reporters who had already dared to write on the subject, among them one whose card I had stashed in my purse on February 9, 2004 in D.C.: "Lisa Reagan, *Mothering Magazine*."

Most impressive of all, however, was the federal contact list. Congressmen and senators initially comprised most of our federal recipients, but then, once again, I spoke with Andrea.

"Lis, I'll email you a list of names and addresses to include. You want to telegraph this whole issue to every Inspector General in the government. You have to be able to demonstrate they all know about this! Health and Human Services, but that's just the beginning. You need to include OGE, GAO, EPA, and PCIE! Make sure you have PCIE down!"

Once again, I was awash in Andrea's federal acronyms. I protested aloud to Andrea who reminded herself that I was a Methodist minister, untrained in federal investigations.

"It stands for President's Council on Integrity and Efficiency, Lis. You want to get them involved in this," Andrea declared.

By the time I received Andrea's suggestions and forwarded them to Kelli Ann, who then integrated them into the OSC Project, the "cc" list included: the Environmental Protection Agency, the Office of Government Ethics, the Federal Bureau of Investigations—Criminal Investigations Division, Homeland Security, the Government Accountability Office, the Department of Justice, the Consumer Protection and Safety Commission, and of course, the President's Council on Integrity and Efficiency and the entire U.S. Congress.

As the "cc" list took shape, so, too, did the letter. I wrote and then Kelli Ann rewrote, and she revised and then I edited. Laura Bono and Lori MacIlwain assisted in final revisions. In a matter of weeks, the letter was stunning for its strength. As the draft neared its final form, we submitted it to the entire circle of Attorney General Parents for input and approval.

As we stayed up half the night, to the chagrin of our spouses, and down-loaded thirty emails three times a day, the OSC Project became less and less a plan and more and more a reality. With a strange mix of excitement and foreboding, I read the final letter over:

April 9, 2004

Scott Bloch, Special Counsel
U.S. Office of Special Counsel
1730 M Street, N.W. Suite 300
Washington, D.C. 20036-4505
(202) 254-3600 (202) 653-5151 Fax

Honorable Special Counsel Bloch,

We, the undersigned parents, have united to advocate for the re-form of the national vaccine program/industry that has unnecessarily exposed our children to unsafe levels of mercury. Mercury, a known neurotoxin, which comprises 49.6% of the antiquated preservative Thimerosal, is used in many pediatric immunizations, flu shots, and Rho-D injections such as RhoGAM. We have clinical data proving that our children have suffered mercury-induced neurological disor-ders due to Thimerosal, and, in realizing that more children succumb daily to this preventable fate, we have resolved to bring this scandal to national prominence. Seeking to enlist your oversight and resources in investigating this serious issue, we make the following charges...

I weighed every word, diagramed every sentence. What followed this opening were nine allegations of significant wrongdoing, which included:

1) The Centers for Disease Control (CDC) is characterized by egre-gious conflicts of interest, which have compromised the safety of the vaccine supply, while putting our nation's children at risk.

2) The CDC, Food and Drug Administration (FDA), and pharma-ceutical companies colluded at the Simpsonwood Retreat Center in Norcross, Georgia on June 7 and 8, 2000.

3) Dr. Verstraeten later denied a link before an Institute of Medicine (IOM) Committee Panel on July 16, 2001, and released a different version of the same study showing no correlation between Thime-

rosal and neurological disorders in the November 2003 *Pediatrics Journal*. The Simpsonwood Transcripts call the veracity of the latter Verstraeten Study into question.

4) Federal and medical authorities including Health and Human Services -Office of Investigations (HHS-OI) and the American Academy of Pediatrics (AAP) incorrectly state that Thimerosal/mercury is out of the vaccine supply. It is not.

5) The methodology of government-sponsored studies of Thimerosal and its connection to neurological disorders in children has been exclusively statistical and epidemiological in nature. Such studies cannot assess the genetic vulnerability of subpopulations.

6) Injecting mercury (Thimerosal) in excess of Environmental Protection Agency (EPA) standards without prior informed consent, represents a significant and widespread violation of civil rights.

Having formulated these and other charges with painstaking care, I was determined that the conclusion of the letter would not lose the momentum provided by speaking for the mothers and fathers of injured children across the country:

"We are convinced there is not a more pressing issue, nationally or internationally, than the epidemic of autism and the devastated lives left in its ruins. The cost of this negligence will be measured economically, intellectually, and politically for years to come...It is tragically ironic that in an era when the American Government is concerned about biological and chemical warfare, our own vaccine supply has been poisoned with a lethal neurotoxin while being administered by the same federal agencies charged with its oversight." [2]

With courage, we parents would soon sign our names to these charges.

As the first week of April arrived, my vocabulary was filled with typical words for a United Methodist pastor such as "confirmation," "baptism," "Maundy Thursday," and "resurrection." When I was not speaking these words as a minister during my official Holy Week duties, I had a very different vocabulary. Late at night, on the internet and over the phone, with other AG Parents from around the nation, I spoke phrases like: "Special Counsel,"

"Press release," "egregious conflict of interest" and "destruction of data." How had I, how had any of us, dared to undertake this level of advocacy? And for me, during Holy Week, of all things!

Some in the Christian tradition referred to these days as Passion Week, and I came to understand my late-night, seemingly never-ending efforts to complete this project as the culmination of the most appropriate Lenten sacrifice I had ever undertaken. Without doubt, beholding the neurological dysfunctions and behavioral symptoms of my own son's mercury poisoning was my crucifixion. As Wesley had marked his eighth birthday without having ever uttered a sentence, still struggling for each syllable and only recently toilet-training, the discrepancy between what I had prayed for and what I confronted each day in the searingly silent blue eyes of my son, provided me with an anger that demanded justice rather than despair, and a resolve that provided focus rather than exhaustion.

"Seth, can you watch the boys for a while?" My husband looked up from his book, puzzled. I never left the house on lovely spring evenings for a walk without taking some assortment of our sons with me. But on this beautiful spring evening, as Easter came so close, not my church work, but my advocacy work had frazzled me. Tomorrow, Good Friday, was the launch date. From around the country, fifteen families would go to their local post offices and each mail a packet to the Office of Special Counsel. Inside each packet would be my federal paper trail of rejection letters, beginning in the year 2000. Inside each package would be the letter of allegation, into which four of us moms had emptied every intellectual and emotional reserve we possessed. Inside each packet would be the signature sheet Kelli Ann had methodically and individually prepared for each of the fifteen families, with a place for our signature and a listing of all the other families who would send their packets under a separate cover. Inside each package would be the fifteen pages of cc's, just as Andrea had suggested. The packages were all addressed to Special Counsel Scott Bloch, the presidential appointee to this office.

As I walked, I swung my arms to and fro, as if I were four, and looked at a blue sky now hinting of the evening's hidden colors as the sun's light crested on the horizon. I hadn't asked for this. I didn't want this. During my childhood, I had seen federal firefights from my vantage point as daughter of a federal scientist. I had watched members of my family, especially my father, do political battle with senators and congressmen. I had seen the toll it took, and I had resolved to myself that such a life was not one that I desired. Instead, I had gone to seminary and become an ordained minister. Still, I would deal with ultimate things, but on a personal level, in a religious setting. I had expected my life to be pastoral, caring for my church, raising my family. I had fallen in love with a contented Scottish man whose quiet strength sustained me. With marriage, I expected my greatest calling to be raising our children.

I tried to discern, in the midst of all this intention, why God would give to me that life which I had so intentionally rejected? How was it that now I, who had sought to avoid federal circles of power, was combating them? Tomorrow, the letters would be mailed. Tomorrow, this project, which Andrea and Dan had dictated to me, and which I and other parents had fulfilled, would be set into motion. Jo and Wendy would soon download the OSC letter across the internet. Those at the highest levels of federal government would know our names, but more importantly, they would know our children's diagnoses: mercury poisoning by the therapeutic use of vaccines.

MAY 2004

"Lisa, I just called OSC." The voice was so excited I had a hard time making out Kelli Ann's words. "Lisa, they're about to close the case. They got all of our packets. They said they weren't the right place to send them. They haven't even studied them! Could Andrea have been wrong?"

"Oh, no, Andrea is not mistaken on matters like this, Kelli."

"Okay, okay, Lisa. I'm going to three-way us with OSC, okay?"

I gulped. "Now? Kelli, I don't have any of my notes in front of me."

I could hear the phone ringing on the other end of the line, as I tried desperately to formulate my thoughts.

"Hello, Office of Special Counsel..."

"Catherine McMullen please..." chirped Kelli Ann.

"Just one moment, please. I will transfer you."

"Hello, Catherine McMullen."

"Hi, Cathy. This is Kelli Ann Davis again. I've also got Reverend Lisa Sykes on the line right now. Can you tell us, again, what is going on with the information we sent you?"

"Well, as I said earlier Ms. Davis, this is not the right office for your complaint. We don't conduct investigations; we only oversee them. And we don't have jurisdiction to authorize an investigation without a whistleblower. We're just going to close the case..."

"What?" On hearing McMullen suggest such abandonment of a critical issue, I had interjected myself into the conversation without thinking. "Have you studied the materials we sent you, Ms. McMullen?" I could not believe that the carefully refined, clearly substantiated allegations we were making could be discarded so perfunctorily.

"Well, you see, this kind of an issue is not ours. We do not investigate."

"Lisa, what about the press release?" Kelli Ann asked me aloud, abruptly interrupting the conversation. "Are all those letters going to go to the wrong place now?"

"Press release?" Catherine McMullen inquired, taken aback. Momentarily another female's voice joined in the conference call from the Office of Special Counsel.

"Hello, this is Tracy Biggs. May I be of some help here?"

Kelli Ann was quick to respond: "Well, yes. We all have children who have been poisoned with mercury. The mercury came from FDA-approved vaccines. There is a major cover-up of this entire issue, and we need you to investigate..."

"We don't conduct investigations, Ms.... er... Ms. Davis, is it?"

"Yeah. But no one else will help us! Maybe that is what we have to say to the press, Lisa. That there is no one in the entire government willing to protect our children... That we have no where to go... What do you think, Lisa?"

"Maybe so, Kelli Ann. We can't stop the letters now. It's too late. The action alert was dropped on the boards this morning..."

"Action Alert?" Tracy seemed as stunned as Catherine.

"Yes, we wanted you to be aware how many Americans realize what has happened to their children. You're about to get hundreds of letters," I explained.

"But... but... this isn't the right office..." Tracy said, almost defensively. "How did you find out about us, anyway?"

Kelli Ann quickly began to answer, "Oh, Lisa's sis..."

"Kelli Ann!" I shouted, to quiet my forthcoming friend. "I have many relatives who work in the federal government, Ms. Biggs. From conversing with them, I think this is precisely the office we need. Do you realize, do you realize what we are doing to our children? We're injecting poison into our babies through FDA-mandated shots! We're maiming one in every hundred male children to the point of disability. And Health and Human Services couldn't care less! This has to stop."

"Okay, okay, Reverend Sykes! We will have a look at the materials you have sent us, okay?"

I sensed that these who spoke for this highest prosecutorial office in the land felt they had just been ambushed. Just what Dan and Andrea had predicted.

CHAPTER ELEVEN

AN UNEXPECTED ALLY

"Seventeen years ago, when an extortionist tried to wring money out of Johnson & Johnson by lacing capsules of Tylenol with cyanide, seven people died. While the government was still considering what to do (sound familiar?), and before the media had time to put the company on the defensive, Johnson & Johnson recalled all Tylenol products. That cost about $100-million and it lost short term sales. But it emerged from the episode with consumer confidence at a higher level than ever, and quickly regained its leadership of the painkiller market.

"The AAP should be dedicated to promptly providing truthful information about this situation to pediatricians. We must follow the three basic rules: (1) Act quickly to inform pediatricians that the products have more mercury than we realized. (2) Be open with consumers about why we didn't catch this earlier. (3) Show contrition.

"As you know, the Public Health Service informed us yesterday that they were planning to conduct business as usual, and would probably indicate no preference for either product. While the Public Health Service may think that their "product" is immunizations, I think their "product" is their recommendations. If the public loses faith in the PHS recommendations, then the immunization battle will falter. To keep faith, we must be open and honest now and move forward quickly to replace these products."

Internal email from Ruth Etzel, M.D., Ph.D., Office of Public Health Science, U.S. Department of Agriculture, July 2, 1999, 10:36 a.m.

MAY 18, 2004

"Guilty as sin." There should have been an exclamation in that statement. There should have been hellfire and brimstone in my voice. But there
was not. My words were uncharacteristically quiet. My words were uncharacteristic. Had I ever felt this furious? I didn't think so.

On the television screen, closer in view than she had ever been in person
during the IOM meetings, was Dr. Marie McCormick, Chair of the Institute
of Medicine Committee. Across the channels of my television, she and other
experts were being interviewed about the newly released findings of the Institute of Medicine after its February 9, 2004 meeting.

"God forgive them!" I almost shouted now, guilty myself of dwell-
ing on the trespass I perceived more than the salvation which I regularly
preached. A mainline Protestant, schooled at Princeton Theological Seminary,
tutored in grace, I had never thought to speak judgment before. In this single
moment, that changed. As I listened in disbelief to their words, I came to
believe that the 2004 Institute of Medicine would face judgment, rather than
mercy, in any kingdom that was to come. For the first time in my life, I proclaimed guilt rather than blessing or forgiveness.

Dr. McCormick appeared tense and detached. When she spoke, I strained
to find any evidence of maternal instinct in her carefully constrained visage.
As she spoke, I sank upon the bed. This waking nightmare could not go on,
and yet the talking heads would not stop. I considered the remote control in
my hand and then thought better of it. I put it down and picked up a pillow,
and threw it as hard as I could at the television which had become an accomplice to the madness of mercury.

"...the committee concludes that the evidence favors rejection of a causal
relationship between Thimerosal-containing vaccines and autism."[1]

I thought back to the most recent meeting of the Institute of Medicine,
whose chair was announcing their findings today. Our efforts at the IOM to
awaken the nation from its tormented sleep could not have failed, could they?
The researchers had spoken so eloquently; the science was gaining such focus;
the mechanisms of mercury toxicity had been so well described. The passion
of us parents had been so evident. Such truth spoken in the nation's ear could
not be overcome by the lie that mercury was beneficial for newborns, could
it?

"Oh, God..." I begged again, in a hushed whisper. I was seeking help. I would have welcomed a thunderbolt. I could not stand these words.

On another channel, further findings of the IOM were praised by more talking heads, each of which seemed to have lost its mind: "In addition the committee recommends that available funding for autism research be channeled to the most promising areas."[2] Resident television medical expert, Dr. Emily Senay, when interviewed about the IOM's conclusions on CBS' The Early Show, parroted the fallacies she had been fed: "They say that looking at some of the genetic research would be very important as an avenue that's very promising."[3]

I roared in frustration, glad no one was within earshot to hear me. I flipped to another channel willing someone, anyone in the press, to ask why a substance considered so dangerous it was illegal to apply to your skin should be deemed safe for injection into the body and blood of pregnant women and newborn children? But no one asked that. No one even asked why we should take the risk when mercury was a completely unnecessary and avoidable part of any vaccine or medicine.

Worse than all that was said and unsaid so far, however, was the IOM's broadcast recommendation that, "Because chelation therapy has potentially serious risks, the committee recommends that it be used only in carefully controlled research settings with appropriate oversight by Institutional Review Boards protecting the interests of the children who participate."[4]

"God, no! They're threatening access to biomedical treatment!" So few parents knew about the mercury. With this statement, how many children would never find their literal burdens—their body burdens of a known neurotoxin—lifted? My mind raced back to how Wesley bit his hands until they bled before we had chelated him. "No," I raged. "No, no, no!"

Was I seeking help for myself or for the children? I was not sure anymore. Ambushed by my anger, I posited that if I ended up in hell, it would not be because I had ever despaired of autism or surrendered hope for my son Wesley. No, if I were to end up in hell, it would be because, in my lifetime, I never found grace ample enough to forgive Dr. McCormick and this Institute for what they declared today.

History, fate or God had placed them at the most important of medical crossroads in history and had given them power to utter but a few words and save hundreds of thousands of newborn minds, intact. It appeared to me that faced with choosing between preserving the medical institution or acknowledging the institution's culpability in mercury-poisoning children, a choice which could subject the institution to legal action, these academics and scientists chose to preserve institutional security rather than newborn life. I doubted I could ever forgive the crass sacrifice offered by defending the mercury instead of the children.

The day following the release of the IOM report was perfectly brilliant, another of those gorgeous spring days. Had God sent it to comfort me? If God had, even such divine care did not assuage the angry wound in my soul. In the afternoon, I was sitting at home, drinking a cup of anemic coffee, reviewing the articles on the IOM decision published in major newspapers. With the *Wall Street Journal* before me, I began to read another article belonging to the vast institutional litany of *"Vaccine-Autism Link Is Discounted"* proclamations.[5]

In contrast to many others, however, this one by Kimberly Pierceall read differently. To my amazement, by the end of the article there were two admissions I could not believe. Spoken for the public record, Dr. McCormick admitted: "The committee doesn't dispute that mercury containing compounds can be damaging to the immune system." More astounding, she went on to advise that parents should choose a Thimerosal-free vaccine if one is available. While such statements would have made sense after the 2001 IOM which found the vaccine-autism link to be "biologically plausible," they clearly contradicted the 2004 IOM's declaration that there was no evidence of harm from Thimerosal-containing vaccines. As I sat and stared at the print in front of me, trying to make sense of such incongruity, the phone rang.

"Reverend Sykes?"

"Yes?" I answered, glad for any distraction from my melancholia.

"This is Tracy Biggs in the Office of Special Counsel."

Not more bad news! I could not take any more bad news right now...

"Yes?" I said, timidly.

"Reverend Sykes, we are about to put out a press release. I wanted you to have a copy of it before we send it out. Can I fax it to you?"

"I don't have a fax here at home. Could you e-mail it to me?"

"Yes, yes, that will be fine."

"A press release?" I finally summoned the courage to inquire, hesitantly.

"Yes, Reverend Sykes. The Special Counsel is putting out a press release on the issue you've brought to our attention."

I drew a quick breath. You don't put out press releases to say you find no merit in the fallacious charges brought to your attention by the unorthodox strivings of a bunch of delusional parents… I dared to hope. Could this be good news?

"Tracy?" I said, sitting down at the kitchen table.

"Yes?"

"I think I'm going to cry…"

"Oh, don't do that…"

Minutes later, I retrieved my e-mail, and shook as I read these words:

"The Office of Special Counsel (OSC) today forwarded to Congress hundreds of disclosures alleging public health and safety concerns about childhood vaccines that include a mercury-based preservative known as Thimerosal, and its possible link to neurological disorders, including autism. Notwithstanding a new Institute of Medicine study released yesterday that concludes there is no link between Thimerosal and autism, the OSC sent copies of the letters to both Senator Judd Gregg and Representative Joe Barton, to ensure that the proper Congressional oversight committees are aware of these serious allegations."[6]

The sentence I prized most, I read over and over again:

"Notwithstanding a new Institute of Medicine study released yesterday that concludes there is no link between Thimerosal and autism, the OSC sent copies of the letters to both Senator Judd Gregg and Rep. Joe Barton, to ensure that the proper Congressional oversight committees are aware of these serious allegations…"

Now, I read the sentence aloud, for fear I was mistaken in what I thought it said. "Notwithstanding a new Institute of Medicine study released yesterday that concludes there is no link…"

"Nothwithstanding…"

I stared at Scott Bloch's words for fear that if I did not, I might awaken and see them no more. Had the Special Counsel, alerted by the OSC Project, been scrutinizing the IOM? Did he suspect the same corruption of which we parents were already convinced? Had he really dared to dismiss their ersatz conclusions out-of-hand?

The world left. I stood there alone with myself and these priceless words in my hand. With each line, I esteemed them more precious:

"It appears the science is inconclusive, not definitive. Based on my limited review of the literature, there appears to be equally qualified experts on both sides of the emotional scientific and medical debate. This strikes me as a far-reaching public health issue that warrants further study and awareness, particularly because it affects the most vulnerable among us."

Yes, yes! The most vulnerable! The unborn and newborn children! For once, I was crying because I was glad. Following the press release was a letter, from Scott Bloch, the U.S. Special Counsel, directed to Congress and addressed specifically to The Honorable Judd Gregg, Senate Chairman of the Committee on Health, Education, Labor and Pensions and the Honorable Joe Barton, House Chairman of the Committee on Energy and Commerce. If the words of the Institute of Medicine has caused me to despair, the words that followed the official seal of the OSC caused me to rejoice! Unlike the Office of the Inspector General, Scott Bloch had weighed our charges about Simpsonwood:

"The disclosures also allege that the CDC and the Food and Drug Administration colluded with pharmaceutical companies at a conference in Norcross, Georgia, in June 2000, to prevent the release of a study which showed a statistical correlation between Thimerosal/mercury exposure through pediatric vaccines and neurological disorders, including autism, Attention-Deficit/Hyperactivity Disorder, stuttering, tics and speech and language delays. Instead of releasing the data presented at the conference, the author of the study, Dr. Thomas Verstraeten, later published a different version of the study in the November 2003 issue of *Pediatrics*, which did not show a statistical correlation. No explanation has been provided for this discrepancy. Finally, the disclosures allege that there is an increasing body of clinical evidence on the connection of Thimerosal/mercury exposure to neurological disorders which is being ignored by government public health agencies."

"He understands!" I shouted to the kitchen. "He knows!" Since reading the Simpsonwood transcripts, I had believed we were sacrificing our children to unsafe vaccines, and so I had written. What I had written, Scott Bloch regarded, because his words ultimately implied indictment:

"I believe these allegations raise serious continuing concerns about the administration of the nation's vaccine program and the government's possibly inadequate response to the growing body of scientific research on the public health danger of mercury in vaccines."

Serious...continuing...concerns...inadequate..." His response to our letter has been as carefully and thoughtfully composed as were our charges, I thought to myself. My mind suddenly returned to a world full of people who did not yet know today's good news—only yesterday's bad. "Whom should I call first?"

I grabbed the phone. I called Kelli Ann, and got her answering machine. I tried her cell and got her voice mail. I knew who I needed to call.

"David?"

"Yes?"

"This is Lisa Sykes. I just received a press release from the Office of Special Counsel pertaining to Thimerosal. May I send it to you? I'd like to get your opinion."

David kept the line open while he downloaded the e-mail containing the Special Counsel's cover letter and press release. He was quiet, reading with great care, as he always did. I waited and waited and hoped and prayed.

"Lisa, I think you have got something very substantial here. This will carry weight equal to or greater than that of the Mercury in Medicine Report. Scott Bloch is calling for Congressional investigation. He is also advertising for a whistle blower in this. Did you notice?"

"Yea. I noticed. At last, someone in a position of power and public trust is trying to help us!"

OSC's press release was picked up by Sharyl Attkisson, the medical and investigative reporter for the Nightly News with Dan Rather. If any of us doubted the importance of what Scott Bloch had dared to do, those doubts were dispelled on May 25, when his explosive words made national news that night:

"... it appears there may be sufficient evidence to find a substantial likelihood of a substantial and specific danger to public health caused by the use of Thimerosal/mercury in vaccines because of its inherent toxicity."

The OSC Project attracted not only Sharyl Attkisson's attention, but also that of Lisa Reagan. Having received one of the packets "cc'd" to the media, Lisa Reagan forwarded it immediately to her editor, Peggy O'Mara, who, upon reading it, called me: "Lisa, we're dedicating an entire issue of *Mothering Magazine* to the mercury issue. Is it all right if we include your letter?"

By August, the OSC Letter of Allegation on which four mothers had worked day and night, and in which fifteen families had invested their literary contributions, approval, energy, names, and some two hundred dollars each in postage, was available in a magazine distributed to every Barnes and Noble, every health food store, and various news outlets around the country.

As news of the OSC project was published, word went out on every electronic board and to every parent advocacy group in existence. The search for a whistleblower was on.

The call I received subsequently from Tracy at the OSC office was almost amusing. "Lisa, we've got parents calling us from all over the country if they ever worked for the federal government. They don't understand the whistleblower must have worked as an employee for one of the federal health agencies. And the faxes—they don't have return addresses—so we can't respond to them all, the fax machines just can't keep up."

At last she said the words I had been waiting for: "We understand the scope of the problem."

I did not know that Tracy was pregnant. Had I known, I would not have feared the allegations we made might have been discarded. No pregnant woman to whom I had ever told this truth found it a matter of negligible importance. In time, when I came to learn Tracy had gone out on maternity leave, I would think to myself, "That's one more safe..."

Along with the call for a whistle blower that went out across the nation, so had my name and phone number; I was getting calls from all over. Among those calls I received was one most extraordinary. An informant, who asked

never to be identified, called me to say, "You need to FOIA* the parameters
of the Immunization Safety Review Committee of the IOM—all the information on how the CDC instructed the IOM to convene and conduct itself.
You'll be amazed at what you find…"

"Brian," I thought to myself. "I have to call Brian!" Brian Hooker was
one of the OSC parents. I jokingly referred to him as 'King of the FOIA'
because he had taken his time and his scientific and governmental know-
how to FOIA the daylights out of the CDC. He had tracked down the most
astonishing communications between CDC and pharmaceutical companies.
He had discovered transcripts and contracts that increasingly threw light on
many dealings at the CDC. Brian, I knew, was the one from whom I needed
to seek help now.

"Brian, this is Lisa. Hi. Can you help me? I need to FOIA something
that we might term a 'parameters document.' I want to know all the instructions the CDC gave to the IOM prior to their first convening. Can you do
that for me?"

Brian sent off the FOIA the next day. When we finally reeled in the line
we cast with this request, we would possess information for initiating many
more investigations, if only someone were willing to uphold the law.

---

*Freedom of Information Act

Chapter Twelve

Hazardous Waste

"All truth passes through three stages. First, it is ridiculed. Second, it is violently opposed. Third, it is accepted as being self-evident."

—Arthur Schopenhauer

June 2004

The OSC Project, and its hard-sought achievement of providing the first sympathetic statement from an appointed federal official, not only got the attention of CBS and *Mothering Magazine*, it also attracted the attention of Lyn Redwood of SafeMinds, one of the first parents to identify mercury as the culprit in autism. Three short years earlier, Lyn and I had dined in Boston just before the 2001 IOM meeting. Seeking to assist me and the parents who conducted the OSC Project, Lyn sorted through the contacts she had made during the years of her advocacy, considering if any of them might fulfill the high criteria necessary to be a whistleblower. With one name in mind, she called me.

"I think you need to talk to a scientist who called me some time ago. His name is Paul G. King. He worked at Walter Reed, and I think he is quite knowledgeable about vaccines."

As soon as we hung up, I dialed the number Lyn had dictated to me. My conversation with Dr. Paul G. King began as many other cold calls I made that spring:

"Hello, Dr. King? This is Reverend Lisa Sykes. I am a United Methodist minister in Richmond, Virginia, and someone who is very concerned about the issue of Thimerosal. Lyn Redwood suggested that I call you. Would you have a few minutes to talk with me confidentially about my concerns?"

I would discover that with Paul, a few minutes were never enough. Dr. King was so knowledgeable about the toxicity of mercury in all its forms, as well as the specific regulatory failures of the FDA, that every conversation was tantamount to an academic lecture on some aspect of the subject. I, the liberal arts double major, tried to absorb all the scientific and regulatory analysis that he imparted to me while one, two, or even three little boys comically crawled over and around my feet.

Paul was enigmatic initially. He answered my non-scientific questions with questions. "Could I be a whistleblower? Well, I don't know. What do you want to accomplish? How could I help you to do this?"

Initially there were very few answers, and yet my intuition told me to follow these conversations and to trust him. Perhaps I was able to be patient because, while I could not speak Paul's language of chemistry, he could speak my language of theology. Interspersed with his cryptic questions were religious professions that I was uniquely qualified to appreciate. While Paul's theological statements perhaps befuddled some, for me, they simply disclosed the deep, but eclectic, faith of someone whose beliefs did not conform to the systematized revelations of just one world religion. Paul would speak of the philosophy of Tao and the Choctaw as readily as the religions of Judaism and Christianity. The creedal statements he made were unorthodox, but so was Paul, both in his candor and his brilliance.

We spoke several times. I got the sense he was testing me, to see if I would remain patient—to judge whether or not he would entrust to me what he knew. After a few of these conversations, Paul declared in his East-Texas accent, "I will help you."

"How, Paul?" I replied, waiting to be enlightened.

"Well, Lisa, you did a great job with the OSC Project. But did you know... did you know that you did the second step before the first one?"

"Second step?" I thought the OSC Project was the only and most daring step we parents-turned-advocates could take. I was wrong.

"So, what is the first step?" I asked, still knowing next to nothing about this man, who, I would come to learn, was an analytical and inorganic chemist, pharmaceutical scientist, and a recognized regulatory consultant.

From our earliest conversations, I discerned that Paul could help the cause of our children, though I did not know how. Paul spoke of a way to advance the cause of the children and to counter the federal government's allegiance to the pharmaceutical companies, an alliance formed at the expense of the health of the nation's children.

"Lisa, go to www.fda.gov, and click on 'Citizen Petition'. You will see that this is a federally established avenue of recourse to force the FDA to re-consider any policy, practice, regulation, or the enforcement thereof. In this case, you can force a reconsideration of the safety of Thimerosal and other mercury compounds in vaccines, serums, and other drugs. Once you file, the FDA only has 180 days to answer your petition, and if you are not satisfied that their conclusion is correct in the eyes of the law, you can take them to court. Now, when you realize they stand in direct violation of the Federal Food, Drug, and Cosmetic Act..."

"The... what?!" I asked Paul, excitedly. He was speaking too fast.

"Didn't you know there's a regulation that states: 'No component of a vaccine shall be toxic...?'"

His words had the bluster of a Baptist preacher on Sunday.

"What! Gosh... well... doesn't that make a lot of sense! You shouldn't put a poison in a vaccine? You shouldn't put poison in a baby? Just imagine that!" I said, feigning surprise. "So, how in the world do they get around the law?" Now, I had become intently serious.

And it was then that Paul began teaching me something even more disheartening than the documented history and toxicity of mercury. "The law is only as good as the persons who enforce it. If those charged with enforcing the law will not, then, what good is the law, Lisa?"

I clenched my teeth. The patriotism that my family had reverently placed in my soul soured once again. Could it be that the law was negotiable? Could it be that all of the fail-safes in the federal system had failed to make vaccines safe? Paul's arguments troubled my spirit and called me, once again, despite the tiredness from a chaotic spring, to undertake yet another season of advocacy.

My pen stopped, and the stream-of-consciousness that was spilling upon the paper in front of me ceased. My somber thoughts were broken by the swell of music. I looked up. Though it might seem irreverent, it was during worship that I had begun to compose the Citizen's Petition. Worship soon concluded, but my argument had not. I continued to write furiously. Those delegates around me judged me dutiful, but they mistook my purpose. The other 2,000 people in the Hampton Coliseum had no idea what I was writing or thinking. And it was not yet time to tell them.

As a clergy delegate to the Virginia Annual Conference of the United Methodist Church, I was grateful to be distracted—distracted from reflecting upon the recent discoveries I found so alarming—by worship. Just like the other clergy and lay delegates from all over Virginia, I had come to Hampton to participate in the governance of our Annual Conference and to share in precious times of worship as one among many delegates and Christians.

One day, I knew, one day after much planning and the building of support, I would bring my cause to the Virginia Annual Conference of the United Methodist Church. Soon, but not yet. For now, it was enough that the church directly supported my pastoral call, and in doing so, that it indirectly supported my advocacy. How often, I pondered, had my religious life and practice saved me from despair? How often, had it given me strength and grace to do what seemed too burdensome? How often had worship, in particular, been the inspiration in my unending crusade to stop the profanity of sacrificing children's lives to illnesses manufactured with mercury?

And how amazing, I thought to myself, that Paul wanted me, a mother and minister, to first attempt placing into words our challenge to the federal government: ban mercury in vaccines and other drugs, or if not, then demonstrate it safe. We knew the federal government, and specifically the FDA, would not do the first and could not do the second. So, it was with my anger refined into a delicate and razor sharp tool that I began to state my case, scribbling it in long-hand upon paper meant to hold notes on the Conference proceedings.

I arrived home from Annual Conference to greet my family and unpack my suitcase. Only after everyone was in bed asleep, did I rescue my writing from my briefcase and smuggle it down to my home office. These papers held six-and-a-half pages of the best argument I could make against mercury to an agency, I believed, to be as corrupt as this element was toxic. I emailed it to Paul, and to those who had so recently agreed to join me to this new and consuming project.

The petition expanded, as Paul took scientific offerings from Mark and

David and Brian, and other edits and additions. Not a month into the petition's creation, I learned that Paul didn't require the normal amount of sleep the rest of us did. Upon receipt of an e-mail message, which I might have sent hours earlier, he would sometimes respond immediately by calling—even if it was well past the normal bedtime of everyone in my house.

"Dr. King, we're all asleep here!" my exasperated husband would say with constrained frustration before putting the receiver down. The numbers on the digital clock often revealed it to be one a.m.. As the petition progressed, I began to stay up later and later, and Seth learned to turn off the ringer to the phone on our bedside table.

This time, thankfully, Paul had not called at midnight or one or two in the morning. This time, Paul had called me midday, when my mind was alert. Somewhere in the midst of yet another hour-long conversation, discussing the contents of the petition, Paul informed me that our team was incomplete.

"Lisa, there's a mom out there that we need to find."

I laughed. One particular mother of an autistic child, somewhere out there. "Okay, Dr. King," I said, pondering how I would search the nation over for one particular mother of an autistic child. "Can you tell me a bit more about her?"

"Yes, I can," Paul replied. "She has a severely affected child. She apparently does not get out much as a result, and so she has amassed articles on the toxicity of Thimerosal by surfing the web. I understand that she has a library of more than a thousand documents."

I was impressed. Impressed by this woman Paul described, and once again, impressed by him. "I've never heard of her, Dr. King! How did you?"

"Oh, I read. I have a lot of time to read. I came across an article about her in some of that reading."

"Okay. Well, she sounds very resourceful."

"And her library of articles is something we need for the petition, Lisa. We must clearly document the current as well as the historical knowledge of Thimerosal's toxicity. I want you to find her."

"I don't know if I can, Dr. King, but I will try." I drew a deep breath, waiting for him to reveal the identity of this woman for whom I would search an entire nation.

"So what's her name, Dr. King?"

"Leslie Weed."

I burst out laughing.

Paul was surprised by my response, and so I explained: "Well, Paul, that was easy! She's in Ponte Vedra, Florida, and she attended the February 9, 2004 IOM meeting. She and I have been e-mailing each other ever since. But I had no idea she had a library of a thousand articles on Thimerosal."

"Lisa, you need to ask her to be part of the petition."

"Done, Dr. King," I said exuberantly, "I'd be delighted to."

"Good. Oh, and Lisa, there's one more thing. I woke this morning with an idea for the name for our group, the Coalition for Mercury-free Drugs. That is what our group is 'for' and an acronym, CoMeD, for that name. After all, getting all drugs to be mercury-free is what our loosely knit group has set out to do. I want the name of our organization to reflect the positive goal we are trying to accomplish."

"CoMeD. I like it, Dr. King. 'Co' also meaning 'with' or 'assisting' and 'MeD' which could be construed as an abbreviation for medicine. CoMeD-helping medicine."[1]

"Leslie, I need your help."

"Sure, Lisa. What can I do?"

Leslie had longed to hold those responsible for the mercury-induced injuries of her youngest daughter, Lanier, accountable and in doing so both advocate for other injured children and protect those children not yet injured. Leslie was a slender and lovely woman, with an elegant and sincere spirit. Of the many mothers whom I had come to know, Leslie was my favorite. She became a close friend, despite miles between us and the immense daily concerns before us, through our electronic correspondence. I had come to know so much about Leslie, her husband Bobby, and their three beautiful daughters, Haley, Carly and Lanier, that I felt as though I knew them all.

Leslie had even confided in me a painful account of her eldest daughter, Haley, who at a young age and in frustration at Lanier's limitations, looked at her mother and demanded, "Mommy, why did the doctor have to poison Lanier?" Exchanging heartbreak for heartbreak, I recalled for her the time when my eldest son Adam, only six, had exclaimed to me, "Momma, if they hadn't put that bad stuff in those shots, I'd have had a really good playmate and friend. But now Wesley can't even talk! That is soooo annoying."

"'Annoying' was the worst word he knew at six, Leslie." I explained, turning quickly away, so he did not see me crying.

Ordinary mothers, with ordinary children, could not understand our loss or our sorrow, but we could understand each other. Leslie had sent me an angel figurine inscribed with the words of Emily Bronte: "Whatever souls are made of, yours and mine are the same." Leslie sent me grace and encouragement, but that was not all.

Even as prepared as I was to do battle with the federal authorities, Leslie was more so. She raided her stores of documents and studies from her assembled Thimerosal library, providing an arsenal of facts to strengthen the petition. Much of the information was so complex, scientifically, that Paul and Mark and David had to judge where in the petition it would best be referenced, but some of it was so simple and so shocking that it required no interpretation for either of us to understand its significance. One beautiful day at the end of June, I fell speechless upon reading one of the documents Leslie forwarded to me that afternoon. As soon as she sent it, she called me so we could review it together.

"Do you see, Lisa?" she asked me, once I had opened the attachment. "The top of the page reads 'Material Safety Data Sheet'.[2] Here are the manufacturer's instructions and information provided to shippers and handlers of Thimerosal, who wear special clothing and latex gloves to transport it, but denied to us parents, even though it's to be injected directly into our children!"

"The first note," Leslie explained, "is 'T+,' meaning 'Very toxic'; N denotes 'Dangerous for the environment.'"

"Yeah, I see," was all I could say in reply, grotesquely fascinated by the information on my computer screen.

"Now if you look down the sheet, you will see that the preliminary information includes these warnings." Leslie began to read them to me:

VERY TOXIC BY INHALATION, IN CONTACT WITH SKIN AND IF SWALLOWED. DANGER OF CUMULATIVE EFFECTS [3]

My anger returned my voice to me once again. "Inhaled? Swallowed? Leslie, the writer of this document never even imagined that anyone would be stupid enough to inject this stuff directly into babies! Look, Leslie—it's labeled as a reproductive toxin under California's Proposition 65! They've known from the beginning what this wretched substance can do to a human being! And they'll warn shippers but they won't warn us parents?"

"Tell parents that there is a poison in their child's vaccine, Lisa? A poison, a neurotoxin and a carcinogen? Why would they do that?" Leslie responded sarcastically.

"This? This is what they injected into my child? This is what my pediatrician shot into my child's thigh? Since when did pediatricians become the chief purveyors of poison to their patients?" My anger consumed me again and again as Leslie, on page after page, pronounced the known danger into which my child had been placed and identified the recognized damage which he had incurred from this poison. My son, her daughter, and how many others, I wondered?

I was dismayed by the varied manifestations that mercury toxicity from Thimerosal exposure could produce. Stunned, Leslie and I discussed the listing provided on this Material Safety Data Sheet:

BRAIN AND COVERINGS (OTHER DEGENERATIVE CHANGES)
BEHAVIORAL (ANOREXIA, HUMAN)
BEHAVIORAL (CHANGE IN MOTOR ACTIVITY)
BEHAVIORAL (ATAXIA)
BEHAVIORAL (COMA)
LUNGS, THORAX OR RESPIRATION (OTHER CHANGES)
GASTROINTESTINAL (NAUSEA OR VOMITING)
KIDNEY, URETER, BLADDER (CHANGES IN TUBULES)
EFFECTS ON FERTILITY (POST-IMPLANTATION MORTALITY)
EFFECTS ON FERTILITY (ABORTION)
EFFECTS ON EMBRYO OR FETUS (FETAL DEATH)
TUMORIGENIC EFFECTS (UTERINE TUMORS)
NUTRITIONAL AND GROSS METABOLIC (CHANGES IN: METABOLIC ACIDOSIS)
TUMORIGENIC (NEOPLASTIC BY RTECS CRITERIA)
TUMORIGENIC (TUMORS AT SITE OF APPLICATION)"[4]

"'Effects on embryo or fetus—fetal death!'" My finger pressed hard against the words appearing on my computer screen.

"I know, Lisa," Leslie sighed, seeking to comfort me. "Now, go down to 'Toxicological information.' Tell me who this reminds you of."

Leslie began to read the Eli Lilly Data Sheet: "Thimerosal may enter the body through the skin, is toxic, alters genetic material... fetal changes, decreased offspring survival, and lung tissue changes... Exposure to mercury in utero and in children may cause mild to severe mental retardation and mild to severe motor coordination impairment."[5]

Again, I sat, staring ahead at the computer screen, speechless.

"That's our children, Lisa," Leslie said to me with an understated heartache that penetrated my silence. "That's Lanier, and that's Wesley."

The next lines upon which my tear-filled eyes fell were these:

TO THE BEST OF OUR KNOWLEDGE, THE CHEMICAL, PHYSICAL, AND TOXI-COLOGICAL PROPERTIES HAVE NOT BEEN THOROUGHLY INVESTIGATED. LICENSE GRANTED TO MAKE UNLIMITED PAPER COPIES FOR INTERNAL USE ONLY.[6]

I wanted to scream; I cursed instead. Mercury poisoning was the single subject which had the power to occasion cuss words from me. "Damn them, Leslie! Damn them for injecting this filth into our children! Damn them for not telling us!" Then, as I at last calmed down, I asked aloud of my patient friend, "Leslie, are we to believe the IOM has never seen this information?"

"They'll wish we had never seen it, once the petition gets filed, Lisa! But there's one more thing I want you to see. I'm sending it to you right now. While you wait for it, make sure you have read the regulatory information here, where it says:

CONTACT A LICENSED PROFESSIONAL WASTE DISPOSAL SERVICE TO DISPOSE OF THIS MATERIAL...THIS MATERIAL AND ITS CONTAINER MUST BE DISPOSED OF AS HAZARDOUS WASTE...AVOID RELEASE TO THE ENVIRONMENT.[7]

"This material and its container must be disposed of as hazardous waste," I repeated into the phone, almost forgetting Leslie was still there.

Fuming at these facts, I waited for the new transmission to download and opened it, almost frenetically. My admiration for Leslie not only as a friend, but also as a detective, was immense. Her library was startling, her soul, savvy. As the parent of a child poisoned with Thimerosal, what could be more shocking than this Material Safety Data Sheet?

"What the heck is this, Leslie?" I opened the e-mail attachment to find a pdf file of a letter on my screen. The top of this page read "Thymerasol

Filtering." The communication originated at Iowa State University in the Industrial Assessment Center and was sent January 9, 1998 at 9:38:31 EST.[8]

"Apparently an assistant at Iowa State was seeking help," Leslie explained. "He was connected with a program to buy-back unused animal vaccines that had gone out-of-date and exchange them for new ones. Trouble is, Lisa, he had discovered there was mercury in the vaccines. Do you see what he says? 'Because of this mercury content, the returned material must be disposed of as hazardous waste.' But you won't believe this... you read it... go on..."

I read the following paragraph aloud to Leslie, though she already knew what it said:

"The current methods of disposal consist of throwing the individual vials of vaccine, container and all, into 55-gallon drums..."

I stopped, waiting for my body to breathe again. At last, I felt my sides expand and lungs draw another breath, and I continued. This time my voice was quivering:

"...which are in turn taken off-site by a hazardous waste disposal firm (This waste stream totaled 9,600 gallons in 1996, at a cost of $600/55 gallon drum.)"

"What?!" My eyes left the page; my hands shook; I was more livid than I had ever been before in my life. "God forgive me, Leslie! Do you mean to tell me if they cannot inject those damn toxic vaccines into our children's arms, then, and only then, they are going to seal them in steel drums and bury them six feet under?"

"That's right, girlfriend."

CHAPTER THIRTEEN

INCRIMINATION

"Never doubt that a small group of committed citizens can change
the world. Indeed, it is the only thing that ever has."

—Margaret Mead

AUGUST 3, 2004

WE WALKED INTO HIS STATELY OFFICE TO BE GREETED IN A SPACIOUS ADMINISTRATIVE
area adorned with memorabilia from North Carolina and beautifully framed
photos of the Edwards' family upon the walls. Bobbie Manning and Leslie
Weed rendezvoused with Kelli Ann and me there, and we mothers were prepared to be outspoken advocates for our children and all others like them.
There, as we awaited an invitation to the conference room with the Citizen's
Petition in hand, we talked excitedly, eager to bring our cause before the
aide of someone who might be the next Vice President of the United States.
Unlike Vice President Dick Cheney, Senator Jonathan Edwards seemed
sincerely interested in examining the issue of Thimerosal.

As we were shown into the sunny conference room, we took seats at
one end of an expansive, polished conference table that gleamed in the light.
Bobbie, a frequent visitor in congressional and senatorial offices, had a
photo of her son, Michael, who had been diagnosed with autism, encased in
a round circular pin affixed to her lapel. Bobbie joined CoMeD to oversee
publicity regarding the Citizen Petition. Among the parents in the advocacy community, no one was better with the press and government officials

than Bobbie. A member of A-Champ as well, Bobbie advocated in the New York area where she lived, and nationally, she sought to enlist new recruits, especially politicians and the press, in the battle against mercury. A-Champ, Advocates for Children's Health Affected by Mercury Poisoning, worked as a parent-led national political action organization.[1]

"The Senator continues to be very interested in this issue, Ms. Davis, and most impressed by your advocacy…"

Kelli Ann smiled and began a presentation of the CoMeD Citizen Petition. She concluded, "We are here to file this Citizen Petition at the federal dockets tomorrow. The FDA is going to have to answer for allowing Thimerosal into our children's vaccines…"

The aide, herself unfamiliar with a Citizen Petition, seemed impressed by the document, if somewhat surprised. How had this group of mothers come to understand regulatory workings of the federal government of which even she was unaware?

For some time, Kelli Ann, Bobbie, and I conversed with the aide. Leslie took time to find her voice in that meeting, but when she did, her appeal was powerful. "I have a daughter who may never talk and may never be independent, but she will never be undefended from the wrong that's been done to her. I will not cease from demanding justice for my daughter. She was poisoned."

The aide listened, her heart obviously moved, as Leslie described Lanier's daily struggles.

"You ladies bring a significant issue before the senator."

"And remember, he promised me a face-to-face," Kelli Ann chided.

"Yes, Ms. Davis. I'm afraid when he did, we were not aware he'd possibly be running for the Vice Presidency. Are there specific things we can do right now to be of help to you?"

I chimed in, pulling the letter from the President's Council on Integrity and Ethics (PCIE) out of my file. "Yes, there is one. We would like for the Senator to write Acting Commissioner Dara Corrigan, the Inspector General for Health and Human Services, requesting that she open an investigation into Thimerosal, as called for in this letter from the President's Council on Integrity and Efficiency."

I handed her the document. On July 21, 2004, Chris Swecker, Chair of the Integrity Committee, had written to me:

"Dear Ms. Sykes:

...After thorough consideration, the IC determined that your complaint did not fall within the IC's jurisdiction because your complaint
did not allege any wrongdoing specifically against the Inspector General (IG)...The IC decided to refer your complaint to Ms. Dara Corrigan, Acting IG, HHS, for review and further action, as appropriate..."[2]

Once again, the aide looked surprised. In her experience, neatly attired,
polite PTA* mothers usually came to this office to request greater educational funding, better health care benefits—things of that sort. But the four
of us were, in ordinary words, calling for an extraordinary investigation into
charges of collusion and criminal conspiracy at the highest levels of the government.

"Here is a copy, too, of the Office of Special Counsel press release from
the end of May," I offered. "You will see here that Scott Bloch refers to
Thimerosal as a 'substantial and specific danger to the public health.'"

And then I pulled out my greatest prize generated by the OSC Project.
It was a piece of HHS stationary, unique among my collection of federal correspondence, for it would be dramatic in its truthfulness. In it, for the first
time, an official of the United States Government, Department of Health and
Human Services, used the word "criminal" to speak of the conflict-of-interest
that plagued our national health agencies and that had created a plague of
mercury-induced neurological disorders among our children. Dated July 19,
2004, it read:

"Dear Reverend Sykes:

...Upon review of the correspondence you provided to the PCIE, in
conjunction with further research into the matter, we have determined
that your above allegation represents a potential conflict-of-interest
issue which may be criminal in nature and therefore falls within the
Department of Health and Human Services (HHS), Office of Inspector General (OIG), Office of Investigations' (OI) authority to investigate.

---

* Parent Teachers Association

...Should you have any questions, you may contact Matt Kochanski
of my staff. Mr. Kochanski is Director of the Investigative Branch for
OI and can be reached at (202) 619-2954.

Sincerely,
Michael E. Little
Deputy Inspector General
for Investigations"[3]

"There is no doubting the credibility of our cause," Kelli Ann concluded,
with eyes and a voice that disclosed both her pain and her resolve.

The aide wrote down Acting Commissioner Corrigan's address as well as
that of Matt Kochanski before we departed, making a preliminary judgment
that correspondence to these officials was something the senator might be
willing to do.

We returned to the Capitol Metro subway stop, giddy with excitement.
"Imagine... imagine if Edwards is elected Vice President! Imagine the Vice
President of the United States calling for an investigation of the poisoning
of our children..." Kelli Ann was thrilled with both this possibility and the
meeting that had just taken place.

On the Metro, we reviewed every word that had been exchanged in the
meeting, and tried to envision what would happen tomorrow. We had come
to Washington, D.C., not only to meet with senators and congressmen, but
also to file an FDA Citizen Petition, a powerful regulatory tool of which few
outside the pharmaceutical industry had ever heard.

"What are they going to do tomorrow when we file this with the federal
dockets?"

After finding our way to Vienna, everyone got into my car and we began
our drive to Chantilly, the Virginia suburb where my brother and sister-in-law
lived.

When we arrived at their house, I rang the bell and then let myself in,
expecting to see my brother, Dan. I tilted my head to the side, still unenlight-
ened and now confused, to see Dr. Mark Geier standing before me, opening
his arms to give me a hug.

"Mark, what are you doing here?" my voice trailed off.

As David, his son, came around the corner into the foyer holding a wrapped box with a bow on top, my benighted mind finally awoke from its slumber. The day had been so full of political activism, any notice I paid to my thirty-ninth birthday had been as fleeting as the morning light in Richmond and Seth's kiss good-bye as we left.

"You're kidding!" I exclaimed out loud. "A birthday party?!"

Soon, everyone was laughing, and after greeting Dan and Andrea and Mark and David, I made my way into the kitchen where the table was full of steamed shrimp, wine, salad, and hors d'oeuvres. It was so wonderfully ridiculous. These parents and scientists, determined to hold several federal health agencies accountable for untold crimes against children, along with my brother and sister-in-law, had planned not activism but reprieve for tonight—just to celebrate the arrival of my middle age! I rejoiced doubly, to celebrate a birthday surrounded by such purposeful friendships and the coming day with its promise of filing the petition at the federal dockets.

As I was in the midst of a lively chat with my brother and Andrea, someone I did not recognize came to stand by my side. He was about six foot, plaid shirt, Texan tie, boots and cowboy hat. He was slightly rotund, and struck me as rather unusual.

"Well, Lisa, I hope you had a good trip up."

"Yes, it's been a great day," I replied, not saying anything about the Edwards' meeting to this unidentified person.

When this man directed his attention elsewhere, I looked at my brother, stumped. "Dan, who is this?" I whispered.

My brother chuckled as I threw him an impatient grimace. The man to my left again rejoined the conversation, and I returned to polite chatter, refusing to admit my ignorance.

Again, when his attention was distracted, I looked at my brother furiously, and demanded in a low, terse voice, "Dan, who is this guy?"

A voice from my left replied, "You don't recognize my voice, do you, Lisa?"

My hand covered my open mouth!

"Dr. King!!!"

My confined mind expanded at last to take in all of the room and all those within it! Of course, this singular man in the room, whom I had never seen before, had to be Dr. King. Yet, my preconceived notion about what Dr. King would look like deafened me to registering the voice with which I had conversed so many times.

"Dr. King!" Unsure whether I should or not, I put my arms about his neck, in thanks for what he had done.

"The cowboy hat threw you, didn't it?" he observed, grinning.

In truth, everything about Dr. King had thrown me. I don't know what I had imagined Dr. King to be like, but whatever it was, it was not the persona before me. Suddenly, the disembodied voice, with whom I had spoken for hours and hours on the phone, had been incarnated.

"Here, I've brought you a birthday present. Unleavened bread..."

I opened a bakery box to see pastries filled with apricot and strawberry jam, between layers of waxed paper.

"I thought if we shared unleavened bread, we might not betray one another..."

I reached out in an attempt to receive not only the gift but also to understand the message that Paul had superimposed upon it. Finally, as this exchange concluded, as my stunned mind recovered, I looked over Paul's shoulder to see a woman, whom I judged to be in her fifties, seated alone upon Dan's sofa. David stood a few paces off, and they were quietly chatting. Her blonde hair was pulled back in a ponytail. She had the prominent cheekbones of one whose ancestry was Celtic, and a face whose shyness was traced with an unrelenting determination. "A tennis champ," I thought. The hair, the expression, gave her identity away.

"Anne?" I asked, certain this time that I was right. She was the third member of the Geier family.

"Yes. Happy Birthday, Lisa."

Just then the phone rang. Dan chatted briefly, and then made an announcement: "Hey Lisa, that was Cliff. He was on his way, but he's had an emergency call. He said to tell you 'Happy Birthday' and he'll see you tomorrow."

Again, I felt such happiness, wonderment and gratitude for this birthday celebration with world-class scientists, nationally renowned lawyers, family and friends.

The old '92 Cadillac Paul drove was wide enough for Bobbie to sit in the front passenger seat and for Kelli Ann, Leslie, and me to fit on the bench seat in back. The petition copies, those with the 1,000 supporting articles and individual copies for congressmen and senators, were carefully packaged and placed in the trunk. Also, beside the boxes of petitions, was a box full of the July-August edition of *Mothering Magazine*, with its coverage of the OSC Project and Wesley's picture on page forty-eight.[4] At my request, Peggy O'Mara sent these to me gratis for the specific purpose of handing them out on Capitol Hill. On this day, she was also sending a reporter to meet us.

We arrived at the address we had been given for the dockets and found ourselves in a satellite parking lot of the FDA's Parklawn Building, a huge glass edifice which, in typical 70's architectural style, had several small and unimposing doorways. Kelli Ann and Paul set off to find a main entrance and determine where we were to enter in order to file the petition. In the mean-time, the rest of us waited by the car and exchanged update calls with Mark and David and Cliff.

As we spoke on our cell phones, a minivan and two gentlemen in blue jeans and t-shirts arrived. As soon as they got out of the van, we noticed the CBS credentials around their necks and the camera equipment inside their vehicle.

"Are you Sharyl Attkisson's camera crew?" I asked.

"Yes," replied the first. "Are you delivering some sort of petition today?" They gazed down at our boxes. "We were told to film you dropping off the document today at the dockets office." Without another word, these gentlemen focused their camera and sound equipment on me as I finished securing the boxes on a dolly.

Mercury in vaccines, mercury in drugs, the poisoning of children with Thimerosal, largely failed to be reported without bias in the American media, and therefore, failed to offend the pharmaceutical company advertisers who patronized the media. *Mothering Magazine*, with its naturalistic philosophy, had been one of a precious few publications bold enough to transgress the voluntary black-out of this subject in the national press. For Sharyl Attkisson to be sending her crew with us today, to shadow us as we filed a document demanding the withdrawal and ban of this neurotoxin, was exemplary inves-tigative journalism and our strongest hope of gaining public awareness.

Mark and David arrived and, then, Cliff. In addition, a brown minivan parked close by, and a pleasant woman in her late thirties got out, inquiring if we were filing a petition today with the federal dockets.

"Are you from *Mothering Magazine*?" I asked.

"Yes," she answered, reaching out her hand to greet me. "I am Rachel Dahlenberg, and I will be following you for today. This is my photographer."

Everyone exchanged handshakes, as Kelli Ann and Paul returned.

"Gang's all here," I chimed in, happily. "So where do we go?"

"We're going to need to drive there. This is the mailing address, but it's not actually where the docket office is," Kelli Ann replied.

With four vehicles, we redistributed passengers. The CBS film crew followed. We retraced several blocks and arrived at a security gate which marked the edge of the FDA campus. Paul spoke to the guard, advising him that we had come to file a Citizens Petition with the dockets. The guard, who seemed almost amused by this entourage of do-gooders, happily opened the gate for us.

At this point, we needed only one complete petition, to which Kelli Ann added all one thousand supportive articles. With spunk in her walk and Bobbie at her side, Kelli Ann carried the box with the petition and strode across the parking lot to a simple three-story building. As they walked, the camera crew filmed them entering the building and then the rest of us who followed. Rebecca and her photographer moved with the television crew.

As we all assembled in the foyer to show photo IDs, sign in, and transit through metal detectors, the guards were astounded.

"Where are all of you headed?" a young woman in uniform asked us, eying the television crew and cameras.

"We're going to dockets," Paul announced, authoritatively.

"All you all going to dockets? Nobody ever goes to dockets! And the cameras too?"

"Yes, all of us," I replied with a smile that could not be contained, no matter how hard I tried.

"Dockets is in the basement. Go to your left, then down the stairs. When you get there, turn left."

We followed the guard's instructions, and exulted in our approach to a room that resembled a small library in an elementary school. Behind us, I could hear the guard exclaiming, "I ain't never seen that many people here to go to dockets before." Once we descended the stairs and turned left, we were in a pedestrian room full of round tables encircled by barrel-shaped chairs, books upon shelves against the walls, and a desk at which one clearly surprised FDA employee sat quietly in uniform.

"We would like to file a Citizens Petition," Paul told the clerk.[5]

The CBS camera crew and the photographer from *Mothering Magazine* were busy recording the simple transaction, as the petition and each article that accompanied it were stamped with the date it was received. Kelli Ann and Bobbie posed as the official copy of the petition was handed over to the clerk.

Now that the FDA had been put on notice that a serious challenge to the legality of Thimerosal had been received and would have to be answered, the Department of Health and Human Services would be our next stop. Not wishing to rely upon internal agency communications to herald our accomplishment, we traveled to the nearest Metro stop and onward to deliver a full copy of the petition to Mr. Tommy Thompson, Secretary for the Department of Health and Human Services.

In a huge and open foyer, with dark wood paneling, a marbled floor, and bright red area rugs, we approached a commanding reception area, staffed by clerks and guards in uniform. Leslie set the complete copy of the petition, documents and all, upon the desk before us. "We are delivering this to Secretary Tommy Thompson," Paul declared.

The guards looked at us, mildly curious. None of them moved.

"You can leave it right there, and we'll send it up to him."

We looked at one another, grinning. I had already called, trying to schedule an appointment, and had been turned down flat.

"No, that won't do," replied Paul. "If we cannot deliver it to the Secretary, then I think you better have a courier come down to pick it up."

The guards looked at each other and then nodded to one of the clerks, who dutifully called upstairs.

"Okay, it will be a few minutes."

We moved to the side of the entryway, taking seats on the red sofa and chairs that were arranged to resemble a small living room without walls, upon the rectangular carpet.

"Well, Cliff, while we are here, tell me, when do you think we will file Wesley's case?"

"I don't know, Lisa. We need to talk about that. Wesley's case is one of the few that has made it through the National Vaccine Compensation Act and is now free to go to civil court. The others have all been frozen in the Act."

My heart skipped a beat. Wesley, I knew, was perhaps one of the best-documented cases of mercury toxicity in the nation. Excellent guidance from Mary since the time of Wesley's diagnosis, and excellent legal advice from Cliff since he had filed Wesley in the Act, meant that Wesley was not only receiving the best medical care available but also the best legal representation possible. The Geiers agreed to be science advisors for Wesley's case and so I had begun to call these four persons "the Dream Team." Now, Wesley was one of only a handful of cases to have been successfully withdrawn from the Act after the requisite 240 days. This meant we were free to take his claim to civil court. A couple cases had already been filed, but were not going well.

"You won't be the first case filed, but you may end up being the first case that wins," speculated Cliff, judging the copious notes and laboratory tests which I had kept since Mary began treating Wesley.

Before Cliff and I made much progress in our conversation, an employee of Health and Human Services appeared before us. "I can take that for you," she said politely.

"Before you do, would you please sign our copy, and date it, to show you have received it from us?" Paul inquired.

"I'll have to check about that," she responded, hesitantly. She consulted with the guards at reception and then had a lengthy phone conversation with someone we assumed inhabited one of the upper levels of this modern building. At last, she returned to the area where we were seated.

"Okay. I can sign it."

Still wondering why we had called for such formality, the young woman accepted the caddy case, with page upon page of our argument against Thimerosal's safety, and article after article chronicling our evidence of mercury's toxicity.

"If Tommy didn't know about the petition before, I'll bet you he knows now," chuckled David, as we pried apart the plate glass doors and walked out into the blinding August sun.

All day long, the conversations I had with this incredible team of parents and experts were rich. I was in the midst of one of these conversations with Mark and David over lunch in Union Station, when I summoned the courage to ask them a question that could only be asked by the ordained minister-mom of an autistic child.

"Would you ever consider meeting with church representatives about this issue?"

To my amazement, the Geiers responded without the slightest hesitation. "We'll speak to anyone, anytime, Lisa. Just say the word."

With time, I would. I would bring them before the social justice agencies and leaders of my denomination. But for now, their willingness was enough. The day was passing, and we needed to leave Union Station and hail taxis to transport us and our boxes of petitions to the Senate Offices on Capitol Hill.

After walking too many corridors to count, we ended the day with a celebration at the Geier's favorite Italian restaurant. As wine was served around the table, we shared the quiet despair of knowing a calamity is happening and being unable to stop it. Today, however, a milestone in the journey had been reached, a line in the sand, drawn. The days of injecting children with poison with impunity were now numbered, and we had only to wait and wonder how quickly the FDA would respond.

"Even just one more day is too long to wait," I thought to myself, recalling how it had become my habit each night to wonder how many children we had lost each day to mercury-induced disability. Naively, I expected the legal wranglings with the FDA would take months, not years. Perhaps, I hoped, when winter next gave way to spring, perhaps then calamity would give way to safety, for all the kids. There was nothing for which I prayed more, except perhaps, Wesley.

Leslie had to fly out early the next morning in order to be home when her daughters began school. After dropping her at the airport as dawn arrived, we once again set out for Washington, D.C. This day, the team would be smaller. Mark and Cliff had to tend to the demands their medical and legal practices, respectively. David, however, was off from college classes and available to meet Paul, Kelli Ann, Bobbie and me at Union Station, as we arrived once again in Paul's vintage Cadillac.

We were eager to deliver copies of the petition to those we considered our strongest political allies serving in the House, Congressmen Dave Weldon and Dan Burton. Yet, because we were being prohibited from bringing our boxes of petitions inside the congressional offices, one of us would have to remain outside with the documents, while the rest of us ventured inside, each carrying the one allocated copy we were allowed to claim as our own.

While we moved through the congressional hallways, tracing paths three times the length that would have been necessary had we been allowed to enter with our documents, Paul sat outside watching over the petitions.

Whenever we needed to replenish our supply, we had only to walk out the door and greet Paul. Surreptitiously, we exited the building, acting as though the guards did not know what we were doing. They reciprocated, acting as though they noticed nothing. It was an odd charade, but well worth it. Though this comic constraint delayed us immeasurably, and caused our feet to ache with countless additional steps, we finally satisfied ourselves that we had paid homage to each of our congressional allies.

"Come on, we need to go now. We're going to be late for the DNC!" Bobbie was intent on arriving promptly for a meeting with Ms. Becky Ogle, the representative for disabilities in the Democratic National Committee.

The taxi we took to the Democratic National Headquarters dropped us off at an entrance made difficult by stairs. Transporting our many boxes into the building proved comical, as we hurried and hoped the rain would not fall. Inside, David, Bobbie, Kelli Ann, Paul and I registered our presence and were sent upstairs to a floor undergoing renovations. When Becky arrived, she was straight-spoken, self-assured, and had a commanding presence; her wheel chair was one attribute among many, and all of them, taken together, seemed only to contribute to her obvious strength.

"The bipolar people were here last week asking for money. You all haven't come asking for money, have you? The pie is only so big..."

We looked at each other. She knew we were autism advocates, but she had no comprehension for what we were advocating. We spoke for a time of autism in general and she continued to assume that we were seeking funding. Finally, I broke into the conversation with a careful bluntness. "Ms. Ogle, we aren't here for money. We are here to stop autism from happening.

We are here to stop mercury from being injected into babies. This isn't just about autism—it's about autism, ADD, ADHD, bipolar, learning disabilities…. We have to stop making people sick."

Becky looked aghast. I pulled out *Mothering Magazine*, and passed it down to her. "These are the charges we have made against HHS, CDC, FDA, and the IOM. You'll see that the U.S. Special Counsel Scott Bloch has found substance in what we say, by his press release on the subject."

Paul quickly began to explain the lack of proof of safety associated with Thimerosal, and David began to describe how the autistic child, who at a young age is perhaps compliant and cute, may become an adult capable of putting his hand through a wall in a rage. The math was frightening when one considered the frequency of autism: "What is our society going to do when all these children grow up? If this doesn't stop, where are we going to place them throughout their lifetime?"

I handed Becky a copy of Wesley's chelation lab results, with the line beside mercury running off the chart.

"Our children have been poisoned with mandated vaccines," I said.

"And Senator Edwards knows how serious this whole issue is," Kelli Ann added. Becky Ogle drew a deep breath and then looked at each one of us around the table.

"I don't understand why you're here," she stopped, her hand to her temple. We looked at each other blankly. Had she not understood what we said? Did she not realize we were here because we desperately needed her help?

"I don't understand why you're here," Becky began again, but this time she continued, with a gutsy impatience in her voice. "Why aren't you out burning down federal buildings and stopping traffic and marching on the Capitol? I don't understand!"

At last, the immensity of this issue became clear to Becky, and now, we knew it.

"Don't think it hasn't crossed our minds," Bobbie answered, her voice strained. "But Ms. Ogle, if we get locked up for civil disobedience, who will take care of our children?"

As we left, Becky promised us one thing. "I'm going to put this on the table before the top strategists in the Kerry Campaign."

With profuse thanks, we left the DNC, thinking that this meeting had brought us full circle. We had begun with an aide in Jonathan Edward's

Office and now finished with a member of Kerry's presidential campaign. We did not seek to support Republican nor Democratic in our political leanings —we sought only to support the children, and them alone. Whoever would defend our wounded children, they would have our vote and our allegiance.

That evening, David returned to suburban Maryland, Paul and Bobbie set off for their home states, and Kelli Ann and I drove to Chantilly, Virginia to meet Dan and Andrea for dinner. Having successfully navigated to the restaurant, we were just parking the car when Kelli Ann's cell phone went off.

"Hello, this is Kelli Ann..."

"Kelli? This is Brian. Hey, I've got some big news here."

Kelli Ann turned to me. "Lisa, it's Brian—he's calling from Washington state..." Then, she resumed the conversation.

"So, yeah, Brian, what is it? ...WHAT? And it says that? You can't...? What don't they want us to see?"

As I listened to Kelli Ann's voice grow louder and higher, I quickly discerned that Brian must have discovered something very significant.

Kelli now was almost shouting: "Three million dollars? THREE MILLION DOLLARS? What the heck for?"

The conversation lasted only minutes, but it seemed like hours, as I heard only half of it, and tried impatiently to fill in the blanks. Kelli Ann became more and more animated and her voice reached a high pitch and remained there. At last, she hung up.

"What, Kelli? What is it?"

"It's the parameters document, Lisa! You know the one you told Brian to FOIA?"

"Yeah! So what did he find out?" My pulse had quickened, just like Kelli Ann's speech.

"The CDC paid the IOM three million dollars, Lisa! Three million dollars to hold the Vaccine Safety Review hearings. What could cost three million dollars? And if the CDC gave the IOM three million dollars, the IOM can hardly declare itself to be independent and unbiased, eh girl?" [6]

AUGUST 2004

Two weeks had passed. Back home in Richmond, Seth and I went out to dinner one Saturday evening. We had just returned to our home and were unlocking the door when the phone began to ring and would not cease. My first thought was that one of my congregation members must have become ill. Then again, I wondered if perhaps it was David with news about lab results on Wesley.

It was neither.

I answered the phone which had continued to sound, so demandingly.

"Lis?"

"Oh, hi Mom!" I said in greeting, surprised by her urgency. When I was out, Mom would generally just leave me a message.

Curious as to what occasioned her intensity, I asked, "Have you been trying to call me for long?"

"Yes, Lis! Don't you know?"

"Know what, Mom?"

"You and your friends were on the CBS Evening News with Dan Rather tonight... Sharyl Attkisson just did the report... about you and your group filing the petition..."

CHAPTER FOURTEEN

TESTOSTERONE

"Today, if you have the courage to reach out to the child poisoned in the womb, across the barrier of a twisted body, across the barrier of slurred or nonexistent speech, you find yourself groping towards the being that does live, somehow, behind the barrier. Envision as you may, though, you can not project the child normal and whole, you can not project the child that might have been, the child not struck by poison. The child itself, can that child ever have recollections of a beginning? That child is an island, rising out of unfathomable depths. We have no way to comprehend."

—W. Eugene Smith and Aileen M. Smith
Minamata, 1956

I DID NOT KNOW, AS WE WERE FILING THE PETITION AND WALKING THE HALLS OF Congress in the summer of 2004, that Mark and David Geier had been captivated recently by a brilliant discovery made by Dr. Boyd Haley, a professor of chemistry and a gentleman farmer from Kentucky who had presented to the Institute of Medicine. Boyd had studied a simple fact: for every one girl diagnosed with autism, there were four boys who suffered with it.[1] What was the clearest difference between boys and girls?

The answer was painfully obvious: the hormones. As a chemist, Boyd knew that testosterone and estrogen had vastly different effects on cells, especially cells in newborns. Based upon this observation, Boyd theorized that hormones might impact the effect of mercury upon living cells. What if,

Boyd wondered, testosterone amplified the toxicity of mercury? For the first time, someone had proposed a logical scientific reason for the fact that autism strikes four boys to every one girl.

Boyd's experiment was as simple as his observation. He took cultured neuron cells in a Petri dish and added mercury, documenting and quantifying the effect. Then, he took an identical Petri dish of cultured cells and added mercury in the presence of testosterone. The result? In the dish with testosterone, there was more death: the mercury killed cells much more quickly and more completely. Boyd had contributed a brilliant and foundational discovery about the association of mercury and autism which, in time, would open a door behind which hope waited for my son and many others.

October 2004

My next trip to Washington, D.C., was October 5, 2004. I juggled my pastoral schedule and placed another minister on call for my congregation so I could attend a U.S. House of Representatives committee meeting convened by Congressman Dave Weldon, the dogged Republican of the state of Florida and a board-certified physician who, along with Congressman Burton of Indiana, gave rare voice to the cause of safe, mercury-free vaccines on Capitol Hill. In this case, his purview as a member of the House Committee on Appropriations extended to oversight of the Department of Health and Human Services. At issue was the shocking addition of the mercury-containing flu shot to the CDC mandated schedule for infants and young children.

From the back of the packed gallery, I watched Weldon's fingers sweep forcefully across his lips, as if trying to contain the words that were forming upon them. With his sculpted cheekbones and broad brow, he seemed both dignified and determined.

In a congressional committee room of the Rayburn Building, at the invitation of Weldon, were those elected congressional politicians charged with overseeing the Department of Health and Human Services and its subordinate agencies. Below their gallery seats at a conference table, sat Dr. Julie Gerberding, Director of the US Centers for Disease Control and Prevention (CDC) and Dr. William Egan, then Acting Office Director, Office of Vaccine Research and Review in the Center for Biologics Evaluation and Review (CBER), part of the FDA, and Dr. Anthony Fauci, Director of the National

Institute of Allergy and Infectious Diseases, National Institutes of Health (NIH).

Weldon moved swiftly to describe his concern as the proceeding began: "I was very disappointed when I discovered in the late 1990's that essentially nobody had done the calculations on the amount of Thimerosal that we were giving infants... And certainly, I was very pleased when then the agency responded by announcing they were going to strip all of the mercury out, go to Thimerosal-free... Why (did you) not work to accelerate the production with FDA of Thimerosal-free before a recommendation was made? It's being phased out, but now we're talking about vaccinating kids again with a Thimerosal-containing product."[2]

Dr. Fauci conceded the congressman's point: "Yes... we all agree, Thimerosal in vaccines needs to go. What we have to do is bridge that gap, as it were, between converting to Thimerosal-free vaccines at a time when we may not have all of the influenza vaccine in a Thimerosal-free form to give to children and the balance of the risk of the influenza versus the risk of the Thimerosal."

I noticed how the exasperation of Congresswoman Nita Lowey, a member of the committee, returned Weldon from his somber and silent ruminations as Dr. Fauci was speaking. In front of a packed assembly, Congresswoman Lowey berated the panel: "I'm really puzzled as, frankly, a grandmother of seven, many of them will be getting vaccinations. All of them will be getting vaccinations. And, Dr. Fauci, you said the weight of evidence, no deleterious effects of Thimerosal. What you said definitively was we're moving towards Thimerosal-free vaccines. And then you said because of public concerns, we are moving towards Thimerosal-free vaccines..."

Dr. Fauci was noticeably uncomfortable and shifted in his seat before offering a one-word response meant to calm: "Right." It did not.

Lowey began again: "I don't, frankly, get this."

Fauci listened as the anger in Lowey's remarks registered in the pitch of her voice: Again, he offered simply, "OK."

Lowey continued as if he had not even spoken: "Because let me just follow-up, if I may."

Trying to be as invitational as he could to the congresswoman, Dr. Fauci again replied: "Sure."

And it was then that Lowey finally found the words to communicate her frustrations: "It seems to me that the NIH, the CDC, and the FDA usually don't take action based upon public concern... I would expect that the FDA and the CDC and certainly your institute take actions and make recommendations based upon scientific evidence."

"Right, right."

Impassioned as a mother and a grandmother and empowered as a congresswoman, Lowey voiced her unbridled disgust with the new influenza recommendation: "So what I don't understand... if, in fact, there's enough scientific evidence to make a clear hypothesis that we should get rid of Thimerosal, then why, why can't we figure out how to increase the production (of thimerosal-free flu vaccine?)

"This reminds me of my conversation the other day, I must tell you, with the Department of Defense. We need 6,000 bullet-proof vests for the men and women that we're sending over to Iraq. We currently have 4,000. And how we, frankly, can send young men and women into a war zone without that equipment on is beyond me. It seems to me we should be able to figure it out.

"And if there's enough evidence to make a clear determination that we should be ridding vaccines of Thimerosal, I wouldn't want any of my grandchildren to take anything. I'm going to make sure they call the doctor and say, 'I want a vaccine without Thimerosal.' And if it's good enough for my kids, it should be good enough for every kid in America. So I don't get it."

I wanted to stand up and applaud. Instead I remained outwardly silent, and inwardly euphoric, thinking that no exchange in this room would be more illuminating than this one. I was wrong. Once again, Congressman Weldon took the lead, this time focusing his astute intellect on an area of expertise that belonged to Dr. Egan, according to his FDA position:

"Dr. Egan, I just want to make sure I understand the history of the safety studies on Thimerosal. I understand they were done in the 1930s. They gave Thimerosal to... people dying of meningitis. They subsequently died with no apparent measurable effect of the Thimerosal. And based on that study, the product was deemed safe and that we really have never had good safety studies done of the preservative, Thimerosal, since that time. Is this true?"

Egan looked ashen.

"Well, I think there actually is a fair bit of data that bears on the safety of the material and doses, you know, the amounts of mercury that can be taken in without observable adverse effect. Yes, those studies that you mentioned, they were done. And they saw no acute short-term effects. I mean, you know, we can't do those kinds of experiments where we just take healthy people and give them Thimerosal until something happens, until they die or whatever and just keep escalating that dose and then say, well, below that, that's safe."

"Do you not realize," I seethed silently, "that the experiment you're describing has already been conducted, and it's called the National Immunization Program?"

Driving home to Richmond that night I tried to find words to express what I had heard. From what illness, I asked angrily, do these officials suffer that they would not only maintain but even increase the mercury that babies are getting through their shots? A troubling and grotesque answer came in the form of a rare psychiatric disorder I had just read about. A parent, usually a mother, secretly induces symptoms of disease in a child so that she can publicly lament over them and receive attention and sympathy. "Munchausen Syndrome by Proxy" became the collective diagnosis I now gave to national health officials intent on administering more and more mercury to the nation's children with no informed consent, all the while issuing alarms about the catastrophic rates that now characterized the autism epidemic.

Neither my anger nor my reasoning was of any help in the face of this institutionalized form of insanity. The flu shot was added to the standard immunization schedule for children, with recommendations for two shots in the first year of an infant's life, each carrying 12.5 micrograms. An average-size baby would get more than twenty-five times the amount of mercury considered safe in these newly required shots. Soon, the flu shots would also be recommended for pregnant women by the American College of Obstetrics and Gynecologists.

Throughout the autumn, the Geiers, impressed by Dr. Haley's work, had continued to study it carefully. Why would testosterone amplify the toxicity of mercury? Boyd had been the first to observe this phenomenon, but he had not explained it. This cipher caused Mark, who recently devoted himself to epidemiology, to return to his first love: biochemistry. A visual thinker, Mark studied what others observed and then sometimes deduced what no one else could see. Perhaps Mark's greatest genius is his ability to decipher biochemical pathways, the succession of chemical steps transforming one substance to another within the body's functioning.

Mark discovered this intuitive ability as he moved through his graduate and doctoral degrees. As early as the 1970's, while a research scientist at the National Institutes of Health, Mark had employed his ability in the field of genetic engineering with spectacular result. He discovered a new biochemical pathway by which milk sugar was broken down in the human body. This accomplishment, along with numerous others, resulted in many accolades, including a congratulatory call from then President Richard M. Nixon.[12]

It was this sightedness Mark now brought to the enigma of mercury and testosterone. How did they interact? Why did the testosterone so increase the toxicity of the mercury?

Diagramming one of the body's pathways, called the androgen pathway, which produces testosterone, Mark began to consider what would happen if mercury were present. "There," he thought, "there!" In the pathway leading to testosterone, Mark recognized that mercury would block a critical step in the pathway that regulates testosterone levels. If this happened, the resulting effect would be like a dam collapsing. Mark realized the unregulated flow of androgens down this pathway would result in elevated levels of testosterone.

Turning to the medical literature, Mark began to search for documented effects of high testosterone.[13] His search yielded notable results. Published articles revealed that high testosterone interferes with the body's ability to excrete mercury by significantly lowering glutathione levels. Quickly, Mark realized that a vicious cycle would be established by introducing mercury into the androgen pathway. Mercury, he reasoned, increases testosterone, and in turn, testosterone makes mercury more toxic by lowering the body's defenses against it.

The more Mark ruminated on his hypothesis, the more autism made sense in terms of its causes. Along with reinforcing Boyd's explanation of the five to one ratio of boys to girls affected with autism, Mark's breakthrough also explained why children with autism often came from families with documented high testosterone levels. Beyond speculating about testosterone's role in the origin of autism, Mark also scrutinized whether high testosterone could be associated with the symptoms of Autism Spectrum Disorders. Here, additional insight came from an unlikely and unexpected source. Professor Simon Baron Cohen, from the Autism Research Center at the University of Cambridge, UK, had for years published that high testosterone could induce the signs and symptoms of autism and that the more severe these autistic characteristics were, the higher the testosterone levels.

Mark began to consider: "If more testosterone increases the severity of autism, then would lowering testosterone decrease the severity?" [14]

Surveying in his mind current biomedical treatments used to treat autism, Mark realized that most shared a common but unrecognized side effect— they lowered testosterone. Ceasing from his ruminations now, Mark grabbed his Physician's Desk Reference, the standard catalog of drugs used by doctors. He located the pages listing drugs to treat high testosterone, and ran his finger down the page until he came to LUPRON® (Leuprolide Acetate), the one which was safest and most effective for treating high testosterone in children. [15]

"That's it," Mark said to himself. "David!" he called from his lab downstairs.

Together, father and son began to search the medical literature for further indications that Mark might be correct. Indeed, the literature indicated he was. By early November 2004, Mark and David had written an article, "*The Potential Importance of Steroids in the Treatment of Autistic Spectrum Disorders and Other Disorders Involving Mercury Toxicity*," which was accepted for publication in *Medical Hypotheses*. In their article, the Geiers described, "…that autistic disorders, in fact, represent a form of testosterone-mercury toxicity, and based upon this observation, one can design novel treatments for autistics directed towards higher testosterone levels in autistic children." [16]

David and I were on the phone late this November night, discussing the petition and the ongoing search for a federal whistleblower as well as the latest articles on Thimerosal. This particular evening, however, while David and I spoke, Mark joined our conversation.

"Lisa, we've been looking at Boyd's work. We've been building on it," announced Mark.

"That's great, Mark," I responded, unsure as to what he was referring.

"Oh, and by the way, we think we've found something significant..." David announced with casualness.

"Significant?" I cautiously asked.

"Yes," Mark answered. "You see, we've just started researching this, Lisa, but it appears that mercury raises testosterone levels. This may be why four boys to every one girl suffer autism. But what is really interesting is this: we conjecture that testosterone lowers the body's ability to defend itself from mercury, while mercury sends the body's production of testosterone into overdrive, so you get a vicious cycle."

"Testosterone? Mark, I've never heard anyone speak of mercury affecting hormone levels in autism before."

"I don't think we have understood it before, Lisa. Dr. Haley's work has opened a whole new area of study, and it is very promising."

"Of course!" I thought to myself. Why had no one ever thought of this before? Testosterone, high levels of it, might predispose a child, especially a boy, to autism.

"What about the one girl who gets autism, relative to the four boys?" I asked.

"Girls have testosterone, too, Lisa." David answered. "Of the girls, it's probably the ones with high testosterone who are affected with autism."

"Fascinating..." I mumbled, as I grabbed for a pen and paper to record the Geiers' discovery that, one day I hoped, would earn them a Nobel Prize in Medicine. Mark continued to explain his discovery, taking time to make sure I understood each part of the theory.

"Now," David added, "If you examine the biochemical pathways, you will see that in the one leading to testosterone there is a crucial step which we know is inhibited by mercury. If a mercury-sensitive child gets massive exposure to this toxin, then this step, which acts almost like a braking mechanism in the production of testosterone, doesn't work. The throttle on this pathway gets stuck in the 'on' position, and the result is too much—too much testosterone. The testosterone reduces the body's ability to excrete mercury, and the mercury produces even more testosterone." [17]

"With all that you have figured out, what is the first step to see if the testosterone is a problem?" I asked eagerly.

"Well, we need to check the serum testosterone level in the blood of a mercury-toxic child. We hypothesize that it's going to be high..."

"And if it is...?"

"Then, we try dropping the testosterone in order to break the cycle. There's a very safe drug on the market that can lower testosterone." Mark offered.

"David, Mark," I said excitedly, "I've got a bold question for you..." I began, unable not to venture my wildest hope. "Forgive me for asking this, but if Wesley fits this profile you're speaking of with the high testosterone, would you treat my son based on your new discovery?"

"Well, Lisa, if Wesley has high testosterone, would you allow us to treat him?"

I wonder if they know, I asked myself, that I'd give my life for a medically sound, medically safe way to help my son?

Hope welled up in my soul as I considered the Geiers' breakthrough and tried to comprehend that my son might be the first to receive it. I had entrusted Wesley to so few and with such care. I had declined the treatment fads that were commonplace in the autism chat rooms. I had been careful, conservative, and conscientious in every treatment option I had pursued for Wesley. My esteem for the Geiers was as great as my esteem for Mary. I would have trusted them with my life, and I would be even bolder now, and entrust Wesley to them.

"Yes, David. In a heartbeat. Of course I would!" In my mind, these scientists had been first acquaintances and then heroes as I learned more of their work: and then allies as they helped with the OSC Project: and then friends as we collaborated with Dr. King on the petition: and now, now they became like family as they offered hope and help to my son.

"Well, Lisa, go and ask Mary to run a serum testosterone level on Wesley. Tell her we are wondering if he has a diagnosis of precocious puberty, simply put, that's early adolescence."

Since we had begun the Methyl B-12 shots, Wesley had become brighter and bubblier. But his energetic disposition since a toddler, of always being on the go, now clearly was hyperactivity. I described my sweet little boy, at times, as a "human super ball" who bounced, light-footedly, across the floors in our home from the time he woke until the time we gave him his medicine at bedtime so he could sleep.

And while the light of his soul shone in his eyes from morning to evening, I still could not hear his voice. Mary referred to Wesley, regarding his inability to speak, as a "kid who won't budge." While she was preoccupied with his unnatural silence, I had become worried about something else. Something I mentioned to no one outside our immediate family. Wesley had begun to masturbate. On those rare occasions when he was still, this was the reason. And even more disconcerting, my eight year-old son had begun to have erections whenever he was in the shower. Was it embarrassment or denial that had caused me to fall silent like my son, at least in regard to describing this part of his condition?

When I entered Mary's office, her questions were all new. She had already consulted with the Geiers by phone. This visit to her office reminded me of that first one, just after Wesley's diagnosis, when she seemed to read my mind and know all my answers to her questions before I opened my mouth in reply.

"Lisa does Wesley have hair on his body yet?"

"Yeah. His legs have peach fuzz, Mary."

"Has he grown rapidly recently?"

"Well, yes. He began shooting up at about seven. It's been a year, and he's almost as tall as Adam who is two years older than he is."

"It's too soon for that kind of growth spurt, Lisa. Does Wesley masturbate?"

"Yes. Lots. I just thought that was part of autism..." Silently, I scolded myself, for having written off symptoms as "autism," without having analyzed them first. In my obliviousness, I was guilty of following the example of mainstream medicine.

"Anything else in way of sexual behavior?"

"He gets erections in the shower, Mary. I never knew why."

"Here's the prescription for the blood, Lisa. I want it run right away."

"Okay, Mary. You know, the Geiers are starting to sound like you! With this new theory about the testosterone, they are beginning to believe that the autism is not so much brain damage as a block in the brain's pathways. They think if we get the testosterone down, and get more mercury out, we may see Wesley coming back."

Mary smiled. "Lisa, I keep telling you. He's all in there!"

God sent me these people to pour hope into my soul until it overflowed. This was mercy, pure and plentiful.

"All message play back," announced the mechanical voice on my answering machine. Two days had passed. The machine beeped.

"Lisa, this is Mary. I've got Wesley's testosterone result back, and it's goo... interesting! Call me."

I could not dial her number fast enough.

"Mary, what's the news?"

"Lisa, the testosterone is absolutely at the top of the range. Call the Geiers. I'm diagnosing Wesley with precocious puberty."

I had already learned how to give a shot to my son. But now, with the small kit of Leuprolide Acetate on the kitchen counter before me, I had to draw the shot also. The pharmacist had given me a quick two-minute lesson in this when I picked up the prescription.

Seth and I looked at one another, unsure what to expect. This first attempt would be a very small test dose, to assure Mary, Mark and David that Wesley would have no allergic reaction to the medicine.

Wesley, very compliantly, lay down, unaware that anything was unusual since he so often received Methyl B-12 injections. I rubbed a patch of skin on his buttock with an alcohol swab and then held the short silvery needle above it. "One, two, three, stick..." By watching, I had learned from Mary how to give an injection, counting aloud so Wesley would not be surprised. There. It was done. Seth and I trained our eyes on Wesley, looking for we-did-not-know-what.

Within minutes, however, we would see what we did not yet know to expect. Wesley, who had gone back to his light-footed bouncing across the den floor, suddenly stopped. His feet made contact with the floor and did not immediately rise again to take another step. In fact, for the first time in memory, my fleet-footed son, who had been in motion from morning to night since he was three, now stopped and sat down on the sofa, completely relaxed. Like his feet, Wesley's eyes also ceased from wandering, jerkily, their gaze incessantly jumping about the room. For the first precious moments in years, we saw our son truly rest and be still.

The television was on and Wesley trained his eyes on the screen, tracking the animated characters with rare clarity. His eyes moved steadily and smoothly as he watched, in great contrast to their previous halting motions. Now, miraculously, my son was still, clearly focused on the visual information before him and his soul seemed so too, as he sat serenely on the sofa, his hands quiet.

It was not until that instant that I realized how much of a burden my son's hyperactivity had been. Almost without noticing, I had become accustomed to tracking Wesley's every movement, never concentrating on merely one thing, but at the very least two: whatever I was doing and my son's perpetual path. Now, just as Wesley had ceased from crisscrossing the room, so I ceased from my constant vigilance for a moment, to breathe in deeply, and welcome the gentle stillness that enveloped my child and myself.

When the television program finished, Wesley wanted out. It was a brilliant blue day with a light wind and a crisp chill in the air. I helped him on with his jacket and sent him into the back yard so I could watch him from the bay window in the kitchen. He had been outside only a few moments when I called Seth. "Honey, have you ever seen him do that before?" I asked eagerly.

"No, never."

Paradoxically, while our son had been a child in constant motion for years, the purposeful use of his limbs had often evaded him. He would sit on the tire swing in our back yard, forlorn, until someone came to push him. It was as if he never realized that the feet which lilted across the floor could also be used to push the swing upon which he sat.

Now, as we looked out the window, we were astonished to see Wesley on the tire swing, laughing and smiling, as it crested first to one side and then the other. His feet traced a path across the dirt only long enough to propel him higher with each revolution of the swing.

"Seth, do you think it's strong enough to hold? Look at how high he's going!"

"Don't worry, Lisa. It'll hold."

I prayed that these changes we saw in Wesley would, too.

CHAPTER FIFTEEN

MORE POWERFUL THAN YOU KNOW

"The world is dangerous not because of those who do harm,
but because of those who look at it without doing anything."

—Albert Einstein

THE CLOCK LOOKED AT ME INTIMIDATINGLY. IT WAS JUST ONE OF THOSE MORNINGS. Getting the first two boys ready for school and out the door had already proved a challenge. Now that Joshua and Adam were off, I had but one task left: to prepare Wesley for departure on a big yellow school bus, one that bore a square, sky blue and white disability symbol on the front. I had already packed Wesley's gluten-free, casein-free lunch, stowed his folder neatly inside his backpack, and zipped up the back of the special harness which he wore on the bus. Then, I looked at his feet, donning socks but sporting no shoes.

"Now, where are they?" I asked myself, sighing loudly.

With the bus due any second, I bounded up the stairs by two's and three's, hopeful to find the wayward sneakers before the driver rejected my sweet sock-footed boy. I raced through Wesley's bedroom, looked under his bed and mine, and then descended the stairs again, only to fly through the coat closet for the umpteenth time.

"They're not in here!" I declared to myself for the last time.

There was nothing to do; it was time to surrender and admit defeat.

I looked at Wesley, who had been watching me and following the frantic path I traced about the downstairs. I found myself again confessing to the gorgeous blue gaze of those inquisitive eyes.

"Wesley," I stated in exasperation, "I've looked everywhere. I can't find your shoes, and without your shoes, there's no way you can go to school."

Oddly, I hadn't even asked Wesley a question, nor queried him for any answer regarding his missing shoes. While his hearing was normal, his processing of sound was not. I might as well have been speaking a foreign language for the past five years, because what I said, especially in sentences, never seemed to register in Wesley's comprehension. That is why this moment left me motionless, despite the distinctive squeaking sound of the bus' brakes heralding its impatient arrival at my front drive.

Momentarily, Wesley focused on me, and then, nonchalantly, got up from his perch on the sofa and walked intentionally past me and into the bathroom.

I thought nothing of it, until he emerged only a second later with his shoes in his hand and a lovely grin on his lips.

"Wesley! You understood me!"

I threw my arms around him in a hug which he resigned himself to accept.

Then, I stooped to the floor, able at last to outfit my son completely for school.

Though it was Wesley's sneaker into which I now placed his foot, at that moment, I felt like Cinderella, having just discovered the identity of the most charming prince I had ever met.

MARCH 2004

While Kelly Kerns had initiated the Attorney General effort, and I had begun the Office of Special Counsel Project, it was Lujene Clark and Dana Halvorson who, in the face of federal inaction, first dared to imagine state legislation to ban mercury from medicine. In Dana's home state of Iowa, they would resolve to protect the children within the boundaries of the plains state, even if the United States Congress would not protect the children nationwide.

As with the Attorney General effort and with the Office of Special Counsel Project, grateful parents enlisted the help of Mark and David Geier with this first effort to secure a state ban on administering mercury-containing vaccines to children under the age of eight.

Mark arrived in Iowa on March 23, 2004, in the crisp cool of spring to be greeted by both Dana and good news.

"Mark, we just won the vote in the senate to ban mercury: thirty to nineteen."

"Oh, is that right?" said Mark, more in jubilation than curiosity.

"Yes, we hope to better it as the bill progresses to the house. For that reason, we are going to be 'calling out' our representatives when we get there and speak with them about the mercury."

At first Mark thought he had misheard Dana, so when she again referenced "calling out" the representatives, he asked her to clarify what she meant.

Dana explained to Mark that in Iowa a constituent could summon their representative from the floor of the house or senate at any time unless a vote was ongoing. A caucus of constituents, all of whom were also parents of autistic children, had arrived from across the state to assure that Dana would be able to "call out" a significant number of representatives to meet with Mark.

As representatives were "called out" by their individual constituents, they were shown to a room where Mark was projecting on the wall the latest scientific studies demonstrating the toxicity of Thimerosal. Following the summons of these Iowa parents, representatives arrived in groups of three and four to hear Dr. Mark Geier. The legislators, many of them farmers by avocation, were impressed that Iowa parents had flown Mark from Maryland to Iowa just to speak to them about this bill.

At regular intervals, as the bell in the House would sound, delegates resumed their voting positions on the House floor. But afterward, they returned, time and time again, to hear more of a morbidly fascinating tale of industrial deceit and unrecognized poisoning.

In addition to enlightening the Iowa representatives on the danger Thimerosal represented to children, Mark was also careful to proclaim to them the historic nature of this proposed legislation. "If Iowa passes this law to ban Thimerosal, it will be the first state in the nation to act so as to protect its children from unwarranted and reckless mercury poisoning." The representatives were enthralled with both Mark's presentation and with the thought that Iowa might take pride of place in setting legislative precedent and in protecting its children from unnecessary harm.

As the workday wore on for the legislators, Mark turned to Dana. "I'm just seeing representatives. I'd like to speak with the Iowa senators as well— the ones who voted against the bill. They need to understand what a cut-and-dry issue this is. We might as well try to build greater support in the Senate, too." Dana quickly agreed and the parents now trekked from one side of the state house to the other to summon senators as well as representatives.

A senior senator entered the room bristling at the interruption of having been called out and impatient to get back to the floor. The senator declared to Mark, "I didn't understand this bill about the mercury. I always vote against a bill if I don't understand it."

"Well, senator, I think I can make this very understandable. Let me explain..." Mark began his presentation for the fiftieth time.

As Mark made the logic and the urgency of the Iowa bill to ban mercury plain, the senator began to yield, listening carefully to each word the doctor from Maryland had to say.

In the moments that would follow, the Iowa house passed the bill by a narrow majority, and the enlightened senator along with others from the Iowa Senate would demand a second opportunity to vote affirmatively on the bill. When the new vote was taken in the senate, the bill passed by acclamation. These legislators, along with Lujene, Dana and Mark made history: they passed the first bill on earth outlawing the practice of giving young children mercury in their medicines.

First Iowa, then California passed bans on giving children and pregnant women mercury-containing vaccines in October 2004. These bills did not have to address the mercury-containing Rho(D) shots, which I received when I was pregnant with Wesley, because only a few months after Wesley's exposure in utero, manufacturers removed the mercury from these products, quietly and without any public announcement. It was the flu shot which now delivered mercury exposure in utero to pregnant women, depriving them of informed consent. Industry and government declared the flu shot effective in preventing the flu, a dubious claim, and the mercury "preservative" in the flu shot, safe—a claim which I already held to be fraudulent.[1]

While I impatiently waited for the FDA to respond to our CoMeD

Citizen Petition, I reasoned, I had no other projects demanding my attention, so why not Virginia? Why not lead an effort in the state of Virginia to do what Lujene and Dana had done in Iowa and what Bobbie Manning, following their example, had done in California? If two states in the Union could ban mercury, why not more? Why not Virginia? I had no idea that this pursuit, which would prove futile and frustrating, would ultimately redirect my efforts and refocus my call to ministry.

Even though Wesley had no words, he could communicate. His gestures, his expressions, his eyes. Wesley was always telling me something. I had only to see it.

The chief aide of my state senator, Walter Stosch, by contrast, spoke with ease. And though he had the gift of speech and great sophistication in his demeanor, I found that he really said nothing. The chief aide responded to my initial call with an invitation to meet and discuss my concerns about Thimerosal.

To that initial meeting, I brought with me the OSC Press Release, the Manufacturer Safety Data Sheet on Thimerosal, the CoMeD Citizen Petition, and countless other documents. The aide seemed to listen intently to everything I had to say, and I was hopeful of gaining the support of my senator through him. This hope intensified when he shared with me the news that he and his wife were expecting a baby boy.

"Then," I replied, "I'm not only here in hopes of protecting all the children in Virginia from unnecessary mercury exposure, but also in hopes that you and your wife will be able to protect your son."

He smiled and nodded, looking through the stack of documents that now weighed upon him as a legislative assistant and as a father-to-be.

Every day, in my email, there were queries from the aide. Most were scientific questions. In order to answer them I would email Mark and David and would receive back a published paper or article or the appropriate scientific reference to answer yet another of the legislative aide's questions.

The energy and time that I spent educating my senator's aide about the danger of Thimerosal were enormous.

After several weeks, I asked to meet with him once again, face to face.

"The legislative session is about to start. Are you going to submit a bill?"

"Well, Reverend Sykes, we are. Now it may not be as encompassing as you want, but we are going to try to submit something in a way we feel it will get through."

"I understand that manufacturing interests are really strong in our state, so if you need to take it step by step, I can live with that. Just so long as we are making progress."

"I assure you, Reverend, that is our intention."

"Good. What is the bill number?"

"I'm afraid I can't tell you that."

"Excuse me... what do you mean 'I can't tell you'?"

"Reverend, we don't want this proposed legislation to attract attention. We've actually put it in a larger piece of legislation, hoping to shield it from too much scrutiny...."

"Okay. So what is the number on the overarching bill, which contains the specific provisions about mercury?"

"I can't tell you that."

"What?!"

"The senator and I believe we need to keep this absolutely confidential. We will track it and speak for it, but we want no one drawing attention to it."

"This legislation is something I want. Surely you don't think I would do anything to hinder it. I just want to see what you've drafted and submitted for consideration by the General Assembly this session."

"I cannot give you that information."

"Well, can I at least see the wording?"

"No, I'm afraid, Reverend, that that would be giving too much away."

I sat for a moment, just staring at this man, exasperated beyond words.

Days passed, and I received a new email from the chief aide.

"The senator would like to know how much mercury there is in circulation in the United States at the present time due to pharmaceuticals containing the preservative Thimerosal."

I clenched my teeth as I read the words. "What is he playing at? What has that to do with anything? Who knows!"

I forwarded the aide's email to a number of "mercury mommas" who advocated, just as I did, and who were also involved in attempts to pass state bills banning mercury.

Lujene, who with her husband Dr. Alan Clark would get a bill passed in Missouri in 2005, fired back the most insightful email:

"Lisa, this is a snipe hunt, and I suggest you not go on it."

The session of the General Assembly in which I had placed my hopes for challenging 'medicinal' mercury in Virginia concluded. I was home on the day I received the aide's call. It was a day in which I thought I had began to recognize a hint of spring in the intensity of the sun's brilliance and the blue sky overhead.

"So, what is the news? What happened with the legislation?"

"I'm sorry, Reverend Sykes. We got nowhere. Nothing passed."

"Nothing? You promised me something. Not everything. Not a complete ban. But something."

All that effort. All for nothing. I reviewed the past months. How could I have educated this political office so well, and yet have nothing to show for it?

"I know, Reverend. There was just no way."

"What do you mean 'no way'? Why would there be 'no way'?"

"Because, Reverend Sykes, your enemies are more powerful than you know."

Standing perfectly still now, I placed my hand on the kitchen counter in front of me. I started to speak several times, but I could not seem to identify any word which to pronounce. There was silence from the other end of the phone.

What have I done, I asked myself, to have an elected official's aide speaking to me this way? It's absurd—positively absurd! I considered for a moment the likelihood that I had fallen into a Stephen King novel, or one by Tom Clancy.

"Enemies?" I finally blurted out. "How can I have enemies when I'm trying to protect children?"

The aide went on to make a response—something about manufacturing, but I was no longer listening to him.

Instead, I found a refrain echoing in my mind, again and again. I wasn't sure how it had formulated there, but the strength in it was undeniable and unforgettable: "...but I have an Ally, and that Ally is more powerful than you know."

As my senator's chief aide finished whatever he was saying, I heard one final declaration from him, perhaps the only concrete disclosure he ever gave me: "This issue has to be put in a box on the shelf, Reverend. It's not time to deal with it yet. When it's the right time, we'll take it off the shelf."

I started to feel undeniably queasy.

"Do you realize children are being disabled by the day? And you're telling me you want to put this issue in storage?"

"If you repeat this, I will deny everything I've said."

As I hung up the phone, I began to wrestle with all the thoughts storming through my brain: "I am a minister. I don't have enemies. The children. Government must protect the children. He knows. I've given him the science. But he won't act. Nothing. No bill. No help. I bet he protected his own son! But now wants to box the issue? Put it on a shelf? Is he mad?"

Suddenly my mind ceased to swirl. That deep and unshakeable refrain began again as if I were speaking it aloud in response to this legislative aide: "I have an Ally, and that Ally is more powerful than you know" and the thought continued now to completion: "and that Ally has an army, and it is called the Church."

History had not only been made in Iowa in 2004; it had also been made in Virginia, only not by the legislature. For me, that year, hopeful news came instead from the Church. At the gathering of the Southeastern Jurisdiction of the United Methodist Church in July, Bishop Charlene Kammerer became the first woman Bishop to be assigned to Virginia. Having served eight years as Bishop of the Charlotte area in North Carolina, she had established a reputation for being an activist and an advocate for children.

With admitted egocentricity, I thought to myself, "God is sending her to Virginia for me."

All that I knew of Bishop Kammerer I learned secondhand through press releases and reports from other clergy. In fourteen years of ministry I never once had reason to seek out a meeting with the Bishop of the Virginia Conference in which I served. My habit had always been to oversee my pastorate, to visit the people, to preach and administer the sacraments, and to minister to the broader community. I had never sought to become involved in the politics of my Conference or to move among its most powerful clergy. I was a small church pastor and very content in my call.

My advocacy, while in keeping with my calling, had always been separate from it, and I was careful to delineate my pastoral role in my congregation from my advocacy as a parent involved in the mercury issue. Only now—having documented my concerns to the highest echelons of national health officials, federal oversight officials, and finally legislators in state government—did I bring my paper trail of federal and state correspondence and my concern for my mercury-injured child before the church.

"Virginia United Methodist Conference. How may I direct your call?"
"Estelle Pruden, please," I requested.
"Thank you," replied the efficient voice at the switchboard.
"Bishop Kammerer's Office..."
"Hello, Estelle. This is Lisa Sykes."
"Why Lisa, how are you?"

It was a genuine question and not just a greeting. Estelle impressed all of us clergy in the Virginia Conference whenever we had occasion to visit the Bishop or contact that office. I did not have to see Estelle today to know that her blonde hair was swept up immaculately, nor that her smile was warm and constant. These things were always true of Estelle, who had managed the office and the schedule of Virginia Bishops for twenty-one years.

"I am well, thank you. Estelle, I am calling with an unusual request. I know the Bishop is extremely busy having just arrived, but I feel I need to meet with her and tell her about my advocacy work on the issue of mercury."

Until now, my philosophy of ministry had always been to avoid notoriety. I told myself, "Do your work. Do it well. Enjoy remaining at the same church for a long time." Indeed, I had sought to discharge my pastoral duties with great competence so that I could remain at the churches to which I was appointed for long pastorates, instead of moving frequently, which is part of a historical legacy from Methodism's founder, John Wesley. By all accounts, I had succeeded in this goal, remaining at my current church for ten years and coming to be regarded as a member of the family by many in my congregations. I valued stability for myself and my family, especially Wesley. Now, however, out of concern for the many children still at risk of being damaged by mercury-containing drugs, I was personally seeking the Bishop's support for a controversial cause that was unknown among my clerical colleagues. I wondered how my advocacy would impact my career. As an ordained minister and as a mother, I needed to share not only the issue but also my call to pursue it with the Bishop who now had authority over me.

Estelle surprised me with her reply. "Lisa, I've heard about what you are doing, and it's very important work. I would like to schedule you to meet with Bishop Kammerer as soon as possible. Let me check her schedule..."

As my appointment with the Bishop approached, I was busy. Along with my testimony and my passion about the importance of protecting children from mercury-containing drugs, I knew I had to offer documentation to the Bishop to support my controversial assertions. If I was about to share with her my conviction that the administration of mercury was criminal and reckless, I needed to be able to prove it. Fortunately, the correspondence I had amassed from four years of pursing officials at various levels of government was plentiful.

With my arms full of files, I arrived at the Methodist Building, well before it was time for my appointment with Bishop Kammerer. I wondered as I waited, "Am I wrong in thinking it's providential that, as I bring this issue to the church, I also bring it to Virginia's first woman bishop?"

Even more striking than this, not only the Bishop but also the Council Director and the Communications Chair for the Conference were women. Would they not understand my passion for protecting the children because they shared with me not only a religious call but also a maternal one? Or was I mistaken to bring my advocacy, considered radical by medical and government authorities, into the open like this? After this meeting, would I be considered too much of a conspiracy theorist by the superior who had authority over me or by my conference which was conservative and mainline? Did I really want to tell my bishop, the very first time I met her, that I believed the pharmaceutical companies were knowingly putting poison in the baby shots? "I'm going to sound like a lunatic," I thought to myself.

"Lisa, can I get you a cup of coffee or tea?"

Had Estelle sensed the worry I felt?

"No, thank you, Estelle. But I did want to thank you for getting me this appointment."

"You're going to like the Bishop, Lisa. She's wonderful." Estelle had a marvelous way of putting people, even pastors, at ease.

"Lisa, tell me about Wesley."

Bishop Kammerer disarmed me of my worry with just a few words. Her voice was deep, tranquil, full of strength and compassion. I knew already she was a grandmother and, too, an Episcopal leader of great accomplishment.

"I love him so much, Bishop, and I see him struggle every day..."

The story flowed out of me without any effort. Bishop Kammerer registered every word I spoke with clarity in her eyes and concern in her voice.

"Bishop, God has surrounded me with the most extraordinary team of physicians and researchers and lawyers, all seeking to save the children from mercury. Most of them are devout Christians, Bishop. Though, not all. You know, the Geiers are scientists of tremendous morality and ethics, but they do not have a faith."

"Lisa, perhaps the Geiers don't believe in God, but it's very clear from what you've said that God believes in the Geiers."

A smile dashed across my face. This Bishop could see the intangible. She could discern the compelling call that had gathered me, Mary, Mark, David and Cliff together. This Bishop was helping me already, tending to my aching heart by listening to how it had broken and, too, by affirming how my call to pastoral ministry had become a call to social justice. I adored her immediately.

"God, you did send this woman to me, didn't you?" I whispered loudly enough for my soul to overhear.

As the hour sped away, I sought to share with Bishop Kammerer the science on the toxicity of mercury, the institutionalized corruption that protected its place in medicine, and even what I had come to consider the CDC's abuse of Simpsonwood by holding there a collusive meeting on Thimerosal—an act which clearly violated the principles of our faith. Finally, I confided in Bishop Kammerer the frightening scope of the danger.

"Bishop, this is not just autism. We believe mercury is causing Attention Deficit Disorder and Attention Deficit Hyperactivity Disorder and many cases of Sudden Infant Death Syndrome. Mercury-poisoning, which occurs while the brain is wiring in our children has one appearance. But when it happens in those who are adults, whose brains have completely wired, it has a different appearance. We believe this is Alzheimer's."[2]

For the first time, the Bishop did not seem to have any words with which to respond to me. Her jaw dropped and as it did so I wondered if she loved someone who suffered with this illness, just as deeply as I loved Wesley, now struggling with autism.

"Bishop, I know what I've said is hard to believe. But for everything I've told you today, you will find the documentation right here, labeled, in these folders."

The stack which I had placed on her coffee table as I entered her office was a foot and a half high. "I would like to ask your permission to bring a resolution before our Annual Conference. I'd like to write a resolution offering a church stance against giving people, especially children, mercury in their medicines."

"Lisa," Bishop Kammerer instructed without any reservation, "Write the resolution. And submit it to the Annual Conference, with the support of any of our boards which you can enlist..."

I was trying hard not to cry in front of my Bishop, though I realized she would not have cared if I did.

"Lisa, I want to pray for you and for Wesley and your family."

She reached out and gently enfolded my hands in hers with the most profound compassion, and as she prayed, once again, an undeniable, unforgettable refrain crossed my mind, so as to etch upon it the words which I had heard before: "I have an Ally, and that Ally is more powerful than the world knows...and that Ally has an army, and it is called the Church."

Chapter Sixteen

Breakthroughs

At that time the disciples came to Jesus and asked, "Who is the greatest in the kingdom of heaven?" He called a child, whom he put among them, and said, "Truly I tell you, unless you change and become like children, you will never enter the kingdom of heaven. Whoever becomes humble like this child is the greatest in the kingdom of heaven. Whoever welcomes one such child in my name welcomes me.

"If any of you put a stumbling block before one of these little ones who believe in me, it would be better for you if a great millstone were fastened around your neck and you were drowned in the depth of the sea."

—Matthew 18: 1-6

FEBRUARY 2005

I was seated around a wooden table in a Sunday school room with six junior high students one Sunday morning. I had begun confirmation class-es—the protestant version of catechism—instructing these youths in United Methodist theology and Church history in preparation for their confirmation as full members of the Church. This rite of passage was one I remembered well from my own youth.

"Who can tell me what 'connectionalism' is?" I asked.

Blank faces stared back.

"Would you like your cell phone if it were able to call, say, only five phone numbers within a two mile radius?"

Immediately, the youth responded to this: "Absolutely not!" I knew already my youth considered their cells phones as integral a part of themselves as an arm or a leg.

"So you want a cell phone that can connect you to the whole world, eh? At least what you know of the world, right?"

They nodded in enthusiastic agreement.

"Well, don't you want a church that can do the same thing? In faith, it's a different 'wireless network,' a network connected by faith, love and prayer that you are a part of. Church congregations connect you, at least in United Methodism, to other church congregations and other believers. And so, if there is something urgent you need to tell the world, you all can go from this church to all the other Methodist churches in Virginia, and from that collection of churches, which we call a conference, to the General Conference, which is United Methodism around the whole world. United Methodism has always led in disaster relief and missionary work and reform efforts, because each member and congregation is connected through its conference to the people called 'Methodist', which is the global church. Now, which Conference do we belong to?"

An intrepid sixth-grader with freckles and red hair piped up, "Virginia, isn't it?"

"That's right, the Virginia Conference is the second largest United Methodist Conference in the world. If you want to get something done through the witness of the United Methodist Church, Virginia is a good place to start."

"Like what, Pastor Lisa?" one of the boys in the class chimed in.

"Abolition. Suffrage. Child Labor Reform. Civil Rights. Temperance. How many of these have you heard about in your history classes at school?"

"All of them," the children responded.

"Well, the Church, and especially the women of our denomination, offered tremendous leadership in each of these reform efforts to make the world a more just place. The Church has often been the conscience of our country, speaking for those who are treated unfairly. We have changed the law of this nation, and we have changed history."

My voice had grown strong and animated. I wondered if I were just instructing my students, or too, reminding myself of these truths as I was beginning the journey I had just described to my class—one from personal concern to global Christian witness.

"Hi, Darlene. This is Lisa Sykes. I'm appointed to Christ Church in the Richmond District."

"Well, hello, Lisa."

Darlene Amon was one of the most accomplished laywomen in the Virginia Annual Conference. She had served as lay leader of the Virginia Conference and the President of its United Methodist Women. Though we had not spoken before, I knew exactly who she was from the impressive speeches she often delivered at Annual Conference. Darlene combined Southern grace with a keen intellect and a warm appeal. She was not only a long-standing leader in the church, with phenomenal gifts in public speaking, but also a military wife, residing in the Norfolk area.

"I'm calling to ask for your help, Darlene. I plan to submit a resolution to the Annual Conference this year and would like to have you as the lay sponsor on it."

"And what is the resolution about, Lisa?"

Darlene was already very familiar with United Methodist resolutions, having sponsored many of them during her leadership in the Virginia Annual Conference. She understood that this was the way to bring an issue properly before the 342,000 members of our denomination who lived in Virginia. Resolutions are voted upon at Annual Conference each June.

"Darlene, it's about mercury in the vaccines, most especially the flu shot which has been recommended for pregnant women and children."

"Mercury?" was Darlene's succinct response.

"Yes, Darlene. I know you wouldn't think that the government would allow a poison into the drug supply, but it has. This is an antiquated mercury-based preservative that's never been safety tested. It's called Thimerosal. My son received so much of it through a shot I got in pregnancy and, then, in his immunizations, that he's been disabled by it. He's actually been diagnosed with mercury-poisoning, though his condition was first referred to as 'autism.'"

"Lisa, I am going to do some research on the subject. Let me call you back next week, after I've made some inquiries."

"Absolutely, Darlene. I'll look forward to speaking with you again soon."

A week had not yet passed when my office phone rang.

"Hi, Lisa, this is Darlene."

I breathed in deep and prayed that I might hear confirmation of Darlene's support in the next few minutes.

"Thanks for calling me back, Darlene, and for the energy you've invested in looking at this issue since we last spoke."

"Oh, not at all, Lisa. You know, you happened to call me last week the day after I got my flu shot."

I gulped, wishing it had been the day before that I might have made Darlene aware before, rather than after, that exposure.

"After you called me, I went down to the naval base to speak with one of the doctors in the infirmary there. He's confirmed what you told me. That Thimerosal was in my shot. That it is mercury. Lisa, everyone warns pregnant women not to eat fish for fear of mercury. But you never hear about this! You go right ahead and put me down as a co-sponsor on the resolution you are writing for Annual Conference."

My heart pounded in my chest. Perhaps Darlene could hear it in my voice, as I thanked her for her support. After a pattern of being denied and refused each time I had requested help from officials in the federal and state government, Darlene's quick and informed response was a joyous change. It also heralded hope, for if one of the strongest laywomen in the Virginia Annual Conference of the United Methodist Church would cosponsor this resolution with me, then likely, the United Methodist Women—the women's organization in our conference and denomination—would support it also.

"Darlene, I don't know how to thank you!"

"No thanks are necessary, Lisa. This is a good thing. It is in keeping with our faith."

"Absolutely." Now, I had not only my first lay support but also a partner for the resolution. Already, there were questions I needed to ask Darlene.

"Darlene, I've thought of two things I want to do, in addition to drafting the resolution to share with you. I'm going to start an email distribution list for leaders in our Conference, and with your permission, I'll begin it with you. Not often, but time to time, when there are significant articles or news pieces, I will email them to this list, so you and others can learn more about the issue. And in addition, I want to make a list of various boards and agencies in the Conference whom I might approach about backing this resolution. I hope it will have great momentum before it even hits the floor of Annual Conference."

MARCH 2005

Jenn Wood, Wesley's third grade teacher, had been euphoric over the recent changes in her gentlest student. She had dispensed with weighted vests which my hyperactive son had worn in what was a futile attempt to keep him seated and focused. They were no longer needed, as he was happy to sit and pay attention to the world of things Jenn was now able to teach him.

Jenn had seen startling changes in Wesley, just as we had at home. With the New Year, these changes were even more dramatic, however, because we had graduated from the test dose of LUPRON® to a timed-release "depo" shot, which Mary gave to Wesley in the office. It was administered with a needle so impressive in length that I could not watch as Wesley was stuck. Remarkably, after receiving the first shot, my son lay down a second time, seemingly in an attempt to request a second one! Clearly, the patient approved despite the needle's prick.

Mary watched him carefully after that first "depo," and immediately she could see improvements in how his eyes tracked objects across his field of view and in his depth perception. After the administration of the shot, which I thought might provoke anger if not outrage, Wesley seemed calm and settled. Not only this, but within the hour as we arrived home, Wesley pulled me to the sofa and wanted to cuddle, snuggling within the curve of my arm —this from a child who had only tolerated occasional touch since he began chelation.

On the day after that first LUPRON® "depo" shot, Jenn had called me, teasingly, declaring, "Okay, I know you've been messing with him. What have you done?"

I cleared my throat, masking a laugh, and said, "What do you mean, Jenn."

I closed my eyes, put my fingers to my lips and breathed in deeply, giving thanks for the change: "Well, he's sitting here in my lap with his arm around my neck, staring into my eyes, and humming a sing-song to me!"

The Geiers' protocol was overcoming the monumental isolation of autism. The change in Wesley, occasioned by the LUPRON®, confirmed what I had always suspected. It was not that these children did not want to be loved. It was that, for some unidentified physiological reason, they could not bear to be held, touched, or caressed. Mary had often said that a mother's caress felt like sandpaper to a child with autism.

Now, the physiology—the pathology—the problem had been overcome, by LUPRON® and a team of researchers who exulted with me in each improvement. Wesley was as snuggly at nine years-old as he should have been as a toddler; he was melting hearts with blue eyes that now trespassed into other's minds and embraces with sheer abandon. Every time Wesley got one of his LUPRON® "depos," he was being recreated and resembled more and more the child I knew God had intended him to be. "Lo, I make all things new," came to mind each time Jenn called me to report on what she was seeing, confirming to me the changes I was watching take place in my son's body and soul at home.

On these nights, I thought I would never get off the phone. I spoke to David, Mark and Paul about my latest observations on Wesley. We went over every clinical detail, every suspicion of my mother's intuition, and when we had covered all there was to tell that particular day, then we would turn our attention from Wesley's treatment to the resolution for the Virginia Annual Conference of the United Methodist Church, which was to be presented in three months in Hampton, Virginia.

David, Mark and Paul all reviewed the resolution I drafted and improved it, adding significant scientific details and regulatory statements to it. Each time they would expand it, I would finesse it, making sure that the science was not too technical and that the words and the sequence of the various "Whereas" clauses flowed well in the minds of all who were non-scientific. This resolution would be long, because I was convinced that it must serve as a teaching tool. It had to inform first and persuade second. While the many "Whereas" clauses comprised the first thirteen paragraphs of the resolution, each composed with the greatest skill and care, it was the "Be It Resolved" conclusion that all of us found most thrilling:

Be it resolved, that the Virginia Annual Conference of the United Methodist Church does hereby call upon the Secretary of Health and Human Services, the Food and Drug Administration, and the Centers for Disease Control and Prevention to come quickly to the protection of the people, especially the unborn and the children, by:

Immediately advocating that mercury-free stocks of vaccines and other pharmaceutical products be prioritized for pregnant women, newborn infants, and children,

Providing an opportunity of informed consent to individuals about to receive mercury exposure through their drugs/pharmaceutical products/ biologics/vaccines, detailing the known risks of its toxicity and Federal Safety Guidelines for Exposure to mercury,

Moving to ban the presence of any mercury compound in a drug/pharmaceutical product/biologic/vaccine, prescribed or over-the-counter, unless the presence of that mercury compound has been proven clinically to have no adverse effects.

With the resolution in final form, I spent part of everyday making calls to church leaders across the state.

"Betty, this is Lisa Sykes. I would like to ask that the United Methodist Women support a resolution Darlene Amon and I will be bringing to the floor of Annual Conference this June."

Betty Whitehurst was a retired missionary and a woman of tremendous spiritual strength. She was also president of the United Methodist Women in the Virginia Conference.

"Lisa, I've heard about the resolution. Please send it to me. I will be happy to present it to the executive committee which meets next month."

As winter gave way to spring, I had placed the resolution before the United Methodist Women, the General Board for Global Ministries—Health and Welfare Division, the Methodist Federation for Social Action, and the Children's Initiative, all United Methodist boards and agencies within the Virginia Conference. With their consideration and votes accomplished, each group to whom I had issued an invitation accepted it without hesitation, as did one I hadn't even known to invite.

"Lisa, this is Martha Stokes, Chair of the Commission on Disabilities."

"Hi, Martha," I responded, not sure as to who she was or why she was calling me.

"Listen, we've heard about your resolution, and the Commission on Disabilities has voted, and we would like to be sponsors as well.

"Oh, Martha, this is just amazing!" I replied, not trying to hide my astonishment. "Everywhere else I've ever taken this issue, the door has been slammed in my face. And now I bring it to the church, and I'm receiving nothing but support and help! I cannot tell you what this means to the cause or what it means to me!"

"You know, Lisa, thank goodness the Kingdom of God just doesn't work the way the world does!"

Sitting at my desk, I answered the phone. On this one day, Jenn was not euphoric; she was not teasing; she was not light-hearted. I could hear the worry in her voice the moment she replied to my "Hello."

"Lisa, Wesley's eyes, just for a second, they rolled back in his head. But then he blinked, and it was okay. And then it happened again, just a couple minutes later. I don't know what's going on. I think you'd better come see."

"Thanks, Jenn. I'll be right there." I grabbed my purse, said something to my church secretary, and headed for the door, almost running.

As I got in the car, I dialed Mary's phone number.

"Mary, I don't know what's happened. Just for a moment, twice now, Wesley's eyes have rolled back in his head. The school just called... No, he didn't lose consciousness, and the teacher tells me he seems fine now, but we just don't know what's going on... I'm on my way to get him right now."

"Lisa, as soon as you get him from school, bring him to my office. I want to examine him right away."

On my way to the school, I made one more call.

"David, we're not sure what's going on..."

The conversation that followed was a carbon copy of the previous one. In the few short moments that were left before I pulled into the school parking lot, David summoned his father to the phone, and I recited the details I had received from Jenn to them both.

"Okay, gotta go. I'm here. I'll call you after Mary sees Wes."

By the time I entered the classroom, Wesley was laughing and smiling, amused to see his mother enter the room in such a hurry.

I went over and knelt by my son to peer into his eyes, as he looked directly at me and began a sing-song.

"It was just like this," Jenn told me, moving her eyes up to the top of her field of view.

"Okay. Anything else I need to know? Any other details?"

"No. That's it. I hope everything is okay, Lisa."

"I do, too. Thanks, Jenn."

When we reached Mary's office, the waiting room was empty, as it was lunch time. Mary had been listening for the door to open, announcing our arrival.

"Lisa, bring Wesley back here."

She moved us directly into one of the examining rooms. Her hands slipped supplely over Wesley's neck and abdomen. She peered into his eyes with a bright beam of light from one of her scopes and then listened to his heart. Nothing was out of the ordinary.

Wesley, fraught with the sudden change in his day, was impatient and sat down upon the floor, whining in protest. I sat beside him, both my arms around his waist, more to comfort myself than him.

When I looked up, I felt my soul being crushed by an awful weight. It was the somber concern of Mary, my favorite physician, who had become a dear friend. She looked down at me and Wesley, and her back flattened against the wall by which she stood. Then slowly, imperceptibly, her knees bent, and the flatness of the wall steadied her while she sank slowly down to the floor beside us.

While Wesley, oblivious to any crisis, watched his fingers dance in front of his face, Mary and I stared at each other, communicating in silence an anxiety which could not be captured in words.

This one isolated incident never recurred, nor were we ever able to determine if it had been triggered by the LUPRON®. David would later conjecture that perhaps this was a literal sign that Wesley's mind was "waking up." Over time, the terror we all felt in those moments was tamed by memory, and both my son's progress and the progress of the resolution toward Annual Conference continued.

APRIL 2005

"Dick, I'd like to invite you to meet with the General Secretary of the General Board of Church and Society in Washington, D.C. on April 22."

Prior to the resolution coming before the Virginia Annual Conference, I'd arranged for 'my' scientists and doctors to present to Mr. Jim Winkler, a member of the Virginia Annual Conference who was also the General Secretary of the General Board of Church and Society. As such, he was the denomination's representative, speaking for the church worldwide on social justice issues.

"I'd like to have you there, if you can attend."

Dick was a wonderful pastor and sage, close to retirement with a white beard, balding head and the presence of the Spirit clearly secured within his soul. Bright, thoughtful, he was always more ready to listen than to speak. A professor of Biblical studies who had taught around the world, Dick was one of the brightest clergy in the Conference.

"You know, Lisa, when you first told me about this issue, I took it to two of my friends. They are a married couple, both toxicologists. You know, they had no idea there was any mercury in the shots. They concur with you that it's a serious problem."

"If only the toxicologists for the government would look at this issue that forthrightly, Dick!"

"April 22, you say? How did you get an appointment with the General Secretary so quickly? It usually takes months."

"I don't know, Dick. I hope that means he understands the gravity of this situation. The scientists and doctor and lawyer I've invited to present are internationally recognized. You will never forget what they have to say."

"Lisa, it sounds fascinating. My calendar is clear for that day. I will be happy to go to D.C. and be part of this gathering."

On the morning of April 22, two vans full of United Methodists from

Virginia, both clergy and lay, as well as Dr. Megson, left Richmond bound for the General Board of Church and Society, located in a building directly beside the United States Supreme Court. With us were Don and Julianne King, filmmakers from Hawaii and parents of an autistic son, Beau. They had flown in to live in my home and shadow my advocacy for two weeks, with cameras rolling. As we arrived in Washington, D.C., rendezvousing with Mark, David, and Cliff, everyone was impressed by the fact that my denomination should own such prime real estate.

On welcoming us into the building, the General Secretary, Jim Winkler explained, "It has always been the practice of the United Methodist Church to buy real estate close to seats of power: in the nation's capitol, in state capitols and around the world. We are here to watch what is going on. How government is functioning... or malfunctioning. We believe our presence here embodies our commitment to impact the world around us for Christ by impacting public policy."

In all my years of pastoral ministry, I had never before been told this.

"You know, Mr. Winkler," I replied, "We have come here because we believe many citizens are being denied not only justice but also their constitutional rights. This generation of children and their parents are being given no opportunity of informed consent as an undisclosed poison is administered to them as part of their medicines."

"And I want to hear more about that, Lisa. Won't you all come this way to the conference room? And call me Jim!" We all took seats around a large conference table in the center of a beautiful sunny room with picturesque views of the diagonal streets and the neoclassical architecture characteristic of Washington, D.C. Scientists, clergy, laity, physicians, the General Secretary as well as a resident bishop were all in the room.

I began the meeting with a prayer and then the Geiers offered their power point presentation. It was not altogether different from the one that they had given in Richmond to the Deputy Attorney General of Virginia, save one thing. I had asked them to go into great detail on the Simpsonwood meeting, with the quotes and an explanation about the illegality of it all. As first Mark and then David read one quote after another from the transcript. Jim Winkler sat forward in his seat, staring intently, eyes not moving from the screen. What I saw on his face was disbelief, as his jaw dropped.

Here, for the first time to my knowledge, the denomination which owned Simpsonwood Retreat Center was officially being informed at its global level, through one of its General Secretaries, what had transpired there nearly five years earlier.

As the meeting progressed, the audience around the table wrestled with the twins of disillusionment and deceit, which they clearly beheld by the time the Geiers had finished presenting. Then, Mary began her remarks.

"You all know, Lisa is a preacher, and she quotes a lot of science. Well, I'm a doctor, and right now, I want to quote some scripture."

Mary, the daughter of a Presbyterian minister and recently recognized by Defeat Autism Now! (DAN) as the physician with the highest rate of patients recovered from autism, knew exactly how to bridge the scientific and theological worlds. Pulling out the Bible which she had brought with her, she read from the Gospel of Matthew:

> "Take care that you do not despise one of these little ones; for, I tell you, in heaven their angels continually see the face of my Father in heaven. What do you think? If a shepherd has a hundred sheep, and one of them has gone astray, does he not leave the ninety-nine on the mountains and go in search of the one that went astray? And if he finds it, truly I tell you, he rejoices over it more than over the ninety-nine that never went astray. So it is the will of your Father in heaven that not one of these little ones should be lost."

Mary, I thought to myself, you know how to preach! Having opened her presentation with scripture, Mary moved through the science of treating a vaccine-injured child. Identifying genetic susceptibilities, treating metabolic imbalances, and employing biomedical treatments were the modern ways Mary practiced an ancient art called healing. As Mary concluded, no one in the room doubted that this physician had been gifted by God for her work.

Cliff was the final one to present. Always affable, always impressive, and a former marine, Cliff was accustomed to laying it on the line: "We all assume vaccines are safe. We all want safe vaccines. The fact of the matter is that the more you start digging into the matter of Thimerosal in vaccines, the more disturbing it is. Frankly speaking, the kids are getting screwed, medically and legally."

I often thought it was the contrast between Cliff's professional and astute demeanor, with the coarseness of what he said in that moment, that shocked those present into realizing this was not just a topic of scientific and medical concern but also a national crisis.

In the weeks that followed, I would hear from many of the attending Virginia representatives that being present for this historic meeting was one of the most life-changing experiences they had ever had.

"Lisa, this is Jenn. You are not going to believe this…" It was April, and Wesley had been on the Geiers' protocol for approximately four months.

The resolution had been submitted for publication in the *Book of Report for Annual Conference*, and United Methodists across the state had a growing awareness that mercury in medicine was cause for alarm. Yet, the excitement I felt at all of this was overshadowed when Wesley's teacher called me this particular afternoon.

"Wesley spoke!" Jenn continued, almost out of breath, as if she had been running. "He spoke today in gym class."

My heart clutched each word that Jenn had said, scared to let any of them go. In one lifetime, how often does a prayer for the miraculous get answered?

"Spoke? Spoke what, Jenn?!"

The words, though racing through the phone from Jenn to me and from me to her, seemed to take forever to arrive.

"He was in gym, Lisa, with Mr. Artis. They were doing sit-ups, and Mr. Artis was counting. Wesley was holding another little boy's feet while he did sit-ups. And when Mr. Artis got to three, he heard another voice joining him, counting aloud. Well, it took 'til seven before he realized who it was—Lisa, it was Wesley!"

"Oh, Jenn!" I shouted into the receiver.

"He got to eleven, and by then everyone was around him. I think maybe they scared him because he stopped," she said, laughing. "But he talked. He talked perfectly normally. Perfect pronunciation. Perfect intonation. Lisa, you're getting him back!"

I hadn't realized I was crying until the tears landed on my hands.

I sighed, unable to speak.

"Lisa, call Wesley's doctors and tell them! Let me know what they say, okay?!"

"Of course. I will! Oh, Jenn, thank you!"

The afternoon was a flurry of phone calls.

"Seth! Seth! Wesley SPOKE... he counted ALOUD to eleven in gym class today!"

"Mom, Wesley SPOKE..."

"David, guess what Wesley did today at school? He TALKED!"

The only significant person I did not call was Mary. Mary had borne the weight of diagnosing Wesley with precocious puberty and treating him with his first LUPRON® "depo" shots. All we had been through together. No, I could not just call Mary. That would not be enough.

It was late afternoon, but I knew she would still be at her office. Upon hearing the news, Mom had come over to keep the boys so that I could drive to the grocery store to buy two bottles of champagne—one for Mary and one for her staff. They had become accustomed to me wandering in with an assortment of desserts for them, but never had the Methodist minister-mom arrived with bubbly!

"Tammy!" I said in an intense but quiet voice over the receptionist's desk. "I've got something for you! We've got to celebrate!"

She looked down to see the bottle of champagne and then looked back at me in a pleasant confusion, a wondering smile crossing her face.

"Tammy, Wesley talked today at school! He spoke! He counted to eleven! Perfectly!"

"Oh, Lisa!" Tammy replied, standing up to put her arms around my neck. She hugged me tight, and then glanced down the hall.

"Let me go see if Dr. Megson is free..."

She returned a second and a half later.

"Lisa, you go right on back, she's just finished with patients for the day."

"Dr. Mary? Have I got some news for you!"

"You do?" Mary's voice crested with anticipation and her smile widened.

"This is for you!" I said, handing her the other bottle of bubbly ceremoniously.

"What's this for?"

"Wesley SPOKE today, Mary! He talked! Perfectly normally!"

"Didn't I tell you, Lisa! Didn't I tell you he was all in there!"

As Mary popped the bottle, for just a moment, there was no sorrow and no sadness and no struggle. Just joy—pure sparkling joy.

As Conference approached, there were more surprises.

"Lisa, this is Carole Vaughn." Carole was in charge of Communications for the Virginia Conference. I knew she must be calling about the upcoming vote.

"Hi, Carol! You know, support for the resolution is really growing. I am sooo excited!"

"Lisa, that's great. In regard to the resolution, I have some news for you. Bishop Kammerer has asked that there be a press conference after the vote."

"Press conference?"

Suddenly, my head was swimming.

"Yes, should the resolution pass, we will hold a press conference. The Reverend C. Douglas Smith of the Virginia Interfaith Center will work with you on it. He will be handling all the arrangements. Will you call him when you have time?"

While we had already conversed often on the phone, I first met Doug face to face in a parking lot at Barnes and Noble. I rendezvoused with him and left my car there that day to ride up to an ecumenical religious event in Washington, D.C. It was not the event that was of great importance for me, but rather the talk-time we would have on both the north and south bound lanes of Interstate 95.

Much of I-95 North was traversed as I told him Wesley's story, start to finish. The gorgeous baby. The miserable toddler. The disabled son.

In conversation with Doug, there was never a spare second. Doug was always probing, inquiring. I could sense him mapping out public relations strategies in his mind with each of the details I revealed to him. His work as a Christian pastor and advocate among Virginia's politicians in the General Assembly seemed to have groomed him well for this foray into national health policy issues.

As we neared our destination, we stopped for a midmorning cup of coffee. "So, Lisa, I think I understand the timeline here. But we need to talk about Senator Stosch."

"Yea? Well, tell me what I need to know, because I never got anywhere with the bill last year."

"Well, that's the thing."

"What's 'the thing,' Doug?"

"I've had my team looking, Lisa, and we can't find a bill. There was no bill. We've searched everything on record from last year. Best we can find is a small provision about mercury in car batteries."

My confusion gave way to disbelief, and my disbelief gave way to anger. I was so angry at Senator Stosch that I could make no reply to Doug. I opened my mouth to begin a sentence several times but failed each time. Finally, a wry smile arrived in place of my scowl, and I just shook my head quietly from side to side. Confronted with more deceit, I figured I could laugh or cry. Laughing seemed the better option.

"Lisa, before we get to the event, there are a couple of questions I need to ask you."

"Sure, Doug. What?"

"Have you ever had an affair?"

"Excuse me?"

I began to laugh again, but then I sensed that while Doug enjoyed the shock value of his inquiry, he was dead serious.

"I'm a United Methodist minister, Doug. No, I have not ever had an affair."

"And your husband, to the best of your knowledge, has he ever had an affair?"

As preposterous as the previous question was, this one was even more.

"No need to be confined to the best of my knowledge, Doug. No. Seth has never had an affair."

"Okay, then. Your father?"

"Where in the world is he going with this?" I asked myself in complete surprise.

"He worked for one of the intelligence branches of the government, right? Did he ever torch any villages?"

"Oh, for crying out loud, Doug! No he did not! He designed counter-intelligence systems. Does that do it, now?"

Despite my impatience, I realized that I was being vetted.

"Yeah. That does it. You know, when this hits, Lisa, you are going to have no secrets. If there are any, I need to know them before anyone else does."

"Well, Doug, you're up to date. What you should know is that, until I discovered that my son had been poisoned with mercury, nothing about me was ever controversial."

Now, he laughed. "You know what we need, Lisa? We need a movie about this."

"Oh, I didn't tell you yet, Doug. There is one. Don and Julianne King are making a movie about their autistic son, Beau, called *Beautiful Son*. They spent two weeks filming me and my family last month."

Dumbfounded, Doug rolled his eyes and just laughed.

"I should have figured."

"Okay, my turn to ask you a question, Doug. How often does an issue like this walk in off the street and set itself down on your desk?"

He needed to think about my question no longer than I needed to think about his before responding.

"Once in a lifetime, Lisa. Once in a lifetime."

Chapter Seventeen

Resolved

Prayer for the Spirit of Truth

From the cowardice that dares not face new truth,
From the laziness that is contented with half-truth,
From the arrogance that thinks it knows all truth,
Good Lord, deliver me. Amen

—A Prayer from Kenya
597 in *The United Methodist Hymnal*

May 2005

As a pastor, I had never gambled on the lottery, but I often gambled on people. There were times I gambled a great deal on a particular person, but had I ever gambled this much? A new front in the war against mercury, months worth of work within my own conference, the hope that the church would come to the aid of the children. I would never have risked it all, had I not known Kelly.

When I picked up the phone to call her, I had intended merely to confide in her my hope that the faith community, through the United Methodist Church in Virginia, was about to make an historic statement on "Protecting Children from Mercury-containing Drugs."

"Pray really hard, Kelly," I entreated my friend and fellow advocate in Kansas. I had first come to know Kelly Kerns through the Geiers. We had spoken about everything, from whistleblowers for the Office of Special Counsel Project to the regimen of supplements she and her husband, Jim, used to help them recover their three autistic children.

"Why, Lisa? What's going on?" she asked, with a voice that I always sensed betrayed the brokenness in her heart.

What must it have been like to lose not one, but three children? I asked myself silently. That Kelly could function, much less advocate, all the while regaining her children from the abyss that is autism, needed no certification in my mind as an authentic miracle.

"Well, we're just a few weeks away, Kelly, from a vote on the mercury issue—a really important vote."

"Vote? Who's voting?"

"My church, Kelly! Actually, it will be the Virginia Annual Conference, of the United Methodist Church, representing 342,000 members..."

"Lisa, are you serious? That's phenomenal!"

"It's better than that, Kelly. If we get this vote, then we send the issue higher. I want a denominational statement against giving children mercury in their medicine. And then I hope we can get other mainline denominations to follow suit, and who knows? World Council of Churches mean anything to you?"

"I... I... I don't know what to say, Lisa! This is amazing!"

"You know, Kelly, in our country, one of the few organizations that has ever been able to challenge the power of national health agencies and change federal health policy is the church. It makes sense, doesn't it? We advocates keep trying to establish a grass-roots network as parents, and yet one already exists that's better organized and more powerful than anything we could create. I believe the church is the way forward. That's the way we will win. We have to give this issue away.

"The church counts each life as sacred. A National Immunization Policy that denies informed consent and accepts collateral damage among our children is something that people of faith and conscience, when made aware of these things, will never accept."

As I spoke, I wondered what Kelly was thinking. I hadn't put my hopes into words for anyone outside my own family or conference to hear. I knew Kelly was a Christian, though, and I hoped this endeavor would make sense to her. Her response affirmed not only my vision of the way forward but also the particular faith community in which I had begun the journey.

"Lisa, you know I'm a Methodist, too. We haven't been back to church in a very long time—you know what it's like trying to handle autism in the midst of a worship service."

"Yeah, I understand, Kelly."

Kelly's voice started to tremble ever so slightly. As long as I had known Kelly, I could sense her pain and her passion very near to the surface of her soul.

"Hey, Lisa, what if I got the resolution submitted out here in the Kansas East Conference, too?"

"I don't know, Kelly. Your Annual Conference, just like ours, will be in June. That's not much time to get it on the agenda or build support for it…"

"Lisa, I could do it. I know I could!"

Kelly was so intense that her voice now quivered. Our conversation had brought me to a most unexpected place. Did I roll the dice? Knowing nothing of Kansas East, and nothing of the Bishop there, did I send Kelly the resolution, and let her see what she could do, last minute, to get it on the floor and passed? I drew a deep breath, hesitating, unsure what to say.

"Okay, Kelly. Here's the plan," I said. "I need to talk with one of the leaders here in Virginia to make sure I can float it to you according to our polity. In the meantime, you make inquiries out there of those in church leadership, to see if it could be submitted at this late date, and more importantly, to consider very carefully if you think it would be passed. We can't afford for the first vote to be anything but a success."

"I'll call you as soon as I know anything."

Susan Garrett, the Council Director for the Virginia Annual Conference, who guided the programmatic ministries of the entire conference, now guided me in the details of the resolutions.

"Susan, I must admit I never learned the answer to this question in seminary. If someone in Kansas East Conference wants to submit my resolution on mercury out there, is that permitted by our polity? Can we share it?"

"Absolutely, Lisa. It's done all the time."

I had my answer. My church's polity would permit it, and Kelly would accomplish it: the historic resolution against mercury would be considered first by a conference of which I knew nothing. Nothing, except for the fact that I trusted Kelly Kerns would make history there.

The Kansas East Annual Conference convened the first week of June at Baker University in Baldwin City, a week and a half before Virginia. It was no longer Virginia but this Midwest United Methodist conference, whose residents referred to home as Big Sky country, that would consider for the first time the historic resolution on mercury.

The theme of the Kansas East Conference was "Come to the Table of Grace." Its members had no idea yet how desperately two mothers prayed we might find a gracious place for ourselves and our cause in that community of faith. Unlike Bishop Kammerer, the newly assigned Bishop in the Kansas East Conference, Scott Jones, neither supported nor opposed Kelly's interjection of this issue into the first Annual Conference over which he would preside. Nonetheless, during opening worship, he might as well have been speaking right to Kelly, as he asked members to think about the plan God had for them as individuals, churches and Christians in the world.

In contrast to Virginia, Kansas East Conference was composed of only 76,000 members. This, I learned from Kelly, was immensely helpful because being a smaller conference Kansas East had fewer resolutions, a more relaxed schedule and was, overall, much more informal than Virginia.

"Lisa, there's not a lot out here but cows and corn," Kelly laughed. "I understand we won't have any trouble introducing the resolution from the floor and bringing it to a vote." Such a strategy in Virginia would have been a long shot at best. Kelly arrived at the Kansas East Annual Conference with hundreds of copies of the resolution, enough to hand out one to each delegate. The motion was introduced from the floor, seconded and then debated. In faraway Virginia, Kansas had become the center of my universe as I sat on my hands and prayed.

The call finally came; I saw Kelly's name on my Caller ID. Kelly was mischievous, teasing me, when I answered the phone with, "Well?"

"Lisa," she said after a long silence, "Unanimous!"

"YES!" Perhaps I had not won over the Institutes of Medicine with the urgency of this issue, but together, David, Paul, Mark, Kelly and I had won over 76,000 United Methodists in Kansas! Perhaps we had not challenged the authority of the National Academy of Sciences yet, but I was determined, that in time we would. Baldwin City, Kansas, was our beginning point.

I threw my head back, closed my eyes, and exclaimed, "Thank you, God, and Ms. Kelly Kerns!" I caught my breath.

"Kelly, tell me, what did the delegates say? What debate was there?"

"Lisa, they just couldn't believe anyone would put poison in a baby shot. The farmers here all said they wouldn't give mercury to their cattle, so why, they wanted to know, are we giving it to our kids?"

"Kelly," I asked, with impatience and excitement, "How is it that Kansas farmers can understand you don't inject cattle, much less children, with a known neurotoxin, and the Ph.D.'s and M.D.'s at the CDC have yet to figure that out?"

JUNE 2005

I arrived for the Virginia Annual Conference in the Hampton Coliseum with a decided flutter in my stomach. I would be addressing a gathering of thousands, and by so doing, inextricably wedding my personal advocacy to my ministerial calling. I welcomed that unity but feared, despite all the preparation and planning I had done, the vote might be contentious.

The fluttering in my stomach calmed the day before the vote with the arrival of Mark and David Geier, Boyd Haley, and Kelly and Richard Kerns. Knowing that the resolution was a scientific as well as an ethical issue, I wanted to have scientists there on the floor in case there were questions that I could not answer authoritatively. They had also come to participate in the press conference the next day, assuming the resolution passed. No one had told me what would happen if it did not, and I had not asked. Now, as I greeted and welcomed some of my dearest friends in the world to the Virginia Annual Conference of the United Methodist Church, I shut that question out of my mind.

I threw my arms around Kelly's neck, congratulating her for the first time in person, "Way to go, girl! I hope I can follow in your footsteps."

"Aw, Lisa," responded Kelly, anticlimactically. "It's going to happen. I can feel it. It's going to happen."

I knew the resolution would be heard sometime in the morning session on June 15. The exact time was impossible to predict, as it depended on the progress of conference business and floor votes on other resolutions. For that reason, Mary Megson and Liz Mumper arrived in Hampton very early that morning. They, too, were part of my expert team, ready to explicate the medical facts and defend the resolution before a coliseum full of United Methodists.

The public address system squealed. "The next resolution is 'Protecting Children from Mercury-containing Drugs.' Would the author please approach the mic?"

"Reverend Lisa Sykes, Christ United Methodist Church, Richmond District, Bishop." I looked up to see Bishop Kammerer, the presiding officer of the Conference. In this role, she was authoritative and decisive, and yet her characteristic warmth was still unmistakable. In meeting her gaze, I recalled her astounding support that day, now months ago, in her office. I also pondered the generosity of the press conference which she, not I, had requested take place only hours from now.

As the author of the resolution, I had three minutes to address conference about it. The speech which I had practiced until I was sick of it came alive as the words came out of my mouth. Just as the speech before the 2004 Institute of Medicine reached its hearers with a power I had not anticipated, so did this one reach the hearts of a people gathered in faith and called to service with an emotion I could not explain.

"Bishop Kammerer, Bishop Chamberlain, Distinguished Guests, Brothers and Sisters in Christ," I began formulaically.

As I reached the opening line of my speech, I noticed a perceptible cry within my voice. Everything that was to follow, I knew, would be preached directly from the exposed heart of a mother whose child had been terribly wounded. Dignity and indignation would be combined in equal portions.

"Of the day of the Lord, the Psalmist says: 'They shall not bear their children for calamity.' That day is not yet! And I stand before you now, because I have borne a child for calamity! Nine pounds, two ounces at birth, startling blue eyes, my Wesley was perfect.

"But by two, my son had ceased to speak. By three, he developed chronic diarrhea that would last for more than a year, and as he approached four, he began to fall on the floor and writhe in pain. Mainstream medicine labeled him 'autistic.'"

My church intern held the poster of Wesley's off-the-chart mercury dump aloft, so the cameras focused on me showed the conference my 'smoking gun' projected upon massive video screens.

"But then, in 2000, based on this lab report, with the mercury reading that runs off the page, researchers diagnosed my four-year-old son with MERCURY-POISONING.

"Only then did I learn that the Rho(D) shot I was given during my pregnancy contained fifty micrograms of the neurotoxin mercury, ten times the EPA exposure limit, fated to cross the placental barrier and lodge in the developing brain of my UNBORN son. I had NO idea."

My voice broke just slightly, outlining the jagged edges which remained in my soul, where it had been torn apart by Wesley's diagnosis of poisoning.

"But that wasn't all... that wasn't all the mercury! Until Wesley turned two, he received more and more of this poison in his vaccines: 162.5 micrograms. I shall never recover from the fact that it was I who held down my mercury-sensitive son so that an 'unwitting' pediatrician might inject him with a known neurotoxin more than a 100 times in excess of EPA safety guidelines."

The atmosphere in the Hampton Coliseum was utterly still, solemn, entranced. Those with empathetic hearts had begun to register the pain in my voice with tears upon their cheeks.

"Today, hundreds of children with developmental issues are spilling catastrophic amounts of mercury in diagnostic tests, as courageous physicians and researchers, like those here today, treat them for mercury-poisoning, enabling the blinded to see, the deafened to hear and the silenced to speak.

"Despite their landmark discoveries and research, mercury, at levels not proven to be safe, continues to be administered to our population in the flu shot and other pharmaceuticals, without any appropriate warning. Officially, the Centers for Disease Control tell us that: one in every six—one in every six American children suffers a developmental and/or a behavioral disorder. My brothers and sisters, *it was not always so.*"

No one moved. No one breathed. Rather, they seemed to gasp.

"We must face the fact that we have before us the most neurologically damaged, the most medicated generation of children to ever live. Injecting toxic levels of a known poison into a person, even a pregnant woman or newborn baby, without any informed consent is a violation of that person, a violation of the Federal Food, Drug and Cosmetic Act, a violation of their constitutional rights, and a violation of the Law of God!

"Where secular society has failed, my brothers and sisters, let us succeed and lead with the spirit and the ethic of Christ, that we might protect our children, and children around the globe, from mercury. Now, my beloved United Methodist Church, may you act... for Christ's sake, and the sake of His precious little ones."

I had not spoken to the resolution, so much as preached it, and now the floor was open for debate. Only one man came forward, a pharmaceutical company employee, to suggest that the church take no official stance on the matter but leave it to individual conscience to occasion any action. I was then granted an opportunity to respond.

"With all due respect to the gentleman who has just spoken," I replied, "Individuals like myself have been trying to take action for years and their individual strength is not sufficient to bring systemic change. This is a moral and an ethical issue, and the church must bring its witness and weight to bear that a grave injustice may be stopped."

The unidentified delegate had no further comment to make. I waited for further questions on the toxicology of mercury or on how Wesley had been diagnosed. No other questions, and more importantly, no other opposition came. Instead, a woman named Tonya Douce, her baby in arms, approached the microphone.

"I serve on the Children's Initiative Committee, and if it hadn't been for Lisa and this resolution, I would never have known to protect my child from mercury..." As she spoke, the infant squirmed in her arms. Her lovely statement continued for several moments, and then there was silence.

"Is the house ready to vote?" the Bishop asked.

"Aye."

"All in favor."

"All opposed."

The resolution passed by an overwhelming majority and with such speed that I could not take in what was happening. At last, the victory dawned on me as Boyd reached out a hand to Mark, and said aloud, "Well, that just went through like a freight train." As the vote was recorded, Doug, from the Interfaith Center, whisked us off to eat before the morning session ended so we might be back in time for the press conference.

I did not see the Bishop until just before we entered the room with the reporters. I approached her, aware that my speech on the floor had been extremely intense.

"Bishop," I began, "I'm sorry if I was too dramatic."

"Lisa," she said, placing her arms about my waist and embracing me, "You were magnificent!"

The tears pooled in my eyes, but I fought to keep them from sliding down my cheeks. I needed to be composed, rational, calm. Seated at a table before reporters and between two of the women I most admired in the world, Mary and my Bishop, I was secured as one of a providential circle, which had now come to include even my Bishop. Her words of concern, addressed to the press, for Wesley and for all children injured as he had been, were beautiful and indelible: "The health and the wholeness which we want for Wesley, we want for all children..." Even though the pilgrimage I had just begun would remove me by great expanses from all that which I thought of as familiar or ordinary, I knew the inspiration I gained from this circle would always secure me from fear.

The week after the press conference, Kristen Gelineau of the Associated Press came to visit me at my home. I gave her copies of all my letters to federal officials and their responses dating back to 2000.

When I awoke on June 26, the phone was ringing with calls from all my fellow advocate "mercury moms" from across the country. The story the AP released to papers across the country was entitled, *Debate Over Vaccines, Autism Won't Die*:

"Even if there were a link, proving vaccines cause autism is another matter, said Dr. William Schaffner, a Vanderbilt University professor and longtime government vaccine adviser. '...Scientific issues are not resolved in the courtroom.'

"Sykes has another place in mind.

"When the federal institution will not respond appropriately, take it to the church," she said.

"Two weeks ago, she convinced the Virginia Conference of the United Methodist church—the largest conference in United Methodism—to pass a resolution calling for the removal of mercury from vaccines and all medicines."

CHAPTER EIGHTEEN

THE ONLY WAY FORWARD

When you get into a tight place and everything goes against you,
till it seems as though you could not hang on a minute longer,
never give up then, for that is just the place and time that the tide
will turn.

—Harriet Beecher Stowe

MY FINGERS SEARCHED FOR SECURITY, CURLED TIGHTLY AROUND THE END OF THE
armrest. My feet were firmly planted on the hollow floor of the plane. Just
as I did not understand the physics which held the plane aloft, so I did not
fully comprehend the strength that brought me to this point. I was still,
breathing deeply of a soulful satisfaction. Outside the plane, the world was
immersed in night. The darkness was made darker by a veil of sheer cloud
that obscured the ground below me, even though I strained my eyes trying to
see it. Somewhere between LaGuardia Airport and home, I noticed below me
pinpricks of light piercing the darkness. How many were there? I couldn't
count them. Not many, yet too many to be denied. Small and yet strong, the
lights illumined by the lives of those below defied the abyss in which I was
suspended. "I've found help," I thought to myself.

APRIL 2006

Now, every time Julie Taylor, the Executive Secretary for Children, Youth
and Family Advocacy in the Women's Division, called me, I remembered the

lights I glimpsed from the plane on my trip back from Stamford, Connecticut. There, I met her for the first time and presented the subject of mercury in medicine to the Social Priorities Committee of the Women's Division of the United Methodist Church. Betty Whitehurst, President of the United Methodist Women in Virginia, notified Julie of the new resolution coming from the Virginia Conference, seeking a ban on mercury in medicine, especially vaccines given to pregnant women and children. Julie, in turn, invited me to this gathering.

While there, I presented to some of the most powerful women in my denomination, whose dedication was equaled by their hospitality. Mark and David helped me to assemble all the necessary power point slides, and carrying my presentation in the memory stick around my neck, I was introduced to a circle of women who had energy, intellect and a passionate commitment to social justice. They came to Stamford, Connecticut, from places all over the world: there was Glory Dharmaraj from India, Esmerelda Brown from Panama, and others whose names were too exotic for me to remember. Along with these who had come so far, were representatives from all over the United States. Mary Baldridge, chair of this committee, and Julie Taylor, who greeted me, both lived in Maryland. Present, too, was Carol Gaston, one of the first UMW leaders in Virginia to whom I had ever spoken about the mercury issue. I did not think to warn this lovely gathering of church representatives that my presentation would shatter many of their preconceptions about the supposed safety in which their children and grandchildren lived.

I began by asking those women gathered in the hotel meeting room, "When you take something lethal, and put it in something lifesaving, does that make the lethal thing safe, or the lifesaving thing, lethal?" My question took them aback as I made the connection between mercury, a known poison and carcinogen, and vaccines, heretofore unquestioned medical tools for saving lives. I began, not with science, but experience: pictures of Wesley in seemingly perfect health, and then portraits of him with purple rings under his eyes, red ears, a white pallor, and a blank gaze, narrated by my description of how I had been an unwitting accomplice in the poisoning of my own son. "Even when the delivery system used to administer a poison is a vaccine, a poison is still a poison," I argued.

"Next," I called, waiting for the screen to change from the picture of my direly sick son to a chart showing the cumulative mercury exposure children in the United States had received through the standard immunizations during the 1990's. Kelly Martini, the Communications Chair for the Women's Division, had dutifully been pushing the button on the projector to advance my slides.

"Perhaps," I reasoned, "She didn't hear me." I said it again, "Next." Again, no response. I squinted through the dim light and finally realized she and most of the other women in the room were busy drying the tears cascading down their cheeks. Lisa, I chastised myself, you should have warned them... but how... I wondered, how do you prepare decent, faithful people for the revelation that we have been maiming our children with mercury for years? My heart broke for them, and theirs, for me. An hour later, the women serving on the Justice Priorities Committee unanimously passed the resolution, "Protecting Children from Mercury-containing Drugs," which Julie had modeled on the Virginia resolution.

As the day concluded and exhaustion began to overtake me, one of the women in the group requested that I join her for a meal in the hotel restaurant before I departed to catch my plane at LaGuardia. As we spoke, the deep gratitude in my heart only increased.

"Lisa," said Esmerelda, the Executive Secretary of Global Concerns within the Women's Division, "My neighbor back home has an autistic son. I had no idea. Let me lift something off your shoulders. You know you told us that the high dose mercury vaccines are still being exported to developing countries like mine?"

I nodded.

"Well, I promise you Lisa, we will let them know. I serve here in New York at the United Nations, and I don't want you to worry anymore. We will let the developing world know."

I put my hands to my face, and struggled with a knot in my throat.

Whenever I think of Women's Division now, I always recall the flight home from LaGuardia. All around me, I noticed pinpricks of light piercing the darkness. How many were there? I couldn't count them. Not many, yet too many to be denied. Small in the darkness and yet strong—these women, now enlightened about the danger posed by mercury in medicine, have defied the abyss which surrounded me and my son.

"I've found help," I thought to myself. "All of these women have seen my darkness. They will help."

AUGUST 2006

One of the steadiest, brightest of these lights was Julie. Since the day she invited me to Stamford, she and I had spoken regularly by phone and emailed even more often. An executive in the Women's Division, she was a professional advocate, moving in religious and secular circles of advocates at the national and global levels. In some ways we were so different. My voice often crested in pitch and rhythm with excitement. By contrast, Julie's voice was ever steady. I discerned that her patient, constant, temperate nature gave her longevity in a field that otherwise would burn out its participants. Julie was my elder in age, but not by much. Her intellectual understanding of social reform movements, however, eclipsed mine utterly. These differences were complimentary, though, as we both had a commitment to social justice, faith, and now, a resolve to safeguard children from mercury.

"Lisa, you've passed the first stage when your opponents ignore you, and the second stage when they ridicule you, and now, well, you are becoming a threat."

I sighed, still uncomfortable with the idea that I, a clergywoman who loved to teach preschool children gospel lessons in chapel, could be seen as anyone's adversary. While I did not think of myself as anyone's enemy, I had begun to accept and consider myself a leader, a leader of a nascent faith-based movement to get mercury out of medicine. With the passage of the resolution, the Women's Division had become the first global organization, consisting of nearly one million members worldwide, to share my fight. Eager to move them from statement to action, I made a landmark proposal to Julie not four months after the resolution passed in Stamford.

"Julie, it's been almost seven years since the meeting at Simpsonwood. I think our denomination needs to learn of what happened there and mark the seventh anniversary of that gathering, since it took place on the premises of the United Methodist Church."

"That sounds interesting, Lisa. Can you write up a proposal and send it to me? I will need to present it to the Board for approval."

By the time I received confirmation from Julie that the proposal had become an event which the Women's Division would sponsor, I had thought up its name: "The Truth is Coming to Light." Though no one would realize, these words recalled for me my hopeful trip home from Stamford on the plane. For everyone else, these words were just evocative enough—just theological enough—to suggest hidden truth and revelation and saving grace. Perhaps even hint of justice. And yet, I reasoned, this title was so straightforward that even those who had no faith would understand its import.

"The Truth is Coming to Light" became the first religious teach-in on the danger of mercury-containing medicines. Julie would focus on moderating the educational presentations of this event, and she would delegate to me the responsibility of crafting its times of worship. This privilege also gave me the opportunity to speak pastorally to those whose children had been injured by mercury and prophetically against those who were responsible for maintaining mercury in the drug supply.

The plans for the teach-in were developing beautifully, but one question lingered stubbornly on my mind: how many children might have been saved had those who gathered at Simpsonwood on June 7 and 8, 2000 acted with honesty? How many children had we lost to mercury-induced disability since then? Tens of thousands? Hundreds of thousands? A million? The question haunted me enough that I expanded the proposal. Now, I suggested the teach-in should be followed by a protest outside the gates of the CDC, that this federal agency might know that some within the United Methodist Church had come to understand what transpired at Simpsonwood in 2000 under its leadership.

The pivotal place of Simpsonwood became even more evident than before, when I was given a copy of an e-mail report written by Liz Birt, Counsel for the Government Reform Committee. As the head legal counsel for Congressman Burton's Mercury in Medicine Hearings, Liz had written to Lauren Fuller, Chief Investigative Counsel for the Senate Health, Education, Labor and Pensions (HELP) Committee on July 15, 2005.[1] She did so because the HELP Committee was taking a cursory look at the mercury issue, in part, due to the OSC Project. The document Liz prepared was her attempt to expose the cover-up of Thimerosal's toxicity. Liz did so not only because she was legal counsel for the Government Reform Committee, but also because she was the mother of a child severely damaged by vaccines. Officially and confidentially, she suggested to Senator Mike Enzi and his committee that the following charges, relating to Thimerosal in vaccines, were appropriate:

I. FDA: Criminal Negligence in failure to regulate the safety and effectiveness of biological products

II. HHS, CDC, and FDA: Criminal negligence in failure to regulate and promote vaccines as provided for under the National Vaccine Injury Compensation Program

III. FDA: Criminal negligence in not instituting a Class I recall of all vaccines administered to infants containing thimerosal in July of 1999 and again in June of 2000 when the results of the VSD were discussed at Simpsonwood.

IV. HHS, FDA, CDC and ACIP employees and contractors: Criminal conspiracy to defraud the government by deception or artifice and to obstruct the wholesome administration of the laws and affairs of the United States.

V. HHS, FDA, CDC, and ACIP employees and contractors: Criminal obstruction of justice.

As soon as I read the document, labeled as confidential and "For Senate HELP Staff Use Only," and saw the mention of Simpsonwood at the center of such serious charges, I forwarded it to Julie. I had no doubt it would reach the highest levels of our denomination's leadership, as astonishing and serious as it was. Neither I nor my denomination was accustomed to seeing the name of one of our spiritual retreat centers identified as the site of criminal negligence, obstruction of justice, and possible federal conspiracy.

As I read over the charges yet one more time, I thought, "This protest at the gates of the CDC will be the beginning of redress for such an abuse of the church's premises and hospitality." More confrontational than the teach-in, the protest would be sponsored by my advocacy group, formed for the Citizen Petition, CoMeD, and another group, known for its amazing expertise in rallies and advocacy, Moms Against Mercury (MAM). I knew MAM better as Amy Carson and Angela Medlin, the North Carolina moms who had helped hold aloft Wesley's chelation chart at the 2004 Institute of Medicine meeting. So, by design, the Simpsonwood event had an elegant reciprocity: the parent community would support the church in its teach-in, sharing their experiences and passion, and the Women's Division would support the parents in protest, adding an overt morality and religious affiliation to the protest.

When announcements of the teach-in and "act of public witness," as Julie called the protest, were distributed by the Women's Division through United Methodist Churches across the nation, Julie and the other officers in the Women's Division quickly learned that they had indeed become lights in the darkness. Letters began to arrive from across the nation from mothers of affected children, most of whom were unable to attend church due to their child's disruptive behavior, but whose mother, aunt, neighbor, or pastor had seen the notice for "The Truth is Coming to Light" at church and passed it on to them. Julie began to collect these letters and share them with the board of directors for the Women's Division.

"The stories, Lisa, the stories are just incredible...what these parents have been through...the letters are coming in from all over..."

"This is front-line mission work, Julie," I replied. "You are doing mission work to those who fight despair everyday. To those who, until your notice came out, thought no one knew or cared."

It was just days before the event. I was busy preparing the meditations and prayers for the worship times, when my office phone interrupted my train of thought.

"Hi Lisa."

It was Julie. We had been speaking numerous times a day. "I bet we need to confer on someone who registered late," I thought to myself when I heard her voice.

"Hi, Julie, are things going okay?"

"Yes, details are all falling into place. But I just got a very interesting call, Lisa."

"Who from?"

"ABC News. And they were asking a whole lot of questions about you and your ordination..."

"Are you talking about the national news, Julie, or a local affiliate?"

"Nightline, Lisa. They want to come to the teach-in."

I was glad Julie could not see me biting my lip. With the exception of Kristen Gelineau, the national press had not been good to our cause. Usually, reporters ignored us. When they didn't, they mischaracterized us as emotional anti-vaccine zealots who had no comprehension how deadly infectious diseases were and no studies to back up our concerns about vaccine safety.

"Nightline... national coverage... Why are they focusing on me, Julie?"

"I don't know," Julie replied, matter-of-factly. "I offered to tell them about the resolutions and the work the Women's Division is doing on this issue, but that's not what they were interested in."

I rested my chin in my hand, considering. Was this going to be a blessing or a curse, and why was Nightline so interested in me specifically? Amidst all the excitement in my soul, there was now, also, anxiety.

As Thursday, June 7, arrived, parents of children diagnosed with autism mingled with members of the United Methodist Women in the Chattahoochee Room of Brooks Lodge at Simpsonwood. While the members of the UMW knew almost nothing about autism, they were expert at legislative advocacy for children and at ministering to "the least of these." To these women with great compassion and faith and ability, parents gave first hand accounts of their lives made tragic when their children were poisoned with mercury from vaccines. And to parents, many of whom clung to their faith fiercely for fear that if they let go, both they and their children would be lost, this community of church women brought concern so genuine that those who had given up hope reached out and took hold of it once again.

After I had finished giving morning devotions, we were to begin the first teaching segment of the day. As we began, I prayed again, this time to myself, to whisper my thanks to God for these with such courage that they would risk their careers to declare the truth so clearly. I knew already that truth-telling, in a time of deceit, could be an electrifying experience. Those who had inspired me, now came to educate a community of church women who suddenly understood themselves to be inspired to act as a collective conscience. There could have been no better match in terms of presenters and audience.

Boyd Haley, who had flown in from Kentucky at my request, was in my mind the "Ross Perot" of the anti-mercury movement. Short in stature but firey, Boyd was indignant at the prostitution of science that let children be poisoned in the name of the National Immunization Program, run by the CDC. I knew Boyd would "tell it like it is," and he did so with his very first words. "Those people here in Atlanta who work at the CDC —they're criminals and they belong behind bars. People who hurt children are criminals, and that's just what those at the CDC are doing: hurting children."

Perhaps at first, those from the church reeled at Boyd's accusations, but there were two undeniable qualities about Boyd: his intellect and his honesty.

He had the ability to describe the most complex science with a farm-boy plainness, which these church leaders could understand well. The longer he spoke, the less anyone doubted what he had to say. And when he pulled out his slides to show that the breakdown in the brain of an autistic child, caused by mercury, was identical to the breakdown in the brain of someone with Alzheimer's, there was an audible gasp. The women understood it was not only children who were suffering from mercury-poisoning.

Boyd finished his presentation, and took his seat. The Geiers, scheduled to present after Boyd, now rose from their seats. Since there was a break while they loaded their slides onto the projector, everyone continued to discuss what Boyd had said. During this intermission, the side door to the lecture room opened and a man and a woman, both nicely dressed with video cameras in hand, entered the back of the room. I looked at them and then at Julie, who moved to greet them. Jon Donvan of Nightline, accompanied by a tall, slender brunette, had just arrived.

Realizing they had timed their arrival to coincide with the Geiers' presentation, I became leery of the motives which brought these reporters here. "Oh, no," I thought to myself. "They're here specifically to get footage for an attack on the Geiers, and they want information about me because Wesley is the first child the Geiers have treated with the LUPRON® protocol. They're going to make us out to be reckless. That's why they weren't interested in the church's work on this issue when they spoke with Julie."

Internally, I felt a certain sense of panic register in the quickening of my heartbeat, but David and Mark, now ready to begin their presentation, were absolutely unconcerned by the intrusion of these reporters. For them, this was a common occurrence. So were attacks upon them in the press. Unbothered, they proceeded through a presentation that I had begun to recognize as an old friend. This time, as before with the General Secretary of the General Board of Church and Society, they lingered with a care that was literally painstaking for all those present, on the original Simpsonwood transcript quotes, spoken in this very same place seven years earlier. As they did, a carefully controlled indignation spread through the spirits of parents and the church leaders alike who listened with intensity. As the Geiers finished their presentation, the conversation among the teach-in participants grew noticeably louder. I could hear tones of outrage in some of the voices.

As I surveyed the room, aware that everyone there now understood why we had come to Simpsonwood to mark this anniversary of the CDC's closed-door meeting, I saw Jon Donvan and the woman with him approaching me.

"Reverend Sykes? Hi. I'm Katie Hinman, a producer for ABC. And this is Jon Donvan." They each extended their hand in greeting.

I welcomed them both.

"I think we got the footage we need for today. We are going to film the rally tomorrow at the CDC. What time will you be there?" Her voice was pleasant, and gentle in pitch. I wondered what she was thinking.

"We will be there at 6:30 am, and the press conference will take place at 9:30. Don't you want to stay and listen to the other presentations?" I offered.

"No, thanks. But we'll see you tomorrow at the CDC." Politely, but firmly, Katie declined my offer.

"They're out to get the Geiers," I thought to myself. I tried not to let my misgiving register outwardly, even though I could not quiet it inwardly.

Mary's presentation followed the Geiers'. Her slides included before and after photos, showing the children in her practice who were recovered, recovering, or at the very least, improving with biomedical treatment. Mary showed slides of intricate metabolic pathways in the body, but then distilled them down to a few simple cause-and-effect relationships that everyone could understand. To illustrate what happened when vitamin A deficiencies were at last identified and treated, and when Methyl B12 was added back into the system of a child who has been "autistic", she showed before and after slides of Wesley.

Those watching "oohed" and "aahed," and I could not help piping up happily, "That one—he's mine!" when a picture of Wesley, beaming, the rose back in his cheek, was projected on the screen. Looking at the difference in him due to Mary's and Mark's care, I knew I had received more blessings by the age of forty than most people received in a lifetime. Mary had been one of the first to declare mercury the culprit in autism. Her care for the children in her practice and her medical giftedness and her courage were obvious. As she progressed through her lecture, I could tell those gathered in the room admired her as much as I did.

After lunch, when everyone once again caught their breath, Paul offered a new approach to the criminality which Boyd had already identified. Paul was an analytical chemist by trade, a pharmaceutical regulator by profession, and a fighter by choice. His consulting business, through which he contracted with the pharmaceuticals, had all but dried up due to his efforts to get mercury out of medicine. This did not discourage him in the least. He merely lived as simply as required by his decreasing income and the continuing fight.

He stood at the front of the room, and closed his eyes conspicuously. Speaking loudly, he said to those assembled, "What do I see? With my eyes closed, what do I see?"

"Nothing," came the obvious reply.

Paul continued to close his eyes. "And if I am the FDA and I keep my eyes shut this tightly, what do I see?"

"Nothing," came a resounding chorus. Paul did not speak about chemistry or medicine. Paul told a brilliant story about how more than a hundred years ago, unsafe elixirs and remedies sold to the American public had caused lots of people to die. It was for this reason, he explained, that the government first created an agency to be sure medicinal products were "pure." From purity, the requirement evolved to safety and then guidelines for judging the safety of a given product were developed and standardized. Paul was radiant, and by the end of his presentation, he had affirmed the accusation Boyd had issued so plainly, placing it in the context not only of the CDC but also its superior agencies, the FDA and the Department of Health and Human Services. By failing to "see" the danger of a poison in the nation's drug supply, placed there by the pharmaceuticals and approved by FDA, the federal government was breaking its own laws and protecting, not the public, but the pharmaceutical industry. In short, Paul attested, they had sold out to big business.

The last presentation of the day was Cliff's. Cliff had come to Simpson-wood despite a huge legal caseload. He was highly regarded among the lawyers who represented children in the Vaccine Act, a specialty in law that most avoided because the Act made it difficult for an attorney to be compensated either quickly or adequately for their work. Gregarious with a good sense of humor, Cliff had all the hallmarks of a Southern gentleman.

Like Paul, Cliff had a simple yet unforgettable gesture by which his audience could remember his presentation. He bent his right arm, and put it behind his back.

"I defend children in the no-fault vaccine compensation program, and if I am to fight to get a child compensation for injuries caused by a vaccine, and you tie one arm behind my back, just how easy do you think it's going to be for me to win?"

He feigned punching, as if in a boxing ring, with one arm.

Quickly, as Cliff described more and more of the procedures and dynamics of the Vaccine Court, established by the National Vaccine Injury Compensation Program, the members of the United Methodist Women came to realize the truth of what Cliff was saying. Most vaccine-injured children who develop autism would never have a claim filed, because their parents were unaware of the program with a statute of limitations that extended for only three years from the onset of the child's first symptom. Since fifty percent of children with autism are not diagnosed until they are four and a half years-old on average, the statute of limitations has usually elapsed before a parent even knows their child has autism.

"While there are almost 5,000 cases in the program," Cliff explained, "there are tens of thousands of children, perhaps hundreds of thousands, who missed the window to file. And how many more whose parents still don't know that the program even exists? And even if you do succeed in finding the program and filing within the statute of limitations, those whose cases are eventually heard have only limited chances for success.

"You see, there is a database at the CDC," Cliff continued. "They use it to say there is no link between the mercury in vaccines and autism. Now while they use it in court, saying their studies on the data disprove any association between vaccines and autism, I, as legal counsel for a child harmed by vaccines, cannot have independent scientists examine the same data to verify the CDC's conclusions or to do further studies. Getting independent researchers to go in and look at the data is nearly impossible. Dr. Geier and David are two of the few who have ever gotten any access, and even that has been restricted. So put me in a ring, tie one arm behind my back, and ask me to defend a vaccine injured child... Do you think I have a chance of winning?"

As Cliff finished, Julie thanked the presenters and called upon Dorothy

Edmunds to pray before the evening meal. Dorothy, the Director of the Women's Division from the Atlanta area, rose to her feet and spoke eloquently.

"We women have a song we sing at many of our gatherings. And there is a line in it that is appropriate to repeat today. It says, 'Our eyes have been opened, and there is no going back.' Would you all join me in prayer, as we give thanks for those who have taught us today, and as we pray for the children? It's true, our eyes have been opened and there's no going back."

Medicine, science, government and the courts have failed our children, I thought to myself. But the church will not fail them.

After dinner, I shared scripture and a meditation with those who gathered in the lecture room, and then I called up a handful of parents and church women whom I had asked to stand on either side of me. In closing this service of worship, I was about to do something more provocative than I had ever done before in my ordained ministry. For me, in this moment, the separation between my advocacy and my ordination would be completely gone.

"We gather here, in part, to redress words that were spoken here seven years ago. Because we gather together as the church, in faith, I thought it only fitting to set the words of mortals along side the Word of God, that we might see the disparity between the two, and seek to find healing and justice for those who have been injured by humanity's words and its desire to hide its own human mistakes. Would you listen to the words spoken here at Simpsonwood seven years ago, and the Word of God which we come to speak today."

In turn, each of the lay readers pronounced their assigned quote from the Simpsonwood transcript, and then I followed with a scripture text:

"Dr. Verstraeten, page thirty-one: 'It is sort of interesting that when I first came to the CDC as a NIS officer a year ago only, I didn't really know what I wanted to do, but one of the things I knew I didn't want to do was studies that had to do with toxicology or environmental health. Because I thought it was too much confounding and it's very hard to prove anything in those studies. Now it turns out that other people also thought that this study was not the right thing to do, so what I will present to you is the study that nobody thought we should do.'"

"... you will know the truth, and the truth will make you free. John 8:32"

"Dr. Verstraeten, page forty: '...we have found statistically significant relationships between the exposures and outcomes (that is diagnoses) for these different exposures and outcomes. First, for two months of age, an unspecified developmental delay.... Exposure at three months of age, Tics. Exposure at six months of age, an attention deficit disorder. Exposure at one, three and six months of age, language and speech delays... Exposure at one, three and six months of age, the entire category of neurodevelopmental delays, which includes all of these plus a number of other disorders.'"

"But Jesus said, "Let the little children come to me, and do not stop them, for it is to such as these that the kingdom of heaven belongs..." Matthew 19:14"

"Dr. Weil, page seventy-five: '...if you consider a dose of 25 micrograms (of mercury) on one day, then you are above threshold. At least we think you are, and then you do that over and over to a series of neurons where the toxic effect may be the same set of neurons or the same set of neurologic processes, it is conceivable that the more mercury you get, the more effect you are going to get.'"

"I call heaven and earth to witness against you today that I have set before you life and death, blessings and curses. Choose life so that you and your descendants may live... Deuteronomy 30:17-19"

"Dr. Verstraeten, page 162: 'When I saw this, and I went back through the literature, I was actually stunned by what I saw because I thought it is plausible.'"

"Do not be overcome with evil, but overcome evil with good. Romans 12:21"

"Dr. Johnson, page 198: 'This association leads me to favor a recommendation that infants up to two years-old not be immunized with Thimerosal containing vaccines if suitable alternative preparations are available...My gut feeling? It worries me enough. Forgive this personal comment, but I got called out a eight o'clock for an emergency call and my daughter-in-law delivered a son by C-Section. Our first male in the line of the next generation, and I do not want that grandson to get a Thimerosal containing vaccine until we know better what is going on. It will probably take a long time. In the meantime, and I know there are probably implications for this internationally, but in the meantime I think I want that grandson to only be given Thimerosal-free vaccines.'"

"I myself will be the shepherd of my sheep, and I will make them lie down, says the Lord God. I will seek the lost, and I will bring back the strayed, and I will bind up the injured, and I will strengthen the weak, but the fat and the strong I will destroy. I will feed them with justice. Ezekiel 34: 15-16"

"Dr. Brent, page 229: 'The medical legal findings in this study, causal or not, are horrendous and therefore, it is important that the suggested epidemiological, pharmacokinetic, and animal studies be performed. If an allegation was made that a child's neurobehavioral findings were caused by Thimerosal containing vaccines, you could readily find a junk scientist who would support the claim with "a reasonable degree of certainty". But you will not find a scientist with any integrity who would say the reverse with the data that is available. And that is true. So we are in a bad position from the standpoint of defending any lawsuits if they were initiated and I am concerned.'"

"If we say that we have no sin, we deceive ourselves, and the truth is not in us. I John 1:8"

"Dr. Bernier, page 113: 'We have asked you to keep this information confidential...So we are asking people who have done a great job protecting this information up until now, to continue to do that until the time of the ACIP meeting...That would help all of us to use the machinery that we have in place for considering these data and for arriving at policy recommendations.'"

"Nothing is covered up that will not be uncovered, and nothing secret that will not become known. Therefore whatever you have

said in the dark will be heard in the light, and what you have whispered behind closed doors will be proclaimed from the housetops. Luke 12: 2-3"

Now, I breathed in deeply, and invited everyone to pray with me, leaving a wide breadth of silence into which they could speak the name of their own child or identify whatever or whomever was on their hearts:

"Lord,

The ways of the world are not your ways.

We ask that you would help us to follow in your ways and not those of the world.

Hear us as we petition you whether aloud or in silence:

Almighty God, Defender, Savior, Rock

We pray for ourselves and for those who have invited us here...

We pray for the children, including our own, whom we name, whether aloud or in our hearts...

We pray for courageous leaders, of every field and discipline, who unswervingly seek your truth....

We pray for those who are parents, and especially for those who parent injured or sick or disabled children...

We pray for those who will speak tomorrow, and those who will speak the day after and the day after, about what you have taught us here...

We give thanks for those whom we have met... those who have shared their stories, their strength, their hopes, and their pain...

We pray for the church, and the community of the faithful, and the witness it gives...

We offer these prayers in the Name of the One that saves us. Amen."

Never in my life had the reading of Scripture and the sharing of prayer seemed as powerful as it was this day. As Julie announced the conclusion of "The Truth is Coming to Light," it was in relief that I found tears on my face. Overwhelmed by all that had been said and received during the teach-in, I was unaware of those around me until Julie put her hand on my shoulder.

"Lisa, you aren't on this journey alone anymore."

On Friday, we rose at 4:30 a.m. for breakfast in the cafeteria. Then we boarded a charter bus provided by the Commission on Disabilities of the Virginia Annual Conference and headed for the front gates of the CDC. Lois Dauway, the Interim Deputy General Secretary of the Women's Division, and Tonya Murphy, the President of the North Georgia United Methodist Women joined us there to speak. For the first time, it was not just beleaguered parents or independent scientists but also bold representatives of the Church who spoke passionately to defend children from the administration of mercury at the gates of the federal agency that continued to defend the mercury rather than the children.

Most of the employees ignored us as they drove into the protected complex, but we all had to laugh as one man in a convertible with its top down put up his windows, in a pathetic attempt to silence the sing-song unison refrains of our shouts: "Hey hey, ho ho, the mercury has got to go!" and "Vaccines should be mercury-free!"

And yet, among those driving past us was the occasional CDC employee, arriving at work, who would give us a thumbs-up, or honk in agreement with the slogans on our posters. Most interesting was one employee, a young woman who, upon seeing our signs with our children's pictures, began to cry.

"They know. There's no doubt, they know…" we said to each other.

As promised, Katie and Jon were there, camera in hand, to record all of this. They filmed us as we politely shouted that our children had been poisoned with mercury, and they captured the leaders of the United Methodist Women standing together with me as we sang "We Shall Overcome." As Katie and Jon prepared to leave the rally, Katie gave me her card.

"Lisa, we want to interview you and the Geiers at their home in Maryland in a few days. And we want you to bring Wesley."

"I'll call you and we can talk about this, Katie. I must tell you that my husband and I are pretty protective of our son."

"We really want you to bring Wesley, Lisa. I'll be in touch, so we can confirm dates."

As the reporters left, and we protestors found ice cold bottles of water delivered by the local United Methodist Women, I thought to myself, "After so much good done here these past two days, are we only going to be attacked by the media again?"

Chapter Nineteen

A Higher Court

"I think casuality is very hard to prove. That is a problem for all potential environmental triggers... **So, the issue is really almost one of ideology or religion, more than it is science.** It is the sense that vaccines are critically important. The principle of "herd immunity", the principle of vaccinating everyone, so that you're not only protecting your child but you're protecting the universe of children. That drives vaccine thinking. Because of that, there is a fear on the part of some in the public health community.... if the public hears that any vaccine is associated with any complications....they will stop getting the vaccines. So, I think there is that view...this is challenging something that is just too important to challenge. So....let's not do the science, let's not pursue the studies..."

—Dr. Bernardine Healy, M. D., May 13, 2008,
Former Head of the National Institutes of Health

As I concluded my women's bible study this particular Tuesday evening, everyone started laughing. Even though my cell phone was on manner mode, they could hear its periodic vibrations as it went off repeatedly.

"The scientists want to talk to you, Lisa!" they teased.

David had learned just when my weekly Bible Study was scheduled to

conclude. What he had not yet realized was that the women gathered there
in the church parlor were never quite done talking by nine o'clock.

"Excuse me," I offered to my circle, concerned that the calls did not stop,
as I moved into the hallway.

"Hello?"

"It's good. It's really good." Even without the usual greeting, I knew it
was David.

"What's good, David?"

"The Nightline report that's coming on tonight. They just posted it on
the web and it's really good."

As I squealed, everyone in the parlor looked my direction.

I had been so careful when I spoke to Katie and Jon in front of the camera
at the Geiers' home more than a week ago. My initial caution only increased
when I asked Katie what the storyline was and she replied that Nightline
wanted to cover how "polarized"—a word I read as "unreasonable"—the
two sides had become in the debate over autism and vaccines.

"I see you are wearing a cross. I know you are an ordained minister.
In that context then, Lisa, who would you say is evil in all of this?" Jon had
asked me, camera rolling.

"That's not mine to say, Jon. I will tell you that clearly there is systemic
evil. How can you inject poison into millions of children without informed
consent and not say that is evil?"

"Lisa, did you let the Geiers experiment on your son?"

I gulped. This is exactly the type of question I had expected and feared.

"Of course not, Jon. The Geiers treated my son for a high testosterone
level. It was an approved medical drug. With it, he has improved immensely."

For an hour and a half, Jon asked me questions. For an hour and a half,
I paused before answering each question, selecting my words with the greatest of care.

Just after I had left the Geiers' home that afternoon, Katie looked at
Mark and David and said, "You know, we didn't get what we wanted from
her."

Back in Richmond by evening, I was overjoyed when the Geiers reported that to me. Katie and Jon had taken even longer with Mark and David, going into careful detail about the LUPRON® protocol, the evidence of conspiracy, the toxicity of Thimerosal.

Well into the afternoon, they would learn from Jon that his older brother was autistic. That helped me to understand the parting comment he had made to me: "If you are right about mercury causing autism, Lisa, I'm going to have to rewrite the book I'm working on."

Though these preeminent reporters had not shown it that afternoon, clearly they had become convinced, or at least fascinated, by our arguments, because the story they aired late Tuesday night after my Bible study was a rare and huge media victory for our side of the debate. The segment aired that night did not make Mark, David or myself out to be lunatics. Instead, it pondered aloud whether the Geiers were "Scientific Saviors or False Hope." They showed footage of Wesley cuddled up with me on the Geier's couch, his eyes bright and aware. The footage of Mark and David recounted their discovery about high testosterone in autism and their medical and epidemiological studies which showed mercury was the cause of the autism epidemic. More astounding yet, on the Nightline website, Katie and Jon provided additional footage from Mark and David's interview, enabling the Geiers to tell a waiting audience the spurious history and science behind Thimerosal, to review in great detail evidence of a conspiracy, and to defend their academic standing. The Geiers, unintimidated by the media, told Katie and Jon exactly what we knew to be true and by some great godsend, it seemed that these reporters understood.

Within the day, the story site, which for an ordinary segment would get a dozen comments, had 431 posts on the website.

"I don't believe it!" was all I could say, as I read the story and eagerly waited for its broadcast that evening.

The Nightline broadcast also announced to the world something I had not revealed, except to my closest friends and my superiors in the church.

"That's right..." pronounced Jon's voice on Nightline. "Lisa Sykes is a reverend, a United Methodist minister, and she is suing the pharmaceutical companies for twenty million dollars..." This was the meticulous estimate arrived at by Wesley's life planner for what his care, over a lifetime, would cost if his recovery did not progress any further.

"Well," I noted to myself, "There's no need to keep news of the lawsuit quiet any longer!" Because Wesley's case was so strong, in medical documentation and expert care, Cliff had formed a coalition of several large law firms to take it to federal court. Federal court promised to be more of a challenge than state court and far more challenging than Vaccine Court. If we could get Wesley's case properly before a sympathetic federal judge, that judge could issue subpoenas for the Vaccine Safety Database and high federal officials, an option not avilable to a state judge and not permitted by the Vaccine Court.

I did not have to debate the issue, nor did Seth. "We want to conduct this case for all the kids, Cliff, and not just for Wesley. If we have a better shot at bringing reforms in federal court, then go to federal court, even if it will be harder."

Harder, I learned, due to the fact that appointments to the federal bench would likely be more easily influenced by elected officials and current policies, both of which favored protecting Thimerosal rather than the children. Though the Vaccine Act clearly stated that a case filed there could be removed on the 240th day and taken to civil court if no action on the case had been forthcoming, Judge Lawrence F. Stengel, in his ruling from the Eastern Pennsylvania Federal Court, had slammed us so hard legally that we could barely see straight afterward. He ruled that the pharmaceutical companies which had manufactured the mercury-containing vaccines given to Wesley were completely protected under federal law from claims of "defect design" and "failure to warn," both relating to the use of mercury in the vaccines and the lack of informed consent given to me. In his opinion, FDA approval guaranteed the shots were safe, even if they contained inordinate amounts of mercury.

There was a final charge, however, and a gutsy one, too: fraud, fraud by these huge pharmaceutical companies for knowingly marketing an unsound, unsafe product. While Judge Stengel reviewed this charge cursorily, he found that we lacked evidence to prove fraud and was not predisposed to grant us "discovery," the legal opportunity to demand documents and depositions from the other side to gather information to support this charge. The case was dead, or so I thought.

"It's bad. It's really bad, Lisa," said David. "The judge killed as much of the lawsuit as he could. All that's left is the claim against the pharmaceutical company that manufactured your Rho(D) shot, and he's sent that case back to the federal court in Eastern Virginia, which is notoriously bad for product liability cases. You're through legally."

Seth and I had accepted this fate, as had all the parents who had been bold enough to try a similar strategy before us. The case was dead. There was nothing we could do. Until someone was fortunate enough to get a sympathetic judge who was not pro-industry, this legal wreckage of cases cast out of court would continue. Cliff would not initiate any action on Wesley's Rho(D) case, as he expected certain defeat if he did. So, with Wesley's Rho(D) case still upon the books, dormant, I turned my attention elsewhere.

"'The Truth is Coming to Light' was a powerful beginning to our advocacy, Lisa," Julie said.

We were reviewing the comments from the event and speaking of the intensity that had been in the room as the church gathered with parents to examine the issue.

"Julie, Beth Fields in the Western North Carolina Conference just got the resolution passed there, too. That's three conferences now as well as the Women's Division, all on record against giving kids mercury in their medicines!"

"We are making a lot of progress, Lisa."

"But I want more, Julie. The urgency in this issue is like no other, at least in my judgment. I've been thinking that we need not just the women of the church but the whole church on board."

"What are you proposing, Lisa?"

"I was wondering if perhaps the Women's Division would submit the resolution on 'Protecting Children from Mercury-containing Drugs' to the General Conference?" This single global decision-making body for the entire denomination of 11.5 million United Methodists convenes only once every four years, and it would gather in Fort Worth, Texas, at the end of April 2008.

There was a thoughtful silence on the phone. Then, after carefully considering what I had said, Julie replied, "I will talk to our board members about this, Lisa. It's possible that we could do that."

In requesting this of the Women's Division, I was seeking landmark action on the part of the United Methodist Women. Had the teach-in and rally in Georgia provided the Women's Division with enough information, enough conviction to stake their fine reputation, which included distinguished leadership on historic issues such as abolition, suffrage, temperance, child labor, and civil rights, on an urgent issue of public health which remained enigmatic and controversial in the contemporary press? Would the Women's Division lead the United Methodist Church to be the first global denomination to decry putting mercury in medicine?

As I waited for news from the Women's Division, Cliff was the one who called with unexpected news. It was late January, and Lent was about to begin unusually early.

"Lisa, the pharmaceutical company that made your Rho(D) shot has motioned for the case to be dismissed. We are going to need to appear in court, and I want you to bring the whole family."

I felt as thought someone had knocked the wind out of me. When I finally spoke it was the simplest question on my mind for which I first found words.

"You want Wesley there, Cliff?"

"Yes, him especially... Adam and Joshua as well..."

"When will this be, Cliff?"

"February 5."

I looked at my calendar and smiled: Shrove Tuesday! What was it about the Holy Season of Lent that always brought such significant developments in the war on mercury?

"Who is the judge, Cliff?"

"His name is James Randolph Spencer, Lisa."

I spent the late hours of that evening googling: "James Randolph Spencer Federal Court Eastern Virginia." When I discovered his biography, I was astounded. "J.D. ...Phi Beta Kappa... Harvard...."

With the next words, my heart almost stopped: "Masters of Divinity, Howard University."

"A ministry degree?" I said aloud to myself. "Judge Spencer attained a Masters degree in Divinity like me?"

I continued, now so excited to think that we might have at least a prayer of success, that I summoned Seth and read the biography out loud to him.

"Seth, it says he was taught by his family to value honesty, integrity and the love of God.... an attorney that entered law because of the Civil Rights Movement. He went into law, it says, 'to punish the wrongdoer...' This judge is a gift, Seth. He is a gift to us, straight from God."

On a pleasant winter day, Seth, the boys, I and my mother arrived at the federal courthouse in Richmond and, passing by, I realized it was right beside the building which housed the office of the Virginia Attorney General.

As we walked along the sidewalk, Seth and I took great pride in all three of our sons, each dressed in suit and tie. Adam walked beside me, Wesley linked arms with his dad, and Joshua chattered happily to his grandmother. "Granna" had agreed to come in order to keep her adoring and youngest grandson happily occupied in the courtroom. Once inside the federal building and through security, we took the elevator to the third floor where we entered a beautiful wood paneled room with a rich red carpet. Between its décor and our attire, I felt as though I had come to church. As I glanced around, this federal courtroom seemed oddly familiar.

"Seth, isn't this the place where you were sworn in as a citizen?" I asked.

"I think so," said my Scottish-born husband. "I never expected to be here again."

Under my arm were coloring books which I gave to Joshua as he sat between my mom and Seth in the courtroom. Wesley snuggled under Seth's arm, comforted and secured by his father's embrace in a strange place. Wesley required no words to convey to those gathered what a gentle spirit he had. As I looked at Wesley, I could not help thinking how extraordinarily beautiful he was. Next to him, I sat down on the bench that reminded me in every way of a church pew. On the other side of me, fascinated by the working of government, was my fourteen year-old son, Adam, who never could understand, though I had tried to explain it to him, how a company could put poison in a baby shot. Finally, seated beside Adam was Cliff, who had been waiting for us while reviewing the copious notes that adorned his legal pad.

"It looks like family week," said the court reporter to Cliff, glancing at all of us. As a number of well-dressed professionals entered the room, Cliff was very intentional to introduce Seth and me to them—three men and a woman. Only after I shook their hands did I realize these were the attorneys for the pharmaceutical companies who had flown hundreds of miles to argue against us before the judge.

"This is all strangely polite," I thought to myself.

"All rise," heralded the officer in the courtroom.

Seth, Mom, and I rose to our feet and then prompted the children to do the same. As Judge Spencer entered the room all was quiet and completely still until he took his seat. I quickly realized the photo of him that I had seen on the internet was many years old. It had portrayed a man in his midlife, but I guessed that the judge before us now was a grandfather in all likelihood. I glance at Judge Spencer only briefly and afterward trained my focus on the lawyers as they came forward to make their arguments.

"In the matter of Sykes v. ..." announced the officer of the court.

The case was entered into the minutes, and lawyers for the pharmaceutical company were given the floor.

"Judge, we know that Thimerosal was considered by the 2004 Institute of Medicine and shown to have no association with autism. In fact, it remains in the flu shot and other products given to pregnant women and children in this country everyday, and the FDA has not seen fit to recall it..."

I stifled my urge to choke out loud. "Why in the world would a lawyer for the pharmaceutical company we were suing use this logic?" I asked myself. If anything, he had only increased the urgency of Wesley's case as a public health issue. In addition, I knew, when Cliff took the floor, he would dispatch the 2004 IOM decision without question.

In contrast to the legal dramas I had watched on television, the courtroom drama playing out before my eyes seemed rather unpolished and inept. I found the lawyers for the pharmaceutical company unimpressive and their arguments riddled with flaws. Of course, I observed everything they said and did through the adamancy of my conviction that mercury had poisoned my son.

As Cliff rose to speak, I prayed silently to myself for him and his words. His presence in the courtroom was remarkable. Cliff was affable yet clearly bright and concise, able to digest words and thoughts quickly and then extract the logic in them with unusual clarity.

"Judge, we can show that the 2004 IOM was compromised, and I might add that its conclusions do not bear on mercury in the Rho(D) shot my client received, but only on mercury in childhood vaccines. We know that the company did not safety test the Rho(D) drug given to Ms. Sykes for safety in pregnancy. In fact, in 1995, it was listed as a class C drug in the Physician's Desk Reference, meaning it had never been tested for safety in pregnant women! As such, this product should never have been administered to Ms. Sykes, except under extreme and extraordinary circumstances. Wesley Sykes should never have been exposed in utero to this known neurotoxin."

I had not expected that I would need to stifle tears, but now I did. Cliff was truth-telling before the judge, even as he had before the United Methodist Women and the parents of autistic children who gathered at Simpsonwood. I wiped away my ambitious tears before they aspired to turn into a torrent.

"Judge, mercury from products like the one Ms. Sykes received is causally related to the autism epidemic. We can show that this product has been marketed illegally. The use of Thimerosal in medicine is clearly fraud. It has never undergone modern safety tests, and when it was given to twenty-two meningitis patients in 1929, they all died. We can demonstrate the adverse events associated with Thimerosal, particularly if you will let us subpoena the Vaccine Safety Datalink database. This court has the power to do that..."

Cliff's voice had risen and with it, so had my hopes. Cliff was challenging the judge to use the power of his federal position and the federal court to clean house at the CDC. It was breathtaking.

The judge listened intently to Cliff as he had the other lawyers, without moving. I tried not to look at Judge Spencer for too long, afraid that he would think I was staring. The power he wielded, however, was mesmerizing.

Cliff continued to intensify his rhetoric. "We do not agree with Judge Stengel that the vaccines are protected by the Act in a case such as this, likely involving fraud. I do not begin to presume, Your Honor, that you would add those vaccine manufacturers into this case, but if you did see fit to do so..."

"Cliff," I shouted inside my head, "You are amazing..." He was hinting to this judge that he might reverse the ruling of the judge in Pennsylvania! "Gutsy, Cliff, really, really gutsy!"

Oral arguments concluded, and we all rose to our feet as the judge rose to leave the courtroom. He had said virtually nothing during the hour we occupied our places there. Now we would wait, but not very long.

Why did I not expect the call as the very first week in Lent ended? It was in keeping with our having graced the federal courtroom on Shrove Tuesday, afterall.

When Cliff called, he was very matter of fact and tremendously modest. "We have won standing. The trial date is set for July 14, Lisa, and will take two weeks..."

After this unexpected revelation, I did not take in anything else Cliff had to say. Wesley's case regarding the mercury in the Rho(D) shot administered to me in pregnancy, which had been sent from Pennsylvania to Virginia, and presumed by all accounts to be dead, had been resurrected, resurrected because of the pharmaceutical company initiating legal action and not we ourselves. Their motion to dismiss had backfired. Cliff had argued and won standing for Wesley in Virginia before a judge whom I felt in my heart was a good judge, a judge who would give Wesley and, through Wesley, all of the children a fair hearing, a just hearing, for the first time.

Neither Seth nor I yet understood what being the lead case in federal court would mean for us nor what it would demand of us.

As Lent progressed, the global gathering of the General Conference of the United Methodist Church neared. As the Conference approached, so did the deadline to submit resolutions for consideration.

"Lisa, we're going to submit the resolution to General Conference." Julie told me, already aware of the excitement this would create in my soul. "Will you draft it as soon as possible? It doesn't need to be as long as the Virginia resolution, but we probably do want it to be slightly longer than the one passed by the Women's Division."

"Oh, Julie, what good news! I'll ask Mark, David and Paul to help, and we will turn it around to you within the week. And I have something else to tell you also. It's about Wesley's case..."

From that point on, the days were merely a blur. I crafted the resolution, even as I answered, in writing, litanies of questions officially issued to me by the pharmaceutical company. Each set of questions was an "interrogatory" and in answering them, I was bound with the same authority as if I were under oath.

"List every physician you or anyone in your family ever saw and explain why..."

"List every pharmacy you or anyone in your family ever used and what prescription was filled there..."

"List everyone who has ever discussed with you that the mercury in Wesley's Rho(D) shot could have contributed to his autism..."

After compiling page after page of information for the pharmaceutical's lawyers, creating the proposed resolution for General Conference was a delight and a joy.

"I want to keep many of the introductory 'whereas' statements, just as in the Virginia resolution," I had told my team of scientists. "But what if we up the ante a little?"

"How?"

"What if we make a part of this resolution that the United Methodist missions, clinics and hospitals around the world will all express a preference for mercury-free pharmaceuticals? If we do, and it passes, then we begin to challenge the assumptions of vaccine manufacturers and the World Health Organization, that they can distribute mercury-containing vaccines without hindrance, whether here or abroad."

"You can do more than that, Lisa," David replied to me. "Why don't we add a challenge at the end of the resolution to other suppliers of vaccines to the world: organizations like the Bill and Melinda Gates Foundation and the Global Alliance for Vaccines and Immunization and Rotary, to follow the lead of the United Methodist Church by also expressing the same preference?"

"I love it! David, write it for me, and let me incorporate it into what we've already done."

After endless revisions, the resolution was completed. It was educational, concise and powerful and reached further than any of the other United Methodist resolutions on the issue because it called the health ministries of my denomination to buy mercury-free whenever possible, and to challenge others to do the same:

And be it further resolved:

That, until mercury is banned from medicine, the medical missions and ministries of the United Methodist Church shall state a preference for mercury-free vaccines over mercury-containing ones and shall communicate this preference to the: Global Alliance for Vaccines and Immunizations, United Nations Children's Fund (UNICEF), Rotary International, and the Bill and Melinda Gates Foundation as well as any other organization from which vaccines are purchased.

I told my small team of scientists, all co-authors of the resolution, "Until this gets voted on, I don't want anyone to know its coming. Not the parents, not the researchers. Nobody. I don't want pharma to hear and have time to derail it. What we stand to gain here is too great to risk anyone's discretion but our own."

Easter had arrived boldly in mid-March. One week later, I was taking in a panoramic view of Richmond's spring from the twentieth floor of a downtown high rise. The flowers were all coming out, and you could see the trees in bloom along the James River, just below. I would have begrudged anyone their request for me to be confined indoors for the first two days of spring's arrival, had it been for any other reason.

I looked to my right. Cliff sat there, beside a court reporter. Both were busy typing on their laptops. I sat at the head of the longest conference table I had ever seen, as a video camera was trained on me and a microphone secured to my lapel.

When I glanced left, I noticed more than a dozen cardboard boxes, each full of manila files. Each file was neatly labeled and contained a selection of papers inside it.

Introductions were made on the record as the video recorded, and then the court reporter looked at me and asked me to raise my right hand.

"Do you swear to tell the truth, the whole truth, and nothing but the truth, "This has to be a dream... wait, no... a nightmare..." I thought to myself.

"I do."

With that, I was on record: "Here begins videotape Number One in the deposition of Lisa Sykes in the matter of Sykes versus Bayer Corporation, filed in the United States District Court for Eastern District of Virginia Richmond Division...Today's date is March 26, 2008. Time on the video monitor is 9:08 am." [1]

I breathed deeply. My goal was to stay calm and level-headed.

A gentleman to my left, a lawyer for the pharmaceutical company, reached down and pulled out one of the files, scanning it at an angle that made it impossible for me to see. He studied the paper before him for some seconds before he finally lifted his gaze to look at me.

"When did—when and how did you become a leader in the movement, Ms. Sykes?"

The lawyer would not address me as "Reverend" no matter the collar I wore and the large cross that hung about my neck. A second lawyer seated further away from me did not speak to or even look at me, but merely whispered in the ear of the first. I answered his question with a question, intent on not misstepping.

"Among the parents or in the church, because they are two different answers…"

"Let's do both. Among the parents first."

I waited until the words accumulated in my mind. "…I became a leader among the parents in 2004, when I began the Office of Special Counsel Project."

"…I've tried to learn things about you, given your prominence in the movement…what you're all about. And the book…"

I knew he was referring to *Evidence of Harm* by New York Times journalist, David Kirby, which had sections devoted to narrating my efforts.

"…at least, says that you ended up with five names of federal employees that you supplied to Mr. Bloch's office."

Slowly, carefully, I corrected him: "That's not completely accurate. We were not supplying names to Bloch's office because they were adamant they didn't conduct investigations. We sought people to call them or contact them as whistle blowers."

The lawyer looked me in the eye. "Who are these people?"

It was time to try his nerves. I sat up very straight in my chair and answered: "When I spoke to these people, I always did so in a pastoral confidence. I identified myself as Reverend Lisa Sykes and told them that our conversation would occur within the bounds of pastoral confidentiality… and I don't feel comfortable right now breaching that."

The lawyer was clearly annoyed but he contained it in the lines upon his brow.

"So you are refusing to answer the question."

Cliff chimed in to my relief, backing me up.

"That's correct."

The silence that hung in the room became heavier.

"But you told them, when you spoke to these individuals, that you were calling them as a minister?"

"Yes."

"So in that sense, this is part of the religious movement that you referred to earlier, and not a parent movement."

I tried my best to explain: "I'm an ordained minister functioning as one of the leaders, of many leaders amongst a parent community that wants change. And I do bring some unique characteristics because I'm clergy."

Perhaps bored now of my banter on this subject, the lawyers changed the direction of their questions. They began to assail the physicians treating Wesley, and the use of LUPRON® to lower his testosterone level.

"Now, did you know—you know that Dr. Geier was not a pediatric endocrinologist, correct, before this treatment was given?"

"Yes."

"And did you also know that Dr. Megson was not a pediatric endocrinologist before you signed the release and he got the first treatment?"

"I'm aware of Mary's specialty as a developmental pediatrician—not a pediatric endocrinologist…"

"Was that an important thing to you, as the parent of a child who is being given treatment for which you were being asked to give a release of legal liability…"

I knew the lawyer had placed before me a question which would condemn me if I answered either "yes" or "no."

"…Mary made a breakthrough in Vitamin A therapy. It was very clear she had capabilities, qualities, and credentials. I found the same to be true of Dr. Geier… both these physicians were able to predict things about my child that were borne out by laboratory tests. That is brilliance… And what we have seen from treatment shows that it's very appropriate…"

During the hours, punctuated only by fifteen minute breaks and lunch, the lawyer would insinuate I was a conspiracy theorist, that I misrepresented Wesley's condition to a variety of people—Seth, Mary, the public school system he attended—and that all my careful observations about my son were wrong. Only once did the lawyer speaking receive what I said about Wesley without questioning it.

"When did Wesley begin to read?"

I responded carefully, despite my pride in Wesley's accomplishments.

"I typed to him last week because I wanted to know that too. I said, 'Wesley when did you learn to read?' And what we got back was, 'I started to read last year.'"

For the only time during the two day deposition, at these words, the lawyer seemed elated.

"Well, that's fantastic. Congratulations. That's great. I know you are very pleased. And I guess this has an impact on what you think Wesley's life can develop into, correct?"

I knew already what the lawyer was doing—trying to minimize any settlement, should we win, by depicting Wesley's condition as less severe and his future as less impaired than it currently was.

"I hope so," was all I chose to say in response, but the lawyer continued: "That's awesome...So there is—you, as a parent, have hope he will actually improve at a much faster rate that he has already done...?"

My heart broke, to have a disingenuous lawyer talking so about Wesley's future. "I hope he will improve. There are still huge deficits."

The day continued on monotonously. I thanked God quietly I had not become a lawyer, especially a corporate one.

"Ms. Sykes, do you contend that there is a conspiracy between the CDC and others with regard to the vaccine program and Thimerosal?"

I breathed in deeply, knowing I would seem delusional before a jury should we get that far.

"I have used the term 'criminal conspiracy' in regard to certain members of national health agencies not being forthcoming about the danger of mercury used in the drug supply and the damages caused."

"And that's your belief," the lawyer followed up, eagerly.

"I do. I do believe so. Yes."

There, I had said it. I knew it left me vulnerable, and so did the lawyer before me.

"And who—who do you think is engaged in criminal conspiracy activity?"

I tried to answer his question without seeming a madwoman.

"Those who, by their offices, have responsibility for drug safety and vaccine safety."

"Would you give me just one name or one office?"

Remembering I spoke as a minister as well as a mom, I sought to be reserved and careful. "...I prefer to let the system judge, and of course, it hasn't; the system, the oversight agencies, judge who is responsible."

The lawyer circled around mentally, and approached again.

"My question to you is who is involved, to your knowledge, either by name or by office held, in a criminal conspiracy?"

I could avoid the eventuality no longer. I had to be specific.

"I think there's a meeting on record of concern where members of, not the whole, but members of FDA and CDC, along with industry executives, attended at Simpsonwood in 2000, that if not conspiratorial, was collusive in what happened at that meeting."

The lawyer let me continue.

"I think there are federal officials who have failed to fulfill their obligation to protect the public... I do believe there's a known neurotoxin in the drug supply, and it's there, and its presence there is very questionable under regulations and American laws."

The lawyer was enjoying his pursuit of my status as a conspiracy theorist.

"Now, let me suggest some names... Dr. Marie McCormick. Do you put her in that criminal conspiracy?"

No longer on the floor of the IOM, still I was sparring with Dr. McCormick.

"Yes, I think she has knowledge and I think the closed door transcripts prior to the 2004 IOM meeting are of concern... there's a statement that they won't set policy in a re-call or such action by the IOM. Causality, causation would be setting policy, so they're not going to do it."

"But you think that's criminal?"

His question seemed more ludicrous than the delusional attribution I sought to avoid. My voice grew stronger and more defiant.

"If it is endangering human lives, American lives, I do think there is something absolutely criminal about having a neurotoxin in the drug supply and keeping it there and letting it be administered with no informed consent."

There was a laundry list of federal officials yet to be named. Worried how my comments might be perceived, I used the lifeline Cliff had given me before we entered: "Lisa if you get stuck and don't know what to do, ask for a break and meet me by the bathrooms at the other end of the hall."

"I think I need a break…"

The lawyer was not surprised.

Reluctantly, he replied, "If you… if that's what you ask for, we'll take a break."

"Going off the record at…" The court reporter once again read the time into the record.

As I walked down the hall and past the receptionist, she looked at me sympathetically. "You doing okay?"

"Yes, I am. Thank you." Just past her desk, in the dim end of hallway, I found Cliff.

"What do I do, Cliff? They want names. They're going to make me look as if I'm neurotic…"

"You know, Lisa, you're not an expert witness. You are just the parent of an injured child. If you think someone is part of this cover-up then go ahead and name them."

I looked at Cliff, beseechingly. This was not the advice I had wanted.

"Okay," I replied, resigned, as I sarcastically declared to myself: "A United Methodist minister names high federal officials for conspiracy! How nice!"

I returned to the meeting room with the long conference table to be greeted by: "And we are back on the record at…" the court reporter read in the time.

And it began again: "Do you allege that Dr. Gerberding at the CDC is involved in this criminal or collusive conduct?"

Okay, I thought, Cliff said to play ball, so here goes…

"I'd have to say yes because she brought the function of vaccine safety directly under her control…"

When I left at the end of that first day, I was relieved about one thing. I called Seth on the way home. "No mention of the General Conference resolution, Seth!" I said joyously. I hope they don't find out about it. The next day, that heartfelt hope was dashed with one of the first questions of the morning.

"And you are presenting a resolution to the General Conference of the United Methodist Church? Do I have that correct?"

"Damn," I said silently to myself, crushed that this lawyer from Alabama had discovered my most closely guarded secret. If he wanted to inquire about my church, I would answer, exactingly.

"No I am not." It was the truth. I would not be presenting the resolution.

"Okay," he responded, catching my game of details. "Somebody that you have been talking or working with is presenting such a resolution to the—to your church general conference?"

I couldn't avoid affirming it now.

"Yes."

"You're involved in that effort?"

"Yes." I felt as though he was accusing me of being embroiled in a terrorist plot.

"And do you think that's an appropriate thing for a church to do when there are federal agencies and even congress, congressional committees that have great competence in the field of science and regulation?"

"This isn't only a matter of science," I almost preached. "It's a matter of ethic, and I think while certain agencies may have greater scientific skill, what we're finding is that the ethic in secular government has failed to protect children and others from harm done by mercury. So the church has grounds to act."

He tried to shake my confidence.

"But the ethical decision is based upon scientific evidence...?"

"Yes."

"...And so how is it that you think the church is competent in a professional sense to make a judgment about ethics... that is based on science or scientific judgment about evidence."

I answered coolly and assuredly: "The church has throughout the history made ethical decisions on secular science."

He surrendered at last. "Well, no doubt, the church has made ethical—taken ethical positions. I agree with that."

He changed the subject quickly.

When my two exhausting days of depositions were over, I called Julie.

"Julie, they know all about the resolution coming before General Conference. Watch carefully, and let me know immediately if you sense any interference."

As the demands for written interrogatories from me increased, as the pharmaceutical company issued subpoenas for every doctor Wesley had ever seen, as Cliff began to negotiate discovery requests with the unyielding bureaucracies of the FDA and the CDC, General Conference came closer and closer. Its theme, "A Future with Hope", was not chance in my thinking. Ironically, neither Julie nor I would attend. There was no way to tell what day of the nearly two-week-long conference the resolution would be presented. So, we both waited expectantly for word from Fort Worth.

On a Sunday afternoon at the end of April as I drove home from church, the Reverend Mary Beth Blinn, a District Superintendent from the Virginia Conference and a former missionary to Red Bird Mission, Kentucky, called me with a precious first update.

"Lisa, the resolution has passed unanimously out of the committee on the God's Nurturing Community. I understand from Martha Stokes who is on that committee that no one even had any questions about it!"

"Mary Beth, that is incredible! Do the delegates down there realize how controversial this is?"

"That doesn't seem to be an issue, Lisa. This is not a controversial topic down here."

After eight years of struggle, I thought to myself, I have finally found the door through which to move this issue. And that door is the Church. The Church doesn't add up liability or calculate the loss in corporate profits when judging the mercury issue. The Church is counting only one thing: the children. Here, if no where else institutionally, the children are important. They are priceless... they are not to be poisoned!

My euphoria was etched in sorrow. Wesley's blue eyes were staring at me from within my own soul. I knew clearly that my mammoth efforts now to save all children from mercury were, in a tragic, constructive way, motivated by my realization that I had not been able to save my own son.

"Mary Beth, thank you so much for letting me know," I said, returning to the world at hand. "I pray the momentum continues. If it does, this General Conference will make history!"

Cliff was in town. The day of my obstetrician's deposition had arrived.

When the judge had first ruled in our favor, denying the pharmaceutical company's motion to dismiss, I had gone to see the obstetrician who delivered both Adam and Wesley. I told the receptionist very specifically that I wanted to make a non-medical appointment to speak with her about a private matter. Despite what I said, I was shown into an examination room when I arrived.

"I'm just going to take your blood pressure," said the nurse upon entering the exam room in which I had been located.

"No, you're not," I said politely but firmly. "I'm not here for a medical visit."

The nurse looked confused, made one more unsuccessful plea, and then finally said, "I will tell the doctor that you refused."

"Fine," I replied, trying to contain my exasperation.

After some minutes, the obstetrician entered the room.

"Well, Lisa," she said in her rolling, jovial voice, "Howareya?"

I smiled. "I am fine, but I am here to talk with you about my second son, Wesley."

"Is he the one diagnosed with autism?"

"Yes. I've brought you some articles relating to that," I said as I proffered her copies of the Office of Special Counsel Press release, a United Methodist News Service article on my advocacy, and the lab showing Wesley's mercury level running off the page.

"Well, Lisa, look at you! You've become quite an advocate."

"I have. I'm seeking to get mercury in medicine banned and recalled. Do you know what Thimerosal is?"

"I think so. That's the mercury-based preservative that was removed from vaccines in the late 1990's right?"

"Well, it wasn't all removed. If you are giving women in this practice a flu shot during pregnancy, you are probably still exposing them and their unborn children to 25 micrograms of mercury through that vaccine. Thimerosal is associated with birth defects, mental retardation, and gross motor difficulties."

She weighed my words carefully and quietly.

"Do you know where else mercury was found in medicine, in the mid 1990's?" I asked poignantly.

She stared, blankly, and moved her head, almost imperceptibly, from side to side.

"Wesley's first hit with mercury came from the Rho(D) shot you gave me at twenty-eight weeks. My patient records show that the brand shot I received contained the maximum amount of mercury of any product on the market."

Her demeanor changed suddenly. She was more tense now, and began taking careful and copious notes on her laptop.

I continued, "Mercury in pharmaceutical products is responsible for autism, ADD, and ADHD. It's never been proven safe. I've been called to stop its administration, and I'm pursuing that right now. Wesley has a case in federal court and the trial date is coming up quickly."

"When is that date, Lisa?" she now asked solemnly.

"July 14. The Federal Court for Eastern Virginia. I am not out to be adversarial with you in any way. I just want to get the mercury out. I don't want any more kids to be hurt as Wesley has been."

I could see the obstetrician was uncomfortable now, both because she realized that this litigation would involve her, and also because she had stayed much longer than her allotted few minutes in this particular examination room with me. Her caseload was backing up.

"Lisa," she replied in a very noncommittal way, "You know, I don't know if what you are telling me is accurate. I'm going to have to research this some. For all I know, you may have your facts confused."

The line sounded like it had been coached, a stock reply given to any patient who raised legal issues.

"I hope you will research this, because this issue bears directly upon the way you practice medicine. This is a tremendous ethical issue..."

"Okay, Lisa," she said, rising to leave the room.

As I moved pass the nurses station toward the door, the OB uncharacteristically yelled past another patient to me, "You are overdue for your pap smear, Lisa! I've checked the chart. Don't let that go."

Her last comment rankled in my mind. It seemed a poor attempt to re-establish her authority over me in all things medical.

What was that? I asked myself. Did she need something that would enable her to bill my medical insurance for an office visit?

Over the next weeks and months, I would speak to the business manager of the practice several times, at Cliff's request. The conversation was always similar.

"My attorney wants your assurance that there is a sticker in my patient chart, as it appears to be from the copies we have, and that the sticker belongs to the pharmaceutical company in question."

"Yes, Reverend Sykes. The sticker is there and it is a sticker for that brand of Rho(D) shot."

Now, with the deposition at hand, it was not me on unfamiliar ground, but the obstetrician. She had met Cliff and the lawyers for the pharmaceutical company at her office.

She addressed them when they first arrived. "Gentlemen, we need to talk…" Cliff sensed that whatever she was about to say was not good.

"Since Lisa contacted the office, we have been researching the procedures of the office and also our inventory records for Rho(D) products. In 1995, when Lisa got her Rho(D) shot, the office stocked two types of this product, from two different companies. It is true that the sticker affixed to Lisa's chart indicates it was your product," she said, motioning to the pharmaceutical company's lawyers. "But, in talking to the head of the nursing staff from that time, I understand that the sticker in the chart was placed there randomly. The nurses just pulled out a sticker from the drawer as a reminder that the shot had been given. It did not necessarily correspond to the shot or brand of shot Lisa received. There is no way to know if the product Lisa got was the product indicated by the sticker or the alternate one in stock at that time, which was also administered by us to our patients…"

Cliff's professional demeanor hid both his tremendous frustration and a feeling that he was about to be physically ill. He sat for a long time without speaking.

"Is this what you are prepared to testify here today under oath?"

"It is," the obstetrician answered.

"Then we are done," declared Cliff—of so much more than just the day's deposition.

With the obstetrician having thrown the identification of the product into question, the suit was over. The depositions, the 200 emails a day Cliff had been fielding, the expert witness reports collected from academics around the country testifying that the mercury in my Rho(D) has significantly contributed to Wesley's autism, were all pointless now.

The case had been over before it ever began, only we didn't know it.

Before leaving Richmond, Cliff stopped by the house. His presence with us seemed more of a preacher paying a call on a parishioner than of a lawyer consulting with his clients. As we gathered around the kitchen table, Wesley came to sit beside Cliff.

"You know, Cliff, I always say, Wesley is an excellent judge of character."

Cliff at last smiled, looking from Wesley to Seth and myself.

"Are you all okay?" asked Cliff, still shell-shocked himself from the sudden halt to a landmark case that had been hurtling toward court.

"We're okay, Cliff. We have a strong faith and a strong marriage," I replied.

"We will be sure Wesley is secure. There's no doubt about that," Seth added, knowing that one of Cliff's goals, and ours, along with occasioning urgent reforms in the manufacture of pharmaceuticals, had been to secure Wesley financially for his lifetime.

"What is it they say, Cliff? Easy come, easy go?" I laughed.

"Only in this case," Cliff responded, "Neither the coming nor the going was easy, Lisa!"

We all laughed.

"It's good to know there is still laughter in this house!" Cliff said, a note of concern still in his voice. Cliff looked exhausted; the case had consumed him and embroiled him in daunting legal skirmishes with national health agencies and mainstream medical officials for three full months. "After I got back to the hotel this afternoon, I was ill. Physically sick. I just couldn't believe the case fell apart like that."

"You know Cliff, the obstetrician's office never once suggested to me that there was any ambiguity associated with the sticker. Not once in all those conversations! I knew the likelihood was we would lose the suit, but I never thought it would be over a bloomin' sticker!"

"I always said, Lisa, if we lost product identification we would lose the suit, and that's just what happened," he replied.

"What about appealing the vaccine case that was thrown out in Pennsylvania, now? Is that possible?"

"Don't do it, Lisa. You'd probably lose, and if you did, then likely the courts would be closed to these cases in every jurisdiction of the country because a decision at the appellate level is considered 'persuasive.' Every judge in the land would follow the legal precedent. We just can't take that chance."

The impossible pace of my life with its depositions, interrogatories, telephone conferences, and legal strategizing suddenly stopped. I was almost grateful for the change. Almost. We had been so close to having national health leaders in court for depositions. We had been so close to informing the press of the existence of the case. We had been so close to getting the best medical and scientific documentation in the world before a court of law, in a courtroom where I had confidence the judge would fairly weigh the evidence at hand.

There was a sorrow in my soul, wrapped in relief. It reminded me of the death of a beloved friend after a long illness. We had nursed this case against the odds, and for a time, we thought we would see it rise up and walk. But, it was not to be. With my faith firmly by my side, I inquired of God why we would be led into the wilderness only to die there. I received no answer. But the demands of my family and my work moved me forward, whether or not I was ready to let go of this hard-fought yet futile challenge to the pharmaceutical industry.

Perhaps prevailing in civil court was an impossibility because the bar was too high and the liability too astronomical. I thought of the mercury-poisoning in Minamata, Japan. Victims of that incident only prevailed after most of their number had died. Initially, as a result of mercury poisoning, whole families were among the casualties and many more were simply stricken by an illness identified as "infectious" by Japan's government. When there was less liability, as the number of surviving victims dwindled, the government and industry could then afford to compensate those who still somehow lived with their poisoning. Then and only then, fifty years later, there had been an admission and a settlement.

"Does justice have to be affordable in order for it to succeed in a society?" I pondered sadly to myself.

Nearly a week had elapsed since the start of General Conference. Sitting at my desk in the office, I was waiting on word from either Mary Beth Blinn or Julie Taylor about the resolution.

"Probably tomorrow morning, Lisa. That's when we expect the vote to come up," Julie had told me in our conversation the previous day. "Those attending from the Women's Division know how much this means to me. I'm sure they will call when the vote is taken."

Over the time we had worked together, Julie's energy and passion for this issue had increased until it equaled mine. In different places, in different roles, we waited together intently for the vote.

As I passed the morning selecting texts for my sermon and ordering curriculum for the Sunday School, I tried futilely not to watch the clock.

The phone rang. The instant I picked it up, I knew it was Julie. I knew it was news. For the first time I ever recall, Julie's steady, calm, even voice was not any of those things. As my mind raced to comprehend the words she spoke with a tremendous rapidity, I understood. "It just passed!" she shouted in a cascade of pitches. "They just called. It just passed this very minute. Overwhelmingly!"

Julie never said the word 'resolution' but I knew exactly what she meant. And I knew exactly what she felt.

"Thanks be to God, Julie, and to you!" I got out these words, just ahead of my tears.

"There weren't any questions, Lisa. No debate. It passed overwhelmingly!"

"The Kingdom sees what the world can't, Julie!" I said, now through a mix of laughter and tears. Both were joyous!

The United Methodist Church had not only made history but also had just become the largest single organization advocating to protect children and the public from undisclosed and dangerous mercury exposure through their medicines. Over eleven million people were now promised to the cause —eleven million people now to educate that each one might become an advocate. How many thousands of hospitals and clinics and missions now would no longer dispense mercury-containing drugs if mercury-free alternatives were available? Already, I knew that the resolution was a promissory note, for millions and millions of children's minds that would never be damaged by this known poison.

The time that elapsed between my greatest defeat and my greatest victory in the war on mercury was approximately forty-eight hours.

The secular press might ignore this, but the religious press would not. The help that the Women's Division had foreshadowed, the conviction that arrived with "The Truth is Coming to Light," the hope contained in the resolution, were now all tokens of triumph to be spread by the faith community. I finished my conversation with Julie unable to thank her sufficiently. At the age of forty-two, I knew precisely what purpose God had for me. I began preaching to myself.

"This is the way forward. This is why I was ordained. Today begins a new, great, social justice movement, led by the church, to protect the public from a known poison. One day, the children will be safe."

In my head, the verse from the prophet Isaiah, that Jo Pike emailed to me so long ago, returned without invitation. Its arrival in my mind was a welcome surprise. As I mouthed these words, at last my soul, picturing the children still in harm's way from Thimerosal, fully believed them:

"But thus says the Lord: Even the captives of the mighty shall be taken, and the prey of the tyrant shall be rescued; for I will contend with those who contend with you, and your children I will save."

                                                    Isaiah 49:25

Epilogue

by Mark Geier, M.D., Ph.D. and David Geier

MERCURY IN THE DRUG SUPPLY IS A UBIQUITOUS SOURCE OF DANGER; AMONG THOSE products which have contained or still contain it are: drugs for the eye, ear, nose, throat, and skin, bleaching creams, cosmetics, tooth paste, lens solutions, allergy tests and immunotherapy solutions, antiseptics, disinfectants, contraceptives, fungicides and herbicides, dental fillings and many other products, especially vaccines. Thimerosal is a vaccine component that is nearly fifty percent mercury by weight. It was used in many vaccines and Rho(D) injections routinely given during pregnancy to Rh-negative mothers. Thimerosal is still used in many vaccines, especially the flu shot.[1]

The rapidly growing use of Thimerosal-containing flu shots are of particular concern to public health. They have recently begun to be recommended for routine administration to pregnant women and/or newborn children. Multiple clinical studies have demonstrated that the administration of Thimerosal-containing vaccines to infants in the U.S. was found to result in increased blood mercury levels with some infants having blood mercury levels in excess of the blood safety limit from the Environmental Protection Agency (EPA), as well as the blood mercury level defined by the Centers for Disease Control and Prevention (CDC) as the threshold level for mercury poisoning. In addition, administration of Thimerosal-containing vaccines to infants in the U.S. was found to induce hair mercury levels in excess of the hair mercury safety limit established by the EPA for significant periods of time during the first several years of life.[2]

All told, researchers have reported that mercury exposures in early childhood from both potential environmental and vaccine sources resulted in some infants receiving in excess of 350 micrograms mercury during the first six months of life. It was estimated that about fifty percent of the total mercury doses to which some infants were exposed came from routinely recommended Thimerosal-containing childhood vaccines. The cumulative exposure resulted in infants receiving doses of mercury in excess of mercury exposure limits established by the EPA, CDC, Food and Drug Administration (FDA) and Health Canada during key developmental periods during the first year of life.[3]

The documentation of such levels is crucial because scientists have long recognized that mercury is a neurodevelopmental poison. This means that mercury exposure can severely disrupt the normal neurodevelopmental processes in the human brain. As a result, mercury may cause problems in normal neuronal cell migration and division, as well as inducing neuronal cell degeneration, and ultimately cell death.[4] Based upon this knowledge, for example, in 1991 a researcher from the National Institute for Occupational Safety and Health (NIOSH) of the CDC reported that organic mercury was among the compounds known to induce behavior disorders such as autism. Subsequently, researchers reported the specific biological effects of mercury exposure on neuronal development to be compatible with brain pathology observed in autism. In addition, published case-reports of patients have described developmental regressions with Autism Spectrum Disorders (ASD) symptoms following fetal and/or early childhood mercury exposure.[5]

Exposure to mercury can cause immune, sensory, neurological, motor, and behavioral dysfunctions similar to traits defining or associated with ASDs, and these similarities extend to neuroanatomy, neurotransmitters, and biochemistry.[6] In fact, in 2008 a scientific consensus statement developed by the Collaborative on Health and the Environment, which defined learning and developmental disabilities as including but not limited to: deficits in learning and memory, reduced IQ, attention deficit-hyperactivity disorder, autism spectrum disorders, and developmental delays, concluded: "There is no doubt that mercury exposure causes learning and developmental disorders..."[7]

FROM AUTISM TO EPIDEMIC

Autism is a lifelong neurodevelopmental disorder that disproportionately affects male children, roughly five males for every female. Autism is characterized by early onset of impairments in social interaction and communication and unusual stereotyped behaviors. Unable to learn from the natural environment as most children, the child with autism generally shows little interest in the world or people around him. Although a few children with autism develop normal and even advanced skills in particular areas, most exhibit a wide range of profound behavioral problems and delayed or undeveloped skills. Further, a child diagnosed with autism may display a range of problem behaviors such as hyperactivity, poor attention, impulsivity, aggression, self injury and tantrums. In addition, many oftentimes display unusual responses to sensory stimuli such as hypersensitivities to light or certain sounds, colors, smells or touch and have a high threshold of pain.[8] Therefore, in the absence of treatment, autism is, in general, a lifelong developmental disability that profoundly affects the way a person comprehends, communicates and relates to others.

In the United States autism is often classified with two related, although less severe, developmental disorders: Asperger's Disorder and Pervasive Developmental Disorder-Not Otherwise Specified (PDD-NOS). Collectively, these three diagnoses constitute the autism spectrum.

Historically, autism is a new disorder first described by Dr. Leo Kanner from Johns Hopkins University among a cohort of children born in the early 1930s. Subsequently, autism remained a very rare disorder affecting less than one in 2,500 children. Starting in the late 1980s/early 1990s, significant increases in the prevalence rate of diagnosed ASDs began to be observed in the U.S. Researchers have been unable to fully explain the increasing rates of ASD diagnosis in the U.S. by changing diagnostic criteria or improved diagnostic systems. In January 2004, an Autism A.L.A.R.M. was issued by the American Academy of Pediatrics, AAP, and the CDC, stating that one in 166 children in the United States suffers from an ASD, and far worse, that one in six children suffers from a developmental and/or behavioral disorder. The most recent survey data from the CDC in 2007 for eight year-old children born in the early 1990s conservatively suggests that more than one in 150 children in the U.S. may have an ASD diagnosis, and that more than one percent of children may have an ASD diagnosis in certain regions of the U.S. Autism is now more prevalent than childhood cancer, diabetes and Down Syndrome.[9] These epidemic rates for ASD diagnoses in the U.S. have apparently coincided with a sharp rise in fetal and infant exposures to mercury.

During mid-1980s, infants received a cumulative dose of 100 micrograms mercury during the first eighteen months from the 25 micrograms mercury in each DTP vaccine routinely administered at two, four six and eighteen months of age. Additionally, during this time, infants may have incurred mercury exposure through breast milk if they were born to mothers with mercury amalgam fillings and/or Rh-negative mothers, since many Rho(D)-immune globulin formulations, given to prevent complications of maternal and fetal blood mixing, contained Thimerosal (10.5 to > 50 micrograms mercury/dose). Rho(D) products were routinely recommended for administration to these mothers within seventy-two hours of birth.[10]

Starting in the late-1980s/early-1990s, the cumulative dose of mercury children received from Thimerosal-containing childhood vaccines/biologics almost tripled. Specifically, a Thimerosal-containing *Haemophilus Influenza* type b (Hib) vaccine (25 micrograms mercury/dose) was recommended for routine administration at two, four, six and eighteen months of age. Furthermore, a Thimerosal-containing hepatitis B vaccine (12.5 micrograms mercury/dose) was recommended for routine administration at birth, two and six months. As a result, an infant could have received a cumulative dose of 237.5 micrograms mercury during the first eighteen months of life. Furthermore, since many formulations of Rho(D)-immune globulins were Thimerosal-containing (10.5 to > 50 micrograms mercury/dose) and were recommended for routine administration to all Rh-negative pregnant women at twenty-eight week gestation starting in the late-1980s/early-1990s (in addition to the recommendation for its routine administration within seventy-two hours of birth), the cumulative dose of mercury received from Thimerosal-containing vaccines/biologics was certainly even higher for many U.S. infants.[11]

By the summer of 1999, the realization that the mercury exposure American infants were incurring through the immunization schedule exceeded some, if not all, safety limits, caused alarm among both private health organizations and public agencies. On July 7, 1999, the U.S. Public Health Service (USPHS) and the AAP issued a joint statement that urged "all government agencies to work rapidly toward reducing children's exposure to mercury from all sources." The statement recommended that Thimerosal be removed from vaccines as soon as possible as part of this overall process. Between 1999 and 2001, many of the Thimerosal-preserved vaccines recommended for children less than six years of age were made available in reduced-Thimerosal ("preservative free") formulations in the US although due to prolonged shelf life and the failure to withdraw Thimerosal-containing vaccines from the market many children were vaccinated with Thimerosal-containing vaccines well into 2002.[12]

Despite the call, issued by the USPHS and the AAP in 1999, to reduce children's exposure to mercury from all sources, Thimerosal was re-introduced into the U.S. routinely recommended childhood vaccine schedule in 2002 with recommendations to administer two doses of influenza vaccine in the first year of life (starting at six and seven months of age) and to vaccinate all children who were six months to twenty-three months of age. In addition, recommendations were made to vaccinate all pregnant women who would be in their second or third trimester of pregnancy during the U.S. "flu" season (December to March) as well as those who have medical conditions that might increase their risk for complications of influenza, regardless of the stage of pregnancy. It is important to note that the significant majority of influenza vaccines have and continue to contain Thimerosal (25 micrograms mercury/dose). Moreover, the 2002 recommendation has been continually expanded to the point that, in 2008, the CDC recommended that all pregnant women should receive an influenza vaccine (without regard to the trimester of pregnancy) and that all infants should receive two doses of influenza vaccine in the first year of life, with one influenza vaccine administered on a yearly basis thereafter until a patient is eighteen years-old.[13] The result of this recommendation is that, as long as Thimerosal-preserved flu vaccines are available, some American children born today will receive almost twice as much mercury exposure from their childhood vaccines than at any time in the past.

FROM DESCRIPTION TO TESTOSTERONE

Epidemiology, the study of disease patterns in human populations, helps to describe the risk of autism, following mercury exposure from Thimerosal-containing vaccines. In several epidemiological studies done in the Vaccine Adverse Event Reporting System, VAERS, a database that has been maintained by the CDC since 1990 as a surveillance tool to evaluate vaccine safety, independent researchers found the more mercury children received from Thimerosal-containing vaccines, the higher was their risk to develop autism and other neurodevelopmental disorders.[14] In these studies, several independent analysis methods were used to examine the potential adverse effects associated with the administration of over 100 million vaccine doses to American children. In a subsequent study, the medical records for almost 300,000 patients in the CDC's Vaccine Safety Datalink, VSD, database were assessed to determine the relationship between mercury exposure from Thimerosal-containing childhood vaccines and neurodevelopmental disorders.[15] Those children receiving higher doses of mercury from Thimerosal-containing childhood vaccines were found to be at significantly higher risk for being diagnosed with autism, ASDs, and other neurodevelopmental disorders.

Researchers from the School of Public Health, Stony Brook University Medical Center, State University of New York, investigated the relationship between mercury exposure from Thimerosal-containing Hepatitis B vaccination in almost 2000 children and developmental disability, based upon examination of data from the CDC's National Health and Nutrition Survey.[16] These researchers observed that their study provided significant evidence for an association between Thimerosal-containing Hepatitis B vaccination to U.S. infants and an increased risk of developmental disabilities. And finally, researchers observed administration of Thimerosal-containing Rho(D) immune globulin preparations to pregnant women significantly increased the risk of autism and other neurodevelopmental disorders.[17]

Not only epidemiological studies but animal model systems have demonstrated ASD-like symptoms in mice, rats, monkeys and hamsters treated with Thimerosal doses mimicking the childhood vaccine schedule.[18] Additionally, numerous clinical studies confirm an association between Thimerosal-containing childhood vaccines and ASDs. Researchers have confirmed elevated levels of mercury among ASD patients relative to controls. This increased level of mercury correlates with decreased levels of glutathione, sulfate, and cysteine, key substances which help the body to excrete mercury. A decreased ability to excrete mercury may explain why children with similar mercury exposure patterns have different clinical outcomes.[19]

Data have demonstrated among individuals diagnosed with an ASD relative to controls: increased brain mercury levels[20]; increased blood mercury levels[21]; increased mercury levels in baby teeth[22]; increased mercury levels in hair samples[23]; increased urinary porphyrins-associated with mercury intoxi-cation[23]; increased mercury in urine/fecal samples[25]; and decreased excretion of mercury through first baby haircuts.[26]

As stated previously, ASDs disproportionately affect male children, roughly, five males per one female, and hence, any causal factors for ASDs must be able to explain this phenomena. In animal models and in human poisonings, males were found to be significantly more susceptible to mercury toxicity than females. Also, in a series of tissue culture experiments, testosterone (the male hormone) was able to increase the neuronal toxicity of mercury (including Thimerosal), whereas estrogen (the female hormone) less-ened the toxicity. Furthermore, while testosterone made mercury more toxic, mercury increased the level of testosterone in the body, initiating a vicious cycle. Finally, mercury exposure was found to significantly increase testos-terone synthesis by inhibiting the conversion of the key androgen regulator metabolite of dehydroepiandrosterone, DHEA, to the storage metabolite of dehydroepiandrosterone-sulfate, DHEA-S.[27]

The overall importance of these phenomena is extremely relevant for patients diagnosed with an ASD because most are characterized by sig-nificantly increased prenatal and postnatal levels of testosterone and other male hormones (androgens), and significantly decreased prenatal and post-natal levels of estrogens. Individuals diagnosed with an ASD also tend to display traits associated with high levels of testosterone and low levels of estrogens, including the following: hypermasculine profiles on many cogni-tive tasks, changes in play patterns, decreased eye contact, decreased social-ization, lower verbal and higher numerical intelligence, and brain hemispher-ic asymmetries. Consistent with this phenomenon, studies of patients with naturally higher testosterone levels were found to display significantly higher numbers of autistic traits than controls.[28]

FROM TESTOSTERONE TO TREATMENT

A clinical trial study of the use of anti-androgen medications in a group of patients diagnosed with an ASD was previously reported.[29] It was observed that the anti-androgen therapeutic agent, LUPRON® (leu-prolide acetate) therapy supplemented with oral ANDROCUR® (cypro-terone acetate), were found to significantly lower androgen levels and help to significantly reduce autistic-like behaviors. It was observed that in some of the patients examined, significant improvements in decreasing autistic behavior occurred within days of administration of LUPRON® such as better sleep patterns, improvement in attention and hyperactivity, and increased socialization. In addition, LUPRON® therapy helped to significantly reduce the clinical symptoms/behaviors associated with elevated levels of testosterone and other androgens in the blood such as early growth spurt, early secondary sexual changes (i.e. masturbation), body and facial hair, and aggressive behaviors that may be observed among some children diagnosed with an ASD. Finally, this androgen-reduction therapy helped to quantitatively significantly lower ASD symptoms measured using the Autism Treatment Evaluation Checklist (ATEC) within about three months of therapy with progress in socialization, sensory/cognitive awareness, and health/physical/ behaviors skills.

In a subsequent clinical study, LUPRON® administration to nearly 200 patients diagnosed with an ASD (from young children to young adults), found significant reductions in hyperactivity/impulsivity, stereotypy, aggression, self injury, abnormal sexual behaviors, and/or irritability behaviors that frequently occur in patients diagnosed with an ASD with few non-responders to the therapy.[30] Further, LUPRON® therapy significantly helped to lower blood androgen levels and was found to have minimal adverse clinical effects. Finally, other drugs with known anti-androgen effects such as ALDACTONE® (spironolactone) may have beneficial effects on patients diagnosed with ASDs, and menstrual-aged females with an ASD diagnosis may benefit from increased estrogen levels provided by YAZ® (drospirenone/ ethinyl estradiol).[31]

Biomedical understanding of autism continues at a quickening pace, allowing for testing and treatment development. Blood and urine testing is essential in understanding ASD situations and working with individual cases. Soon, even more information may now become available, helping to make better differential diagnoses and perhaps identifying causal contributing factors. This is an encouraging time with important possibilities for all who live and work with autism.[32]

Information on testing and treatment clinics across the U.S. can be found on the web at: www.asdcenters.com. If you are not internet connected, information is available by calling (301)989-0548.

Afterword

Same Song, Second Verse

As *Sacred Spark* went to press in February 2009, parents of vaccine-injured children and national autism organizations once again faced another devastating betrayal as federal health officials quietly blocked sixteen million dollars in previously approved funding for vaccine-autism research. Created in 2006 by Congress through the Combating Autism Act (CAA), the Interagency Autism Coordinating Committee (IACC), was charged to pioneer a national autism research agenda—inclusive of the investigation of vaccines and their components in relation to autism. However, in an unannounced vote on January 14, 2009, IACC government representatives reversed their decision to fund studies on vaccine-autism research despite approval of the same studies at their prior meeting on December 12, 2008.

"The bureaucrats responsible for this scandal are on the wrong side of history and it's hard to not attribute an obstructionist motive to their act since vaccine-autism research has already entered the realm of mainstream science. Serious scientists (except those tied to the vaccine industry) no longer debate whether vaccine-autism research should be done, but rather how it should be done, and by whom," stated Robert Kennedy, Jr. and David Kirby in the Huffington Post.[1]

"These days, being opposed to vaccine-autism research puts one outside of the 'mainstream' and let's be clear, supporting such research in no way makes one 'anti-vaccine'—that charge is a tired, diversionary charade—an ugly lie perpetrated by vaccine industry allies and their blind supporters," wrote Kennedy and Kirby.

Not surprisingly, the re-vote was initiated by the IACC's representative from the Centers for Disease Control and Prevention (CDC), and pushed through by the IACC Chair, Dr. Tom Insel, Director of the National Institute of Mental Health of the National Institutes of Health (NIH). Dr. Insel admitted that the Department of Human Health and Services (HHS), agencies —including the NIH and CDC—have a conflict of interest in conducting vaccine-autism research due to over 5,000 autism lawsuits pending in "Vaccine Court" against the HHS.[2] Unlike most federal advisory committees, the IACC is dominated by government representatives occupying twelve of the eighteen committee seats. Of the six civilian members, five voted to retain the vaccine research. The lone dissenting public member resigned from her organization, Autism Speaks, the night before the meeting. Autism Speaks issued a statement denouncing her vote.[3]

Considered the world's largest mainstream autism group, Autism Speaks also condemned the potentially illegal maneuvering of federal officials: "We are angered and disappointed by this last-minute deviation in the painstaking process of approving the Strategic Plan. Members of the autism community have worked tirelessly during the last two years to develop a plan that would set the stage for significant progress and discoveries for autism research over the next five years," said Bob Wright, co-founder of Autism Speaks and former CEO of NBC-Universal and Vice President of General Electric.[4]

"In a matter of minutes, the Federal Members of the IACC destroyed much of the good will that had been established during the course of this process. Because of this surprise tactic, we now have a plan that is tainted and cannot be supported by the autism community," stated Wright in a press release.

Generation Rescue, the autism advocacy group headed by Jenny McCarthy, has consulted with a prominent Washington, D.C. law firm to assess possible legal recourse for multiple violations of the Federal Advisory Committee Act (FACA) committed by the IACC. Generation Rescue says it began seeking legal counsel during the summer of 2008 when it became increasingly apparent that federal officials affiliated with the IACC were in violation of FACA rules.[5]

SafeMinds, whose president Lyn Redwood served on the IACC committee, and Autism Speaks have withdrawn their support of the IACC Strategic Plan for Autism Research. The groups are also demanding that the incoming

HHS Secretary investigate the IACC's action and reconstitute the committee, including removal of NIMH as its lead agency.[6]

The refusal of our federal government, which legislates and mandates mass vaccination and spends 300 billion dollars on vaccine promotion, to close vaccine safety research gaps sends a dangerous message that will only increase parents' concerns about vaccines. Research determining total health outcomes from multiple vaccinations, with toxicants like mercury, aluminum, formaldehyde, and antigens, will require a comprehensive study of vaccinated versus unvaccinated populations to assess the long-term effects of vaccines. Such a common sense study is one the CDC's own former Director, Dr. Julie Gerberding, has stated could and should be done.[7]

Despite the appearance of an old, tired song being played out in early 2009, independent studies continue to go forward, with or without approval and aid of our tax-funded federal health agencies. Even President Obama stated on the campaign trail last year: "We've seen just a skyrocketing autism rate. Some people are suspicious that it's connected to the vaccines. The science right now is inconclusive, but we have to research it."[8]

As the psalmist wrote, there is always a new song to sing. Parents who wish to join the movement of hope and healing for all children are encouraged to find more information and support at these national groups:

CoMeD http://www.mercury-freedrugs.org
Autism Action Network (AAN) http://autismactioncoalition.org
Autism One http://www.autismone.org
Autism Research Institute http://www.autismresearchinstitute.com
Generation Rescue http://www.generationrescue.org
Heal Every Autistic Life (HEAL) http://www.healautismnow.org
Moms Against Mercury, http://www.momsagainstmercury.org
National Autism Association (NAA)
    http://www.nationalautismassociation.org
National Vaccine Information Center http://www.nvic.org
NoMercury http://www.nomercury.org
SafeMinds http://www.safeminds.org
Schafer Report http://www.sarnet.org

...continued

Talk About Curing Autism (TACA)
  http://www.talkaboutcuringautism.org
U.S. Autism & Asperger Association http://www.usautism.org
Unlocking Autism http://www.unlockingautism.org

CHAPTER TWO MERCURY

1. Megson MN. "Is Autism a G-alpha Protein Defect Reversible with Natural Vitamin A?" *Medical Hypotheses,* 2000, 54(6):979-983.

2. Farfel Z, Bourne HR, Iiri T. "The Expanding Spectrum of G Protein Disease." *New England Journal of Medicine,* 1999;340(13):1012-1020.

3. McGinnis WR. "Oxidative Stress in Autism." *Alternative Therapies in Health and Medicine,* 2004;10(6):22-36.

4. Faustman EM, Silbernagel SM. Fenske RA, Burbacher TM, Ponce RA. "Mechanisms Underlying Children's Susceptibility to Environmental Toxicants." *Environmental Health Perspectives,* 2000;108(Suppl 11):13-21.

Bernard S, Enayati A, Redwood L, Roger H, Binstock T. "Autism: A Novel Form of Mercury Poisoning." *Medical Hypotheses,* 2001;56(4):462-471.

5. Gasset AR, Itoi M, Ishii Y, Ramer RM. "Teratogenicities of Ophthalmic Drugs. II. Teratogenicities and Tissue Accumulation of Thimerosal." *Archives of Ophthalmology,* 1975;93(1):52-55.

6. Westphal GA, Schnuch A, Schulz TG, Reich K, Aberer W, Brasch J, Koch P, Wessbecher R, Szliska C, Bauer A, Hallier E. "Homozygous Gene Deletions of the Glutathione S Transferases M1 and T1 are Associated with Thimerosal Sensitization." *International Archives of Occupational and Environmental Health,* 2000;73:384-388.

7. On October 1, 1988, the National Childhood Vaccine Injury Act of 1986 (Public Law 99-660) created the National Vaccine Injury Compensation Program (VICP). The VICP was established to ensure an adequate supply of vaccines, stabilize vaccine costs, and establish and maintain an accessible and efficient forum for individuals found to be injured by certain vaccines. The VICP is a no-fault alternative to the traditional tort system for resolving vaccine injury claims that provides compensation to people found to be injured by certain vaccines. The U. S. Court of Federal Claims decides who will be paid. Three federal government offices have a role in the VICP: the U.S. Department of Health and Human Services (HHS); the U.S. Department of Justice (DOJ); and the U.S. Court of Federal Claims (the Court). The VICP is located in the HHS, Health Resources and Services Administration, Healthcare Systems Bureau, Division of Vaccine Injury Compensation.

8. From: Maurice R. Hilleman, To: Dr. Gordon Douglas. Vaccine Task Force Assignment. Thimerosal (Merthiolate) Preservative – Problems, Analysis, Suggestions for Resolution. Merck, 1991. pgs 1-7.

9. U.S. Department of Health and Human Services, National Vaccine Injury Compensation Program, Statistics Reports.

http://www.hrsa.gov/Vaccinecompensation/statistics_report.htm

10. Geier D, Geier M. "The True Story of Pertussis Vaccination: A Sordid Legacy?" *Journal of the History of Medicine and Allied Sciences,* 2002;57:249-284.

CHAPTER 3 CHELATION

1. Forman J, Moline J, Cernichiari E, Sayegh S, Torres JC, Landrigan MM, Hudson J, Adel HN, Landrigan PJ. "A Cluster of Pediatric Metallic Mercury Exposure Cases Treated with Meso-2, 3-dimercaptosuccinic acid (DMSA)". *Environmental Health Perspectives*, 2000;108:575-577.

Bradstreet J, Geier DA, Kartzinel JJ, Adams JB, Geier MR. "A Case-control Study of Mercury Burden in Children with Autistic Spectrum Disorders." *Journal of American Physicians and Surgeons*, 2003;8(3):76-79.

Geier DA, Geier MR. "A Clinical Trial of Combined Anti-androgen and Anti-heavy Metal Therapy in Autistic Disorders." *Neuroendocrinology Letters*, 2006;27(6):833-838.

Geier DA, Geier MR. "A Case Series of Children with Apparent Mercury Toxic Encephalopathies Manifesting with Clinical Symptoms of Regressive Autistic Disorders." *Journal of Toxicology and Environmental Health*, Part A 2007;70:837-851.

CHAPTER 4 AN UNEXPECTED INVITATION

1. Letter. From: Dr. Kathryn C. Zoon, Director, Center for Biologics Evaluation and Research, To: Lisa K. Sykes. April 23, 2001.

2. SafeMinds, www.safeminds.org. The Coalition for SafeMinds (Sensible Action For Ending Mercury-Induced Neurological Disorders) is a private nonprofit organization founded to investigate and raise awareness of the risks to infants and children of exposure to mercury from medical products, including thimerosal in vaccines. Safe Minds supports research on the potential harmful effects of mercury and thimerosal.

3. National Academy of Sciences, Institute of Medicine, Immunization Safety Review Committee. "Thimerosal-Containing Vaccines and Neurodevelopmental Outcomes." Public Meeting, Monday, July 16, 2001. The Charles Hotel, One Bennett Street, Cambridge, Massachusetts. Transcript online at: http://www.iom.edu/Object.File/Master/8/176/Transcript7-16.pdf.

CHAPTER 5 A REAL AND PRESENT DANGER

1. United States National Academy of Sciences. Press-Release. "Link Between Neurodevelopmental Disorders and Thimerosal Remains Unclear." October 1, 2001. Washington, D.C.

2. Geier DA, Mumper E, Gladfelter B, Coleman L, Geier MR. "Neurodevelopmental Disorders, Maternal Rh-negativity, and Rho(D) Immune Globulins: a Multi-center Assessment." *Neuroendocrinology Letters*, 2008;29(2):272-80.

Geier DA, Geier MR. "A Prospective Study of Thimerosal-containing Rho(D) Immune Globulin Administration as a Risk Factor for Autistic Disorders." *Journal of Maternal-Fetal and Neonatal Medicine*, 2007;20(5):385-90.

3. Grandjean P, Budtz-Jorgensen E, Steuerwald U, Heinzow B, Needham LL, Jorgensen PJ, Weihe P. "Attenuated Growth of Breast-fed Children Exposed to Increased Concentrations of Methylmercury and Polychlorinated Biphenyls." *Federation of American Societies for Experimental Biology Journal*, 2003;17(6):699-701.

Amin-Zaki L, Majeed MA, Greenwood MR, Elhassani SB, Clarkson TW, Doherty RA. "Methylmercury Poisoning in the Iraqi Suckling Infant: a Longitudinal Study Over Five Years." *Journal of Applied Toxicology*, 1981;1(4):210-4.

4. Geier MR, Geier DA. "Neurodevelopmental Disorders After Thimerosal-containing Vaccines: a Brief Communication." *Experimental Biology and Medicine*, (Maywood) 2003;228(6):660-664.

5. "Vaccines and the Autism Epidemic: Reviewing the Federal Government's track Record and Charting a Course for the Future." Hearing before the Committee on Government Reform, US House of Representatives. One Hundred Seventh Congress, Second Session, December 10, 2002. Government Printing Office, Washington, DC.

CHAPTER 6 SIMPSONWOOD

1. "Scientific Review of Vaccine Safety Datalink Information." June 7-8, 2000. Simpsonwood Retreat Center. Norcross, Georgia. Official Transcript, 1-259. Dr. Verstraeten, page 31.

2. Ibid., Dr. Verstraeten, pages 40-41.

3. Patrick Killough. "Cherokees and Christians in North Georgia: the Christ Doors of Simpsonwood." *Ashville Tribune*, October 24, 1997.

4. Scientific Review of Vaccine Safety Datalink Information. June 7-8, 2000. Simpsonwood Retreat Center. Norcross, Georgia. Official Transcript, Pgs 1-259. Dr. Weil comment p. 75.

5. Ibid., 151.

6. Ibid., 161.

7. Ibid., 162.

8. From: Maurice R. Hilleman, To: Dr. Gordon Douglas. "Vaccine Task Force Assignment. Thimerosal (Merthiolate) Preservative – Problems, Analysis, Suggestions for Resolution." Merck, 1991: 5.

9. Ibid., 1.

10. "Scientific Review of Vaccine Safety Datalink Information." June 7-8, 2000. Simpsonwood Retreat Center. Norcross, Georgia. Official Transcript, 1-259. Dr. Verstraeten: 162.

11. Ibid., 199-200.

12. Ibid., 207.

13. Ibid., 229.

14. Ibid., 247.

15. Ibid., 113.

16. National Immunization Program, Office of the Director, Centers for Disease Control and Prevention. To: Roger Bernier, From: Gayle Hickman. Subject: Transcription of Consultant Notes. June 10, 2000: 1—24.

17. Ibid., 3.

18. Ibid., 4.

19. Ibid., 4.

20. Ibid., 14.

21. Ibid., 20-21.

22. Email. From: Dr. Verstraeten, To: Dr. Orenstein, Dr. Cordero, Dr. Bernier. Subject: "Notes on last week's expert meeting." June 12, 2000, 3:55 PM.

23. Email. From: Dr. Chen, To: Dr. Stehr-Green, Dr. Bernier, Dr. Chu, Dr. Verstraeten. Subject: "RE: IMPORTANT—PLEASE READ—Draft of Simpsonwood meeting." June 13, 2000, 12:04 PM.

24. Email. From: Dr. Bernier, To: Dr. Chen, Dr. Stehr-Green, Dr. Chu, Dr. Verstraeten. Subject: "RE: IMPORTANT—PLEASE READ—Draft of Simpsonwood meeting." July 11, 2000, 4:25 PM.

25. Email. From: Dr. Verstraeten, To: Dr. Grandjean, Dr. Chen, Dr. DeStefano, Dr. Pless, Dr. Bernier, Dr. Clarkson, Dr. Weihe. Subject: "RE: Thimerosal and neurologic outcomes." July 14, 2000, 10:42 a.m.

CHAPTER 7   PICKING UP THE PIECES

1. Patricia A. D'Itri, Frank M. D'Itri. "Mercury Contamination: A Human Tragedy." *A Wiley-Interscience Publication*; 1977: 129-136.

2. Ibid., 197-201.

3. Ibid., 15-28.

4. Waly M, Olteanu H, Banerjee R, Choi SW, Mason JB, Parker BS, Sukumar S, Shim S, Sharma A, Benzecry JM, Power-Carnitsky VA, Deth RC. "Activation of Methionine Synthase by Insulin-like Growth Factor-1 and Dopamine: a Target for Neurodevelopmental Toxins and Thimerosal." *Molecular Psychiatry*, 2004;9(4):358-70.

5. National Autism Association. www.nationalautismassociation.org. The mission of the NAA is to educate and empower families affected by autism and other neurological disorders, while advocating on behalf of those who cannot fight for their own rights.

CHAPTER 8   A PROVIDENTIAL CIRCLE

1. Geier MR, Geier DA. "Thimerosal in Childhood Vaccines, Neurodevelopment Disorders, and Heart Disease in the United States." *Journal of American Physicians and Surgeons*, 2003;8(1):6-11.

2. Wilson, Steve. Chief Investigative Reporter for WXYZ. WXYZ Series (Parts I-V). Detroit, Michigan. www.wxyz.com.

3. Bradstreet J, Geier DA, Kartzinel JJ, Adams JB, Geier MR. "A Case-control Study of Mercury Burden in Children with Autistic Spectrum Disorders." *Journal of American Physicians and Surgeons*, 2003;8(3):76-79.

James SJ, Cutler P, Melnyk S, Jernigan S, Janak L, Gaylor DW, Neubrander JA. "Metabolic Biomarkers of Increased Oxidative Stress and Impaired Methylation Capacity in Children with Autism." *American Journal of Clinical Nutrition*, 2004;80(6):1611-7.

CHAPTER 9   INSTITUTIONAL DENIAL

1. National Academy of Sciences, Institute of Medicine, Immunization Safety Review Committee. "Vaccines and Autism." Public Meeting, February 9, 2004. National Academy of Sciences Auditorium, 2100 C Street, NW. Washington, DC. Official Transcript: 4.

2. Ibid., 6-7.

3. Ibid., 18-60.

4. Ibid., 100-101.

5. Email. To: Dr. Chen, From: Dr. Miller. Subject: "RE: UK vaccine schedule and Thimerosal exposure." June 26, 2001, 11:25 AM.

Email. To: Dr. Miller, From: Dr. Chen. Subject: "FW: UK vaccine schedule and Thimerosal exposure." June 26, 2001, 22:47.

6. National Academy of Sciences, Institute of Medicine, Immunization Safety Review Committee. "Vaccines and Autism," Public Meeting, February 9, 2004. National Academy of Sciences Auditorium, 2100 C Street, NW. Washington, DC. Official Transcript: 111.

7. Ibid., 124.

8. Ibid., 167.

9. Ibid., 167.

10. Ibid., 207-208.

11. Ibid., 225, 232.

12. Ibid., 258.

13. Ibid., 289-290.

14. Ibid., 335-336.

15. Ibid., 338-339.

CHAPTER 10   THE OFFICE OF SPECIAL COUNSEL PROJECT

1. Letter. From: Matt Kochanski, Director of the Investigative Branch for the Office of the Inspector General for Health and Human Services, To: Lisa K. Sykes. March 11, 2004.

2. Letter: From: Seth and Lisa Sykes from Virginia, Kelli Ann and Jim Davis from North Carolina, Scott and Laura Bono from North Carolina, Bob and Lori Krakow from New York, Michael and Bobbie Manning from New York, Jo Pike from South Carolina, Brian and Marcia Hooker from Washington, Jeff and Karen Trelka from Washington, Lee and Dana Halvorson from Iowa, Linda and Kerry Weinmaster from Kansas, Alan and Lujene Clark from Missouri, Christian and Lori McIlwain from North Carolina, Michael Wagnitz from Wisconsin, Arnie and Rita Shreffler from Missouri, and Nancy Hokkanen from Minnesota, To: Scott Bloch, Special Counsel, U.S. Office of Special Counsel. April, 9 2004.

CHAPTER 11   AN UNEXPECTED ALLY

1. US Institute of Medicine. Immunization Safety Review: "Vaccines and Autism." Washington, DC: National Academy Press, 2004. Executive Summary: 7.

2. Ibid., 12.

3. "Autism, Mercury Link Disputed: Doctors Say No Connection Found, Parents Disagree." CBS/AP News. May 18, 2004.

http://www.cbsnews.com/stories/2004/05/18/health/main618142.shtml

4. US Institute of Medicine. Immunization Safety Review. "Vaccines and Autism." Washington, DC: National Academy Press, 2004. Executive Summary: 14.

5. Kimberly Pierceall. "Vaccine Autism Link Discounted." *Wall Street Journal.* May 19, 2004: D3.

6. U.S. Office of Special Counsel. Press Release. "OSC Forwards Public Health Concerns on Vaccines to Congress." May 20, 2004.

CHAPTER 12 HAZARDOUS WASTE

1. Co-Med. www.mercury-freedrugs.org. The Coalition for Mercury-free Drugs is a 501(C)(3) not-for-profit group. We are dedicated to reducing the mercury-exposure risks, for the unborn, infants, children, adolescents and adults, from all mercury-containing medical products to which they are, or may be, exposed. We support and, when we can, assist the efforts of all those who share any part of our mission, vision, or values.

2. Merck. Safety Data Sheet. Thimerosal. Date of Issue: 7/28/03:6.

3. Sigma Chemical Co. Material Safety Data Sheet. Thimerosal. Valid 11/2002 – 01/2003: 1.

4. Ibid., 3.

5. Eli Lilly and Company. Material Safety Data Sheet. Thimerosal. Effective Date: December 22, 1999: 2

6. Sigma Chemical Co. Material Safety Data Sheet. Thimerosal. Valid 11/2002 – 01/2003: 3.

7. Ibid., 4.

8. Email. From: Timothy S. O'Neil, to: p2tech@greatlakes.net. Subject: "Thymerasol Filtering." January 9, 1998, 9:38 AM.

CHAPTER 13 INCRIMINATION

1. Autism Action Network, formerly A-CHAMP. www.autismactioncoalition.org. AAC is a national, non-partisan political action organization formed by parents in support of children with neurodevelopmental and communication disorders. We are dedicated to advancing public policy issues affecting our children, protecting their human and civil rights, educating the public and media, supporting candidates sharing our goals in state and federal elections, and holding accountable those in government who do not act in the best interest of our children.

2. Letter: Chris Swecker, Chair, Integrity Committee, President's Council on Integrity & Efficiency. To: Lisa Sykes. July 21, 2004.

3. Letter: Michael E. Little, Deputy Inspector General for Investigations, the Office of the Inspector General for Health and Human Services, To: Lisa Sykes. July 19, 2004.

4. "We the Parents... Hurt and Angry Moms and Dads Get Political." *Mothering Magazine,* July-August 2004: 48-51.

5. Co-MedCitizen'sPetition.http://www.fda.gov/ohrms/dockets/dockets/04p0349/04p0349. htm.

6. Department of Health and Human Services, Public Health Service, Centers for Disease Control and Prevention. Inter/Intra-Agency Agreement with the National Institute of Health to Establish a Vaccine Safety Review Panel from 8/1/2000 through 9/30/2003 for $2,043,000. Payable Agreements.

CHAPTER 14   TESTOSTERONE

1. Haley, BE. "Mercury Toxicity: Genetic Susceptibility and Synergistic Effects." *Medical Veritas,* 2005;2:535-542.

2. US House of Representatives, Committee on Appropriations, Subcommittee on Labor, Health and Human Services, and Education. Hearing on, "Influenza Vaccine Issues." October 5, 2004. Washington Transcription Service. Official Transcript: 10.

3. Ibid., 11.

4. Ibid., 11.

5. Ibid., 11.

6. Ibid., 11.

7. Ibid., 11.

8. Ibid., 12.

9. Ibid., 12.

10. Ibid., 18.

11. Ibid., 18.

12. Merril CR, Geier MR, Petricciani JC. "Bacterial Virus Gene Expression in Human Cells." *Nature* 1971;233:398-400.

Petricciani JC, Binder MK, Merril CR, Geier MR. "Galactose Utilization in Galactosemia." *Science* 1972;175:1368-70.

13. Xu E, Suiko M, Sakakibara Y, Pai TG, Liu MC. "Regulatory Effects of Divalent Metal Cations on Human Cytosolic Sulfotransferases." *Journal of Biochemistry,* 2002;132:457-62.

Ryan RA, Carrol J. Studies on a 3beta-hydrosteroid sulphotransferase from rat liver. *Biochimica et Biophysica Acta,* 1976;429(2):391-401.

14. Manning JT, Baron-Cohen S, Wheelwright S, Sanders G. "The 2nd to 4th Digit Ratio and Autism." *Developmental Medicine and Child Neurology,* 2001;43:160-4.

Baron-Cohen S, Knickmeyer RC, Belmonte MK. "Sex Differences in the Brain: Implications for Explaining Autism." *Science,* 2005;310:819-23.

Knickmeyer RC, Wheelwright S, Hoekstra R, Baron-Cohen S. "Age of Menarche in Females with Autism Spectrum Conditions." *Developmental Medicine and Child Neurology,* 2006;48(12):1007-8.

"Elevated Rates of Testosterone-related Disorders in Women with Autism Spectrum Conditions." *Hormones and Behavior*, 2007;51(5):597-604.

Kickmeyer RC, Baron-Cohen S. "Fetal Testosterone and Sex Differences in Typical Social Development and in Autism." *Journal of Child Neurology*, 2006;21:825-45.

15. Tanaka T, Niimi H, Matsuo N, Fujieda K, Tachibana K, Ohymam K, Satoh M, Kugu K. "Results of Long-term Follow-up After Treatment of Central Precocious Puberty with Leuprorelin Acetate: Evaluation of Effectiveness of Treatment and recover of Gonadal Function. The TAP-144-SR Japanese Study Group on Central Precocious Puberty." *Journal of Clinical Endocrinology and Metabolism*, 2005;90(3):1371-6.

16. Geier MR, Geier DA. "The Potential Importance of Steroids in the Treatment of Autistic Spectrum Disorders and Other Disorders Involving Mercury Toxicity." *Medical Hypotheses*, 2005;64(5):946-54.

17. Geier DA, Geier MR. "A Prospective Assessment of Androgen Levels in Patients with Autistic Spectrum Disorders: Biochemical Underpinnings and Suggested Therapies." *Neuroendocrinology Letters*, 2007;28(5):565-73.

Geier DA, Geier MR. "A Clinical Trial of Combined Anti-androgen and Anti-heavy Metal Therapy in Autistic Disorders." *Neuroendocrinology Letters*, 2006;27(6):833-8.

Geier DA, Geier MR. "A Clinical and Laboratory Evaluation of Methionine Cycle-transsulfuration and Androgen Pathway Markers in Children with Autistic Disorders." *Hormone Research*, 2006;66(4):182-8.

Geier DA, Geier MR. "A Case Series of Children with Apparent Mercury Toxic Encephalopathies Manifesting with Clinical Symptoms of Regressive Autistic Disorders." *Journal of Toxicology and Environmental Health*, 2007;70(10):837-51.

Prudova A, Albin M, Bauman Z, Lin A, Vitvitsky V, Banerjee R. "Testosterone Regulation of Homocysteine Metabolism Modulates Redox Status in Human Prostate Cancer Cells." *Antioxidants and Redox Signaling*, 2007;9(11):1875-81.

CHAPTER 15   MORE POWERFUL THAN YOU KNOW

1. State of Iowa: 2007 Merged Iowa Code and Supplement, Title IV Public Health, Subtitle 2 Health-Related Activities, Chapter 135, Department of Public Health, 135.39 B, Early Childhood Immunizations. Approved by the Governor on May 14, 2004.

State of California: CHAPTER 837. An act to add Article 9 (commencing with Section 124172), "Mercury-Containing Vaccines" to Chapter 3 of Part 2 of Division 106 of the Health and Safety Code, relating to vaccinations. Approved by the Governor on September 28, 2004.

2. Attention Deficit Disorder:

Cheuk DK, Wong V. "Attention-deficit Hyperactivity Disorder and Blood Mercury Level: a Case-control Study in Chinese Children." *Neuropediatrics*, 2006;37(4):234-40.

Young HA, Geier DA, Geier MR. "Thimerosal Exposure in Infants and Neurodevelopmental Disorders: An Assessment of Computerized Medical Records in the Vaccine Safety Datalink." *Journal of the Neurological Sciences*, 2008;271(1-2):110-8.

Geier DA, Geier MR. "A Two-phased Population Epidemiological Study of the Safety of Thimerosal-containing Vaccines: a Follow-up Analysis." *Medical Science Monitor,* 2005;11(4):CR160-70.

Geier DA, Mumper E, Gladfelter B, Coleman L, Geier MR. "Neurodevelopmental Disorders, Maternal Rh-negativity, and Rho(D) Immune Globulins: a Multi-center Assessment." *Neuroendocrinology Letters,* 2008;29(2):272-80.

Infant Deaths:

Rohyans J, Walson PD, Wood GA, MacDonald WA. "Mercury Toxicity Following Merthiolate Ear Irrigations." *Journal of Pediatrics,* 1984;104(2):311-3.

Fagan DG, Prichard JS, Clarkson TW, Greenwood MR. "Organ Mercury Levels is Infants with Omphaloceles Treated with Organic Mercurial Antiseptic." *Archives of Disease in Childhood,* 1977;52(12):962-4.

Axton JHM. "Six Cases of Poisoning After a Parenteral Organic Mercurial Compound (Merthiolate)." *Postgraduate Medical Journal,*1972;48:417-21.

Alzheimer's Disease:

Pendergrass JC, Haley BE, Vimy MJ, Winfield SA, Lorscheider FL. "Mercury Vapor Inhalation Inhibits Binding of GTP to Tubulin in Rat Brain: Similarity to a Molecular Lesion in Alzheimer Diseased Brain." *Neurotoxicology,* 1997;18(2):315-324.

Pendergrass JC, Haley BE. "Inhibition of Brain Tubulin-guanosine 5-triphosphate Interactions by Mercury: Similarity to Observations in Alzheimer's Diseased Brain." *Metal Ions Biological Systems,* 1997;34:461-78.

Leong CC, Syed NI, Lorscheider FL. "Retrograde Degeneration of Neurite Membrane Structural Integrity of Nerve Growth Cones Following In Vitro Exposure to Mercury." *NeuroReport,* 2001;12(4):733-7.

CHAPTER 17   RESOLVED

1. Virginia Annual Conference Resolution. The United Methodist Church. http://www. vaumc.org/repository/AC2005/BOR2005.pdf

CHAPTER 18   THE ONLY WAY FORWARD

1. Memo. From: Liz Birt, J.D., L.L.M. and James Moody, J.D. to Lauren Fuller, Chief Investigative Counsel U.S. Senate Health, Education, Labor and Pensions (HELP) Committee, Re: Timeline, July 15, 2005. Available online at www.generationrescue.com.

CHAPTER 19   A HIGHER COURT

1. Lisa Sykes et al. Plaintiffs vs. Bayer Corporation Defendant. Case Number CV460. The United States District Court for the Eastern District of Virginia, Richmond Division. March 26, 27, 2008 videotaped deposition of the reverend Lisa Sykes, a plaintiff, taken at the instance of the Defendant, before Helen B. Yarbrough, RPR, CCR, a Notary Public for the State of Virginia at Large, beginning at 9:08 a.m., at the law office of Hunton & Williams, 951 East Byrd Street, Richmond, Virginia; said deposition taken pursuant to the Federal Rules of Civil Procedure.

Epilogue

1. Geier DA, Sykes LK, Geier MR. "A Review of Thimerosal (Merthiolate) and Its Ethylmercury Breakdown Product: Specific Historical Considerations Regarding Safety and Effectiveness." *Journal of Toxicology and Environmental Health, Part B: Critical Reviews* 2007;10(8):575-596.

2. Geier DA, King PG, Sykes LK, Geier MR. "A Comprehensive Review of Mercury Provoked Autism." *Indian Journal of Medicine and Research*, 2008;128(4):383-411.

3. Bigham M, Copes R. "Thiomersal in Vaccines: Balancing the Risk of Adverse Effects with the Risk of Vaccine-preventable Disease." *Drug Safety*, 2005;28(2):89-101.

4. Geier DA, King PG, Geier MR. "Mitochondrial Dysfunction, Impaired Oxidative-Reduction Activity, Degeneration, and Death in Human Neuronal and Fetal Cells Induced by Low-level Exposure to Thimerosal and Other Metal Compounds." *Toxicological and Environmental Chemistry* (in press).

5. Geier DA, King PG, Sykes LK, Geier MR. "A Comprehensive Review of Mercury Provoked Autism." *Indian Journal of Medicine and Research* 2008;128(4):383-411.

6. Ibid.

7. Collaborative on Health and the Environment's Learning and Developmental Disabilities Initiative. LDDI Scientific consensus statement on environmental agents associated with neurodevelopmental disorders; 2008:1-35.

8. Austin D. An Epidemiological Analysis of the 'Autism as Mercury Poisoning' hypothesis." *International Journal of Risk and Safety in Medicine*, 2008;20(3):135-142.

9. California Department of Developmental Services. *Autistic Spectrum Disorders: Changes in the California Caseload – An Update: 1999 through 2003.* Sacramento, CA: April 2003.

Austin D. "An Epidemiological Analysis of the 'Autism as Mercury Poisoning' Hypothesis." *International Journal of Risk and Safety in Medicine*, 2008;20(3):135-142.

10. Geier DA, King PG, Sykes LK, Geier MR. "A Comprehensive Review of Mercury Provoked Autism." *Indian Journal of Medicine and Research* 2008;128(4):383-411.

11. Ibid.

12. Ibid.

13. Fiore AE, Shay DK, Broder K, Iskander JK. Uyeki TM, Mootrey G, Bresee JS, Cox NS; Centers for Disease Control and Prevention (CDC); Advisory Committee on Immunization Practices. Prevention and control of influenza: recommendations of the Advisory Committee on Immunization Practices (ACIP), 2008. *Morbidity and Mortality Weekly Report, Recommendations and Reports,* 2008;57(RR-7):1-60.

14. Geier DA, Geier MR. "A Meta-analysis Epidemiological Assessment of Neurodevelopmental Disorders Following Vaccines Administered From 1994 Through 2000 in the United States." *Neuroendocrinology Letters,* 2006;27(4):401-13.

Geier MR, Geier DA. "Neurodevelopmental Disorders After Thimerosal-containing Vaccines: a Brief Communication." *Experimental Biology and Medicine (Maywood),* 2003;228(6):660-4.

Geier DA, Geier MR. "An Evaluation of the Effects of Thimerosal on Neurodevelopmental Disorders Reported Following DTP and Hib Vaccines in Comparison to DTPH

Vaccines in the United States." *Journal of Toxicology and Environmental Health, Part A* 2006;68(15):1481-95.

Geier DA, Geier MR. "An Assessment of Downward Trends in Neurodevelopmental Disorders in the United States Following Removal of Thimerosal from Childhood Vaccines." *Medical Science Monitor,* 2006;12(6):CR231-9.

Geier DA, Geier MR. "A Two-phased Population Epidemiological Study of the Safety of Thimerosal-containing Vaccines: a Follow-up Analysis." *Medical Science Monitor,* 2005;11(4):CR160-70.

Geier D, Geier MR. "Neurodevelopmental Disorders Following Thimerosal-containing Childhood Immunization: a Follow-up Analysis." *International Journal of Toxicology,* 2004;24(6):369-76.

Geier DA, Geier MR. "An Assessment of the Impact of Thimerosal on Childhood Neurodevelopmental Disorders." *Pediatric Rehabilitation,* 2003;6(2):97-102.

Geier MR, Geier DA. "Thimerosal in Childhood Vaccines, Neurodevelopment Disorders, and Heart Disease in the United States." *Journal of American Physicians and Surgeons,* 2003;8(1):6-11.

Geier MR, Geier DA. "Early Downward Trends in Neurodevelopmental Disorders Following Removal of Thimerosal-containing Vaccines." *Journal of American Physicians and Surgeons,* 2003;11(1):8-13.

15. Young HA, Geier DA, Geier MR. "Thimerosal Exposure in Infants and Neurodevelopmental Disorders: an Assessment of Computerized Medical Records in the Vaccine Safety Datalink." *Journal of the Neurological Sciences,* 2008;271(1-2):110-118.

16. Gallagher C, Goodman M. "Hepatitis B Triple Series Vaccine and Developmental Disability in U.S. Children Aged 1-9 Years." *Toxicological and Environmental Chemistry,* 2008;90(5):997-1008.

17. Geier DA, Mumper E, Gladfelter B, Coleman L, Geier MR. "Neurodevelopmental Disorders, Maternal Rh-negativity, and Rho(D) Immune Globulins: a Multi-center Assessment." *Neuroendocrinology Letters,* 2008;29(2):272-80.

Geier DA, Geier MR. "A Prospective Study of Thimerosal-containing Rho(D) Immune Globulin Administration as a Risk Factor for Autistic Disorders." *Journal of Maternal, Fetal, and Neonatal Medicine,* 2007;20(5):389-90.

Holmes AS, Blaxill MF, Haley BE. "Reduced Levels of Mercury in First Baby Haircuts of Autistic Children." *International Journal of Toxicology,* 2003;22(4):277-85.

18. Hornig M, Chian D, Lipkin WI. "Neurotoxic Effects of Postnatal Thimerosal are Mouse Strain Dependent." *Molecular Psychiatry,* 2004;9(9):833-45.

Olczak M, Duszczyk M, Mierzejewski P, Majewska MD. "*Vaccine Preservative, Thimerosal, Causes Wide-spread Neurodevelopmental Disturbances in Young Rats.*" Presentation at International Conference, Autism and Vaccinations: Is There a Link? October 25-26, 2008. Warsaw University, Poland. Conference Proceedings: 22.

Laurente J, Remuzgo F, Avalos B, Chiquinta J, Ponce B, Avendano R, Maya L. "Neurotoxic Effects of Thimerosal at Vaccines Doses on the Encephalon and Development in Seven Day-old Hamsters." *Annals of the Faculty of Medicine, Lima, Peru* 2007;68(3):222-237.

Hewitson L, Lopresti B, Stott C, Tomko J, Houser L, Klein E, Castro C, Sackett G, Supta S, Atwood D, Blue L, Rhite ER, Wakefield A. "Pediatric Vaccines, Influenza, Primate

Behavior, and Amygdale Growth and Opioid Legand Binding." Friday, May 16, 2008: International Meeting for Autism Research (IMFAR).

Wakefield A, Stott C, Lopresti B, Tomko J, Houser L, Sackett G, Hewitson L. "Pediatric Vaccines Influence Primate Behavior, and Brain Stem Volume and Opioid Ligand Binding." Saturday, May 17, 2008: International Meeting for Autism Research (IMFAR).

19. Geier DA, Kern JK, Garver CR, Adams JB, Audhya T, Geier MR. "A Prospective Study of Transsulfuration Biomakers in Autistic Disorders." *Neurochemical Research* (in press).

20. Sajdel-Sulkowska EM, Lipinski B, Windom H, Audhya T, McGinnis W. "Oxidative Stress in Autism: Elevated Cerebellar 3-nitrotyrosine levels." *American Journal of Biochemistry and Biotechnology,* 2008;4(2):73-84.

21. DeSoto MC, Hitlan RT. "Blood Levels of Mercury are Related to Diagnosis of Autism: a Reanalysis of an Important Data Set." *Journal of Child Neurology,* 2007;22(11):1308-11.

22. Adams JB, Romdalvik J, Ramanujam VM, Legator MS. "Mercury, Lead, and Zinc in Baby Teeth of Children with Autism Versus Controls." *Journal of Toxicology and Environmental Health, Part A* 2007;70(12):1046-51.

23. Fido A, Al-Saad S. "Toxic Trace Elements in the Hair of Children with Autism." *Autism* 2005;9(3):290-8.

24. Geier DA, Geier MR. "A Prospective Assessment of Porphyrins in Autistic Disorders: a Potential Marker for Heavy Metal Exposure." *Neurotoxicity Research,* 2006;10(1):57-64.

Nataf R, Skorupka C, Amet L, Lam A, Springbett A, Lathe R. "Porphyrinuria in Childhood Autistic Disorder: Implications for Envionrmental Toxicity." *Toxicology and Applied Pharmacology,* 2006;214(2):99-108.

Geier DA, Geier MR. "A Prospective Study of Mercury Toxicity Biomarkers in Autistic Spectrum Disorders." *Journal of Toxicology and Environmental Health, Part A* 2007;70(20):1723-30.

Austin DW, Shandley K. "An Investigation of Porphyrinuria in Australian Children with Autism." *Journal of Toxicology and Environmental Health, Part A* 2008;71(20):1349-51.

Nataf R, Skorupka C, Lam A, Springbett A, Lathe R. "Porphyrinuria in Childhood Autistic Disorder is Not Associated with Urinary Creatinine Deficiency." *Pediatrics International,* 2008;50(4):528-32.

Geier DA, Kern JK, Garver CR, Adams JB, Audhya T, Nataf R, Geier MR. "Biomarkers of Environmental Toxicity and Susceptibility in Autism." *Journal of the Neurological Sciences* (in press).

25. Geier DA, Geier MR. "A Case Series of Children with Apparent Mercury Toxic Encephalopathies Manifesting with Clinical Symptoms of Regressive Autistic Disorders." *Journal of Toxicology and Environmental Health, Part A* 2007;70(10):837-51.

Bradstreet J, Geier DA, Kartzinel JJ, Adams JB, Geier MR. "A Case-control Study of Mercury Burden in Children with Autistic Spectrum Disorders." *Journal of American Physicians and Surgeons,* 2003;8(3):76-79.

26. Adams JB, Romdalvik J, Levine KE, Hu LW. "Mercury in First-cut Baby Hair of Children with Autism Versus Typically-developing Children." *Toxicological and Environmental Chemistry,* 2008;90(4):739-753.

Holmes AS, Blaxill MF, Haley BE. "Reduced Levels of Mercury in First Baby Haircuts of Autistic Children." *International Journal of Toxicology*, 2003;22(4):277-85.

27. Geier DA, Geier MR. "A Prospective Assessment of Androgen Levels in Patients with Autistic Spectrum Disorders: Biochemical Underpinnings and Suggested Therapies." *Neuroendocrinology Letters*, 2007;28(5):565-73.

28. Baron-Cohen S, Knickmeyer RC, Belmonte MK. "Sex Differences in the Brain: Implications for Explaining Autism." *Science*, 2005;310(5749):819-23.

Geier DA, Geier MR. "A Prospective Assessment of Androgen Levels in Patients with Autistic Spectrum Disorders: Biochemical Underpinnings and Suggested Therapies." *Neuroendocrinology Letters*, 2007;28(5):565-73.

29. Geier DA, Geier MR. "A Clinical Trial of Combined Anti-androgen and Anti-heavy Metal Therapy in Autistic Disorders." *Neuroendocrinology Letters*, 2006;27(6);833-838.

30. Geier DA, Geier MR. "A Prospective Assessment of Androgen Levels in Patients with Autistic Spectrum Disorders: Biochemical Underpinnings and Suggested Therapies." *Neuroendocrinology Letters*, 2007;28(5):565-73.

31. Geier DA, Geier MR. "Autism Spectrum Disorder-associated Biomarkers for Case Evaluation and Management by Clinical Geneticists." *Expert Review of Molecular Diagnostics*, 2008;8(6):671-4.

32. Ibid.

AFTERWORD

1. Kennedy, Jr., Robert and Kirby, David. "Autism, Vaccines and the CDC: The Wrong Side of History." The Huffington Post, January 27, 2009.

2. Internet Alert. The Autism Action Network. "Protest Federal Autism Committee's Deceitful Reversal on Vaccine-Autism Research." February 3, 2009. http://www.autismactioncoalition.org

3. Press release. Autism Speaks. "Autism Speaks Withdraws Support for Strategic Plan for Autism Research, Decries Unexpected Change in Final Approval Process Calls for New Administration to Restore the Intent of Combating Autism Act to Respect and Value Community Input." January 15, 2009. http://www.autismspeaks.org

4. Ibid.

5. David, Kelli Ann. "Generation Rescue Seeks Legal Advice on IACC Violations." The Age of Autism, The Daily Web Newspaper of the Autism Epidemic. January 19, 2009. http://www.ageofautism.com

6. News Release. "SafeMinds: Federal Members of Advisory Committee Block Vaccine-Autism Research." Age of Autism, The Daily Web Newspaper of the Autism Epidemic. January 16, 2009. http://www.ageofautism.com

7. Television interview. House Call with Dr. Sanjay Gupta, CNN. March 29, 2008.

8. Hughes, Virginia. "Autism Research Expected To Prosper Under Obama." January 30, 2009. Simons Foundation Autism Research Initiative. http://www.sfari.org

Biographies

Rev. Lisa Sykes currently serves as the associate pastor of Welborne United Methodist Church, Richmond, Virginia. She graduated from the University of Virginia, where she was an Echols Scholar, in 1987, and from Princeton Theological Seminary in 1990. She was ordained in the Virginia Annual Conference in 1990 as a probationary deacon and in 1992 as an elder in full connection. She has served the Virginia Annual Conference of the United Methodist Church for almost twenty years. Lisa married her husband, Seth, in 1989, and they have three sons: Adam, Wesley and Joshua. Wesley was diagnosed with autism in 1998 and with mercury poisoning in 2000. Since that time, in addition to being a wife, mother, and minister, Lisa has become an advocate for safe, mercury-free vaccines and for children with disabilities. She is president of CoMeD, Inc., a 501(c)3 nonprofit dedicated to the elimination of mercury from medicine.

Mark R. Geier has a M.D. and a Ph.D. in genetics. He is board certified in genetics by the American Board of Medical Genetics and is a Fellow of the American College of Epidemiology. Dr. Geier is founder of ASD Centers, LLC, and has been in clinical practice for more than 29 years. Dr. Geier is president of the 501(c)3 non-profit Institute of Chronic Illnesses, Inc. and is a founder of the the 501(c)3 nonprofit CoMeD, Inc.

Dr. Geier was a researcher at the National Institutes of Health for ten years. He was also a professor at the Johns Hopkins University and at the Uniformed Services University of the Health Sciences. Dr. Geier has addressed the Institute of Medicine of the U.S. National Academy of Sciences, the U.S. State Department, the Government Reform Committee of the U.S. House of Representatives, and numerous other professional meetings. Dr. Geier has authored over 100 peer-reviewed medical studies, and recently, has co-authored more than fifty peer-reviewed medical studies on vaccine safety, efficacy and policy. In addition, Dr. Geier has authored more than twenty peer-reviewed medical studies on patients diagnosed with autistic disorders. His research has won awards and has received national and international media coverage.

Dr. Geier has participated in the evaluation and treatment of more than 600 patients diagnosed with autism spectrum disorders. He has served as a scientific reviewer for autism grants for the U.S. Government. Dr. Geier has a patent pending for the treatment of patients diagnosed with autism spectrum disorders. Dr. Geier has also been involved in vaccine/biologic litigation.

DAVID A. GEIER is president of MedCon, Inc. and is vice-president of the non-profit 501(c)3 Institute of Chronic Illnesses, Inc. David is a founder of the non-profit 501(c)3 CoMeD, Inc. He graduated with honors from University of Maryland with a B.A. in biology and a minor in history. He has been a researcher scientist at the National Institutes of Health.

David has co-authored approximately fifty peer-reviewed medical studies on vaccine safety, efficacy, and policy. He has received critical acclaim from his colleagues for his research on vaccines by winning the "Stanley W. Jackson Prize," which is given to authors having the best paper in the preceding three years in the Journal of the History of Medicine and Allied Sciences published by Duke University. He has addressed numerous professional meetings, and has recently twice co-addressed the Institute of Medicine of the United States' National Academy of Sciences on vaccine issues.

Over the last few years David, as a member of the Institute of Chronic Illnesses, has been studying and publishing on the relationship of genetic, biochemical and hormonal changes in autism which has resulted in new insights as to the cause and treatment of autism and other chronic illnesses. Overall, David has authored more than twenty peer-reviewed medical studies on patients diagnosed with autistic disorders. David has a patent pending for the treatment of patients diagnosed with autism spectrum disorders. David has also been involved in vaccine/biologic litigation.

"Sacred Spark is an extraordinary account of one mother (who happens to be a minister) who becomes tenacious in her advocacy for her own son who has autism and mercury poisoning. She also has become a fierce advocate for children and parents everywhere who live day in and day out with the complex, debilitating, and painful effects of autism spectrum disorder. I would encourage everyone who is concerned about the grim statistic that one out of every 150 children being born in the U.S. today will be diagnosed with some form of autism to read this book and pick up the work of advocacy that will be needed to prevent mercury poisoning and autism."

—**Bishop Charlene Kammerer**, Resident Bishop
Virginia Conference, The United Methodist Church

"Lisa Sykes interweaves her compelling personal experience in healing her son's vaccine injury with a faithfully accurate account of the public controversy over the dangers of mercury in vaccines, all powerfully tied together by her calling as a Minister in the United Methodist Church."

—**Robert J. Krakow**, Esq., Parent

"Sacred Spark is a book to be read by all who are interested in the causation, treatment and politics involved in the recent autism epidemic. Nothing is more important than for our citizens to be educated about the damage that is classified as autism, but is really a toxic response of infants exposed to specific neurotoxins. This book details many of the occurrences and issues surrounding the theory that vaccines played a major role in the epidemic of neurological illnesses our children are suffering with today."

—**Boyd E. Haley**, Ph.D. Professor Emeritus,
University of Kentucky Chemistry Department

"The church can provide a moral compass in the modern world. With our current knowledge of the individual nature of the human genome, this story explains why we need to reassess our "one size fits all" approach to vaccines. Lisa's struggle to heal her vaccine damaged son with (gluten free) loaves and fish (oil) and toxin removal is compelling. This book reads beautifully and is Shakespearian in scope."

—**Mary Megson**, M.D., FAAP.
Pediatric & Adolescent Ability Center

Printed in the United States
141604LV00001BC/2/P